Bruce Nicholls writes from an intimate knowledge of international affairs, having served as Australia's Trade Commissioner to India, Germany, Switzerland, China and finally, Hong Kong, where he was also Commissioner for Australia. He was President of the Australia-China Chamber of Commerce & Industry and a Trustee of the Committee for Economic Development of Australia and is the founding chair of public policy forums in Sydney & Melbourne. He is a vocal champion in the cause of allowing good public policy to rise above political toxicity and a promoter of civil discourse, free thought and free speech. This is his 5th book. His books have won wide literary acclaim, including the Newspaper House Annual Literary Award and other accolades.

To Steve, Mike, Ellie, Maddie, Billie and Lucas –

'May the world you inherit be more hopeful than the one I leave you, and may your moral compass ever seek true north' – Dad / Pa

My thanks also to Edmund Burke (1729 – 1797) and to Plato (BC 500) whose prescient philosophical warnings left us the following:

'The only thing necessary for evil to triumph is for good men to do nothing'

Edmund Burke

'The price of indifference to public affairs is to be ruled by evil men'

Plato

Bruce Nicholls

THE PLATO PROPHECY

AUSTIN MACAULEY PUBLISHERS™
LONDON • CAMBRIDGE • NEW YORK • SHARJAH

Copyright © Bruce Nicholls 2023

The right of Bruce Nicholls to be identified as author of this work has been asserted by the author in accordance with sections 77 and 78 of the Copyright, Designs and Patents Act 1988.

All rights reserved. No part of this publication may be reproduced, stored in a retrieval system, or transmitted in any form or by any means, electronic, mechanical, photocopying, recording, or otherwise, without the prior permission of the publishers.

Any person who commits any unauthorised act in relation to this publication may be liable to criminal prosecution and civil claims for damages.

A CIP catalogue record for this title is available from the British Library.

ISBN 9781035810529 (Paperback)
ISBN 9781035810536 (ePub e-book)

www.austinmacauley.com

First Published 2023
Austin Macauley Publishers Ltd®
1 Canada Square
Canary Wharf
London
E14 5AA

This book would not have been possible without the support and counsel of many people. Chief among them was my wife, Annie, whose unwavering support, advice and assistance was critical, as was her excellent editing of my superfluity - with the deftness of a former PR executive. Thank you darling.

To my special friend, the late Paul Barratt AO, former Australian Secretary of Defence, Secretary of Agriculture and Deputy Secretary of Trade who, at the time of writing, had lost his battle with a brain tumour... Paul, you were a giant amongst men, a wonderful friend, an inspiration and a mentor. Fifteen years ago, Paul joined me in forming the QUAFFERS Public Policy Forums (Quarterly Assembly of Fine Fellows, Epicureans & Raconteurs) with my other dear friend and deputy chairman, Rob Hobart. Their leadership, wise counsel and input into our policy deliberations have informed much of this book. I also recognise the many friends and colleagues who joined me in forming Quaffers' and marched with me towards a more civil discourse.

I particularly recognise the contribution of the late Charles Jamieson AO, former head of the Australian Trade Commission, the many guest speakers who informed our debates and are referenced in this work, the Royal Automobile Club of Victoria, for its wonderful hosting and support of our institution in its splendid halls, and my old friend, Dr David Cunneen, who gave me fearless advice and editorial suggestions.

Table of Contents

Prologue	12
Chapter 1: The Winds of Change	14
Chapter 2: A Sleeping Dragon Wakes	19
Chapter 3: Are We Sleepwalking into Disaster?	32
Chapter 4: A New World Order	39
Chapter 5: 'Lebensraum' and Territorial Ambition	46
Chapter 6: War and Peace	55
Chapter 7: What Happened to Lao Pengyou?	64
Chapter 8: China's 'Belt and Road'—a Roman idea	74
Chapter 9: Democratic Dysfunction—A New Malaise	79
Chapter 10: Is Democracy Dying?	86
Chapter 11: Democracy Versus Autocracy	98
Chapter 12: Re-Aligning a Troubled World	107
Chapter 13: Free Speech	113
Chapter 14: Political Correctness — "I Feel, So I Must Be Right"	133
Chapter 15: Could Democracy Use a Makeover?	144
Chapter 16: Public Policy and Public Order	150
Chapter 17: Without Policy Clothes, Democracy Walks Naked	158
Chapter 18: Can Policy Rise Above Politics?	164

Chapter 19: Toxic Language—Hate Speech, Virtue Signalling and
           Other Toxicity   168

Chapter 20: Money and Democracy   185

Chapter 21: 'Policy Flat-Earthers'   196

Chapter 22: Who Governs—Politicians or Bureaucrats?   204

Chapter 23: Fiscal Governance   210

Chapter 24: Can Democracy Prevail?   221

Chapter 25: Accountability—A Window into Democracy   227

Chapter 26: The Right to Vote   230

Chapter 27: Does Democracy Look the Same Everywhere …
           And Does It Speak with the Same Voice?   238

Chapter 28: Is a Democratic Person a Capitalist or Socialist?   244

Chapter 29: Welfare Versus Self-Reliance   252

Chapter 30: Reaching Across the Aisle   266

Chapter 31: Climate Change—A Case Study in Public Policy   271

Epilogue: The Year 2050   287

Annexure   297

The price of indifference to public affairs ... is to be ruled by evil men.
Plato 500 BC

Prologue

I *search for a lighthouse to guide my path and light my gloom. I find none. My trusty pilot, Western Leadership, is nowhere to be found. An eerie silence tells of an approaching storm but is interrupted momentarily by a clanking sound. It is the sound of the scales of justice, rattling and creaking on their hinges. The wind picks up, and Lady Justice's blindfold is blown from her eyes. It is replaced by a surgical mask, protecting her nostrils from the stench of democratic decay. A new mask covers her mouth and nose, gagging her speech and allowing only a muffled protest. She surveys a bleak landscape and spies another, distant set of scales, measuring the balance of power, which tilts to the east.*

Two large animals—a dragon with blazing eyes and a bear, stand tall, holding hammers and sickles and laughing at a group of western leaders, sprawled at their feet. Boris's buffoonery gives way to Trumpian tackiness and is soon eclipsed by Biden's befuddlement. Meanwhile, another person, Civil Discourse, wants to join in, but is savaged by the talons of political toxicity. His protests are censored by cyber police and politically correct storm-troopers. Voters, too, have been silenced, replaced by a new, cyber electorate with digital megaphones, who invade our information highways with their spin and impose their unedited swill upon us all. Where are the guardians of democracy? None can be found!

This bleak landscape is imaginary, but it could become real if we remain indifferent to the dysfunction which now threatens democracy, and which has compelled me to write this book. To balance its narrative, I have decided to write it standing on the shoulders of some philosophical giants, so their thoughts about democracy and freedom might guide my pen.

I chose Plato first, who said: *the price of indifference to public affairs is to be ruled by evil men.* Marcus Aurelius, Rome's great emperor and administrator next, who codified public policy, launched it as a science, and was kind enough to write down his thoughts for us. His splendid example taught generations of future leaders that public policy not only makes nations great but is essential to keep them so. I chose Voltaire, who said *I may not agree with you, but I defend to the death your right to a different view!* Then Abe Lincoln, who said democracy was *Government of the people, by the people and for the people*, followed by John Stuart Mill, who said democracy was *government with the moral authority of the people*. And finally, Confucius, who said: *When you plot revenge, be sure to dig two graves.* (If you speak with a toxic tongue and a dark heart, be very sure of your facts.)

Chapter 1
The Winds of Change

Democracy is two wolves and a lamb, voting what to eat for lunch.
Andrew Napolitano

Buffeted by the storm-winds of change, particularly by changes in the way we now communicate with each other, our democratic ship of state has arguably been blown off course and is sailing into unchartered waters. Our democratic institutions, too, which had their genesis in a different age and were tempered in a different furnace, are being sorely tested. The good ship *Democracy* is facing strong headwinds and listing dangerously, sometimes to port; sometimes to starboard, for want of a deep keel to keep it steady, upright and on course. Subtle dysfunctions are appearing—like cracks in a great ship's hull.

They include political toxicity, which reached new heights during the Trump Presidency, the rise of a vocal minority whose strident voices now instruct us how to think, speak and behave *correctly*, and a hailstorm of what I will call *democratic detritus*; discarded truth, fake news and unedited cyber commentary, which is poisoning our civil discourse. Democratic detritus and unedited cyber-swill now clog our information highways, and as democracy grapples with this emerging dysfunction, those nations with different values, like China, continue their relentless progress towards greater prominence in world affairs. Has democracy lost its ascendancy as a system of government?

It certainly appears to have lost its global leadership, and arguably its cohesion, as it struggles to address new challenges.

Where is the leadership which so resolutely defeated Hitler's Nazism and Japan's imperialism? We could use some of that! At the conclusion of World War II, when democracy had prevailed over evil, our democratic leaders paused to take stock. At pains to avoid the mistakes of Versailles, which had arguably caused the war, they began judging the vanquished in sober courts, like the one established for the purpose in Nuremberg, which so powerfully showcased the triumph of good over evil. Those western leaders stood in the smoke and rubble of a war-torn landscape and planned new institutions, to bring hope and order to a troubled world. They established global referees—the UN, the International Court of Justice, the WTO and others—to enforce a rules-based world order and regulate fairness across a vast, global domain, protecting everything from human rights to trade practices.

Where are today's champions of democracy ... leaders of that ilk determined to face down the challenges of these troubling times? They are nowhere to be found. Distracted and menaced by petty domestic issues, western leaders are busy at home, wrestling with politics that divide, rather than unite and failing to bring direction to our stumbling democratic world. The rise of China, the chaos of Brexit and a new isolationism imposed by the coronavirus have conspired to suck oxygen out of western leadership, creating a vacuum which China, Russia and others are delighted to fill. Meanwhile, the institutions which once provided a safe fundament for democracy appear to have lost their muscle, prompting many observers to question whether democracy is losing ground as a preferred system of government.

There is little doubt that democracy is struggling as it tries to make sense of the identity politics and petty obsessions which beset it. At this moment in history, democracy needs purpose, leadership and gravitas more desperately than ever. It may be time for men and women of good conscience to come together in a common cause, instead of allowing the present political toxicity to set them at each other's throats. To join hands across the political divide and face down a more insidious threat than that which offends our parochial political egos—the foreign forces which threaten democracy's very survival.

As it struggles against new headwinds, the good ship democracy groans. Its timbers shriek a cry for help, begging us to review its architecture, to deepen its keel and to set it back upon a steady course. In this fast-moving era, we may need to re-image the institutions and values that underpin democracy; not just the ballast which has always kept democracy upright—liberty and justice—but also the changing relationship between people and their rulers. Just as the English barons of old did, we subjects may need to become a little incensed. To rise-up, redefine and reshape the relationship between ourselves—we citizens—and our rulers. To make democracy 'fit for purpose' in a contemporary world.

We should do so, for history has shown us that democracy is not a rigid construct. It is, at best, a work in progress. Its longevity is fragile and, if it is to survive, its' structure must bend in strong headwinds and be supple enough to resume a sturdy shape. But if we hope to reform its present architecture, we must first understand its history and evolution.

An Uncertain Genesis, A Patchy History and A Clouded Future

A giant intellect once said … "Democracy will not last. It will create a culture of entitlement." Those prescient words were spoken some 2,500 years ago, in BC 500, by no less a figure than Plato. He may have been right, and his observation moves me to ask this: 'With what authority do we arrogantly assert that democracy is the best form of government?' It cannot be so. Rome was not a democracy, but its' Plutocracy was the most successful and longest serving continuum of government in history. Modern China, ruled by a central elite and buttressed by the blunt force of its military, seems to fit the ancient Roman model of government more closely. The rise and fall of Rome should remind us that great nations only persist when they are buttressed by military might (measured by a nation's defence budget, by its military technology and by the strength of its alliances).

When Athens fell, in BC 400, it arguably took 1,615 years before the flame of its small, nascent democracy—more like a local Shire Council—was reignited. That flame sputtered back to life in 1215, when angry men signed the Magna Carta, ensuring that "No man shall be seized or imprisoned except by the lawful judgement of his equals." Democracy doesn't always last, but its strong undercurrent flows like a persistent river and re-emerges, sometimes subtly, sometimes explosively like a geyser, to defeat tyranny and oppression. Public records show that democracy had a renaissance during the second half of the 20th century. According to the UK's 'Freedom House', in 1941 the world had just 11 democracies. By 2015, that number had grown to 123. But how many would pass John Stuart Mill's test? When Yeltsin and Gorbachev reshaped the Soviet Union, there was a brief sense of euphoria. The world held its breath, praying that Russia might finally join the democratic fold. Sadly, today's Russia, under Putin, looks more like Hitler's Germany. The absurd elections which pretend to choose Russia's leaders are emulated by many other, so-called democracies which are fakes. Whose ballots are directed by an influential, and usually corrupt elite. We should be proud of our Westminster system and of the close variants of it, but vigilant that they remain strong enough to withstand the winds of change.

The world's greatest and most influential exemplars of democracy and open government—Britain, France and the United States, were forged in the fires of oppression, uprising and social revolution, arguably beginning with Magna Carta, before traversing the battlefields and political bulwarks of the French Revolution, the War of Independence and other social upheavals. But not all democracies have had to endure such a bloody birth.

Australia's democracy, for example, emerged gently from the colonial loins of mother-England, when Western democracies were fewer in number and typically headed by a monarch or a president. Australia's democracy simply flowed, like an easy birth, without an epic struggle for freedom. Later, it took a huge loss of life on a distant cliff-face to give that young democracy a sense of its own identity. Like the young conscripts clinging to the cliffs of Gallipoli, Australians still cling to the ANZAC legend, forged in that bloody battle from its acts of heroism. This belies the fact that the Gallipoli campaign was a military disaster, concocted by British generals, who reputedly used Australian troops as cannon fodder.

Gallipoli may have given Australians a new sense of nationhood, but that sense came at a terrible price and was a shaky foundation for a fledgling democracy. Gallipoli was a foreign cause, not an Australian one, and Aussie troops marched to a British, not an Australian drum. With no independence struggle of its own, its bloodless transition from colonial serfdom to an independent democracy was unremarkable. Its constitution borrowed unashamedly from the British and US models, oblivious to the epic human struggles, historic battles and legal precedents which had so brutally shaped Britain's and America's democracies. Australia could choose the best of each without firing a single shot.

That experience demonstrates that democracy can evolve in many, different ways but is always shaped by the shifting sands of a dynamic world, which change beneath its feet. So, if our contemporary democracy is to survive its current buffeting, it must be a living one, able to bend and adjust to meet the times. It must always be a work in progress, always seeking answers to the perennial question: *"what constitutes good government?"* For good government is not just about maintaining social order. Any dictator can do that. In the final analysis, it is about guaranteeing a people's personal freedoms, personal happiness, and a safe environment for them to raise their children.

In that context, Magna Carta, rather than the Greeks, is the democratic fundament I turn to for guidance, for Magna Carta illuminated a dark world. It defined, for the first time, the relationship between a ruler and his subjects, the human rights of individuals, including the right to a fair trial and judgement by one's peers, the right to own property, and other indelible rights which survive as basic planks in our law. It follows that 'government by the will of the people' is only as good as the laws which underpin personal freedoms, elevate a society and encourage a nation's people to laugh, to dream, to hope and to aspire. Those things can only be delivered by rulers who place good public policy above self-interest.

While contemporary democracy struggles to rediscover itself, there is a new kid on the block who is not playing by our democratic rules. Not so much a kid, as a great dragon which has been roused from a deep sleep and whose hot breath we may soon feel! That dragon, China, has not always been so confident or so strident. Only four decades ago, it was emerging from a dark chapter in its history. Mao-suited comrades cycled through foetid streets and alleyways with a dull look of hopelessness in their eyes. A nation with one third of the world's population and enormous, latent potential had, for half a century, languished in the backwaters of global affairs, as foreign turmoil and cultural revolution took it backwards, killing science, learning and ambition and reducing its citizens to a drab oneness.

Our journey to understand how the world is changing, where that change is coming from and what it heralds, must therefore begin by revisiting the rise of China.

Chapter 2
A Sleeping Dragon Wakes

We choose to die on our feet rather than live on our knees.
Themistocles

On the morning of 1 July 2021, I woke to the sound of my bedside alarm, paddled into the kitchen, made a coffee and turned on the television. The ABC had promised live coverage of a major pageant in Beijing's Tiananmen Square, to mark the 100th anniversary of the founding of the Chinese Communist Party, and I had thought the event a spectacle worth watching. I had been told some 70,000 Chinese officials, carefully chosen guests and a display of military paraphernalia would be crammed into the square. Broadcasters from around the world—CNBC, the BBC, Deutsche Welle, NHK-Japan and others—had been invited to cover the event.

As one who had lived and worked in China, who spoke Mandarin, who had been emotionally invested in China's progress for over 40 years and who followed, sometimes with awe but increasingly with dismay, its rapid rise, I was consumed by a sense that I might witness a seminal moment in history, like the moment Neale Armstrong's boot made it's impression on the moon's surface, that would linger in the consciousness of a global audience for generations to come.

At 10 am Eastern Standard Time, Chinese President Xi Jinping alighted from a stately black *Hong qui*—a hand-built stretch limo reserved for China's leaders. Xi then mounted an impressive dais adorned with a nest of microphones and turned to face a carefully orchestrated display of might, arranged across the expansive stage before him. Military personnel stood sentinel-straight in sparkling white service-dress. Excited Chinese youths waved patriotic flags. A display of mobile missile launchers and military weaponry proclaimed China's arrival as a great power, and heroic banners—featuring comrades in Mao suits with hammers and sickles hung from towers—recalling the Communist party's humble, peasant roots.

A taciturn President Xi Jinping radiated gravitas and power, as his steely gaze traversed the surrounding spectacle. His choice of wardrobe—an immaculately tailored Mao suit—reminded the world that Mao Zedong, a peasant Emperor, had been the father of modern China, albeit one who had led a rag tag army of ill-equipped revolutionaries, as it retreated across rugged mountains in a bitter struggle to survive and live to fight another day. Mao's long march had cost many lives, and the cultural revolution which followed Mao's elevation to its first Chairman and head of state, had sadly seen China stagnate, for nearly 50 years.

Nonetheless, Mao had commenced another sort of long march—an ideological one, and his successors, from the first to open China's hitherto closed doors—Deng Xiaoping—through to Xi Jinping, had nourished Mao's fragile roots, nursed the fledgling communist state to adulthood, then boldly lifted millions of China's citizens out of poverty and dramatically repaired its historic loss of face. On this mid-summer's morning in Beijing, Xi's purpose quickly became apparent. His language was calculated to inspire a new nationalism and to warn a nervous global audience that China was back, was a superpower and was a force to reckon with.

"China will not accept sanctimonious preaching from those who feel they have the right to lecture us," said Xi, referring to the US, and "we would never allow any foreign force to bully China. Anyone attempting to do so would find themselves on a collision course with a great wall of steel, forged by over 1.4 billion people.

"The victory of our new democratic revolution has put an end to China's history as a semi-colonial, semi-feudal society, to the state of total disunity that existed in old China, and to all the unequal treaties imposed on our country by foreign powers and all the privileges that imperialist powers enjoyed in China. Through tenacious struggle, the Party and the Chinese people have shown the world that the Chinese people have stood up, and that the time in which the Chinese nation could be bullied and abused by others has gone forever. In the process, we overcame subversion, sabotage, and armed provocation by imperialist and hegemonic powers, and brought about the most extensive and profound social changes in the history of the Chinese nation.

"A century ago," he continued, "China was declining and withering away in the eyes of the world. Today, the image it presents to the world is one of a thriving nation, that is advancing with unstoppable momentum towards rejuvenation."

Xi then spoke generally about taking "strategic steps" towards securing the "second centenary goal":

"We will make sure the destiny of China's development and progress remains firmly in our own hands," he said, and explained that China's 'two centenary goals' were to "build a moderately prosperous society in all respects by 2021" and "to build a modern socialist country that is prosperous, strong, democratic, culturally advanced and harmonious" by 2049, the 100th anniversary of the People's Republic of China."

* Extracts of Xi's speech are given at Attachment 1, end of this book. Xi's grand plan for China included promoting high quality development, building strength in science and technology, modernising its military and training its personnel to world-class standards to ensure national security. In a speech which lasted over an hour, Xi related the history of Chinese Communism, but he conveniently neglected to mention darker chapters in its history, like the Cultural Revolution, or China's humiliation by British and other invaders during the Opium Wars. The humiliation which these had brought had left indelible hurt and offense in the Chinese consciousness, which was still palpable in Xi's China, and had left an indelible stain on British and western morality which could never be removed.

"The Communist Party and the Chinese people will move confidently forward in broad strides along the path that we have chosen," Xi said. *"We will make sure the destiny of China's development and progress remains firmly in our own hands."*

On the special administrative region of Hong Kong, Xi said China would *"ensure social stability",* and on Taiwan, that it would seek *"peaceful national reunification"* (a much gentler strategy than he had espoused just six months earlier, when he *"did not rule out reunification by force"*).

Xi's address was a bold statement, not just to his captive audience in Tiananmen Square, but to a global audience, putting them on notice that China, like its symbolic imperial dragon image, was on the move and would sweep aside all foreign interference in its affairs. As the West grappled with its own, internal and cross-border dysfunctions—with the coronavirus pandemic, with Brexit and with a growing US democratic malaise—the centre of global political gravity was shifting irrevocably from a Pan-European to an Asian-Pacific theatre, with an Indo-Pacific appendage. China was marching confidently, and relentlessly, forward while western democracies stumbled over the detritus of their own, internal political dysfunction.

The ceremony in Tiananmen Square was good theatre. Its' significance was made more poignant by China's increasingly terse diplomacy, and by the sudden rise of its massive naval, air and land-based forces—a development which rivalled Hitler's *guns or butter* strategy. Xi may have understated China's extraordinary economic miracle, but the world was acutely aware of it. It was on notice that the status quo had ended and that a new chapter—one of Chinese Empire—had begun.

The pomp and majesty of China's aspirations for a renewed empire were laid bare by Xi for all the world to see, in much the same way as ancient Chinese silks were displayed to foreign merchants from far off markets who once travelled China's ancient silk road in search of its treasures. Western observers were left in no doubt that China was on the move again. But the West remained divided about whether China's ambitions were likely to fan new winds of war or whether they could be 'managed', to allow a gentler assimilation of China into a rearranged world order—an order which China seemed to be planning, not just for itself, but for all of us.

After viewing the spectacle, I was persuaded that the West is, indeed, witnessing the evolution of a new world order and that the rise of a new, more adept autocratic power—an effective counterpuncher—will pit a demonstrably more effective system of government against democracy. Like the tectonic plates which rub beneath the earth's crust, these two different systems of government are bound to abrase and to generate heat and tectonic tension which must somehow find release. Hopefully, that will not be in the form of a global conflict, but only a naïve fool would rule that out. Is democracy ready for this contest? I doubt it.

In Defence of China

It would be churlish to make this narrative one-sided ... to ring alarm bells about the rise of China while forgiving Western hegemony and exploitation of China over past several centuries and make China's new assertiveness the greatest sin of all time. Guilt about the aggressive actions of one side or the other—the East or the West—over the past two centuries must be acknowledged honestly, not left hanging like a sword of Damocles over China's head alone. For there is much guilt to be apportioned and much of it on the western side of the balance sheet. I offer the following defence of China in the hope that it might encourage the search for a middle ground of reason, and a peaceful pathway to a new world order.

Any nation preferring civilisation over barbary, must first favour peaceful coexistence over conflict, stability over war, and respect for the cultures of others over xenophobia. A global contract, albeit an intrinsic rather than a written one, exists between all nations. Its clauses, express or implied, must reflect civilised values and safeguard each nation's right to its own sovereignty and to peaceful coexistence with others sharing our planet, whatever the respective systems of government. But utopian ideals like that usually disappoint when compared with reality. Life is not a dull, straight-line progression. It throws curve balls at us all the time and disappoints. But despite their utopian nature, one hopes that the following words, spoken in 1963 by U Thant, a Burmese diplomat and former Secretary General of the United Nations, might inspire all those whose moral compasses still point towards true north:

"I wonder if people ever pause to ask themselves this question: What is the alternative to peaceful coexistence?"

When U Thant spoke these words, atomic bombs were sufficiently developed to ensure the destruction of mankind, so the answer was too terrible to contemplate. Between 1945 and 1963, the United States and the USSR had conducted numerous tests in the atmosphere—the United States in places like the Marshall Islands, Britain at the Maralinga site in South Australia, about 800 kilometres north west of Adelaide, and the USSR, in the Novaia Zemlia archipelago, north of the Ural mountains. The severe environmental damage caused by these bombs, the most powerful ever to be exploded in the atmosphere, and the realisation that they were a monstrous blight that could end humanity, made international cooperation to eliminate nuclear testing essential. When U Thant spoke, he was remarking on a 1963 treaty banning nuclear weapons tests in all global environments—the Test Ban Treaty. Two key states—France and China—refused to sign. They continued their tests and continued to release their radioactive isotopes into the atmosphere.

The banning of tests back then was in the context of a cold war and the threat of a nuclear exchange between Russia and the United States. In the context of today's geopolitical realities, a different threat has evolved, in a different geopolitical theatre, Asia, or more correctly the Indo-Pacific, with China the main protagonist. How have we come to this, and how has China, once the bastion of Confucian pacifism and accord with nature, changed its philosophical face so profoundly?

In 2021, the population of Asia was 4.6 billion, representing an astonishing 59% of the world's 7.8 billion people. Mainland China's share of this was 1.45 billion, almost one quarter of our planet's human passengers. That proportion of humanity must surely command our attention, if not our cultural respect. Moreover, we must never forget China's magnificent historic contribution to human culture, to civilisation more generally and to man's knowledge (or technology). It is unmatched in the annals of history. The list of China's contributions still astounds me:

Paper; printing; lacquer; the wheelbarrow; the bell; the compass; the iron plough; the crossbow; bricks; the water wheel; the seismograph; the trace harness for horses and oxen, paper money; the cannon; the mechanical clock; rice cultivation; playing cards; the fishing reel; sericulture; fireworks, gunpowder; riding stirrups; dental amalgam; oil wells; the kite; the toothbrush; noodles (and arguably spaghetti, if it is true that Marco Polo took it back from China to Italy); petroleum as fuel; chopsticks and other eating implements; green tea; acupuncture; a range of medicines and surgical procedures, including inoculation; Zu qui (soccer); suspension bridges, soyabean meal, soy sauce, sails (to harness wind power at sea), stringed instruments (the Chinese lute); cast iron; toilet paper and surprisingly, since they didn't travel far abroad, the ship's rudder.

This summary, found in a recent research paper, was not exhaustive. It failed to mention other significant contributions. The writings of Chinese General Tsung Zu—whose '*Art of War*' remains prescribed reading in military academies all over the world, comes to mind. So, too, does Chinese opera, which dates back centuries, as does the university system of higher education, including the ancient requirement that one pass an exam at each level before ascending to the next level of learning. China has left a remarkable legacy for mankind, which we must forever respect.

China, Too, Can Aspire to Greatness

China has the same right as any nation to aspire to greatness. The same right as the ancient Romans had, the Macedonians under Alexander the Great, the British at the height of their empire, and the United States, at the zenith of its global influence. As nations rise, xenophobia towards them is a common reaction—simply a part of the human condition when people feel threatened. While the West must avoid the urge to imagine dark clouds on the horizon where none appear or to leap to the assumption that the rise of China is ominous for humanity, it must also be alert to a rising threat that China does not disguise in either its language or its ambition. A more generous response would be to celebrate, rather than fear a vibrant contribution by China to world affairs ... in technology, in the arts and sciences etc. and China's emergence from a dark chapter in its history. We should also be moved to celebrate the huge improvement in the human condition of its people.

Despite China's many achievements over the centuries, Xi Jinping was right about the previous dark periods in its history. For much of its history, China's people suffered poverty, serfdom and endless regional conflict, which plagued the lives of simple village dwellers. In pre-history, most Chinese people just wanted to get on with tilling their rice paddies, or with their lives as artisans, working on looms, in carpentry or blacksmithing. Those who were not court officials, or scholar gentry lived a subsistence life or were poorly remunerated foot soldiers. China's history has thus always been somewhat turbulent, with one province rising up against another in seething battles for domination during the *warring states* era. Back then, China lacked a vision of itself as a nation. Instead, it was a hotch-potch of tribal-cultures in search of a ruler to give it social cohesion and a national identity.

In feudal times, when leaders emerged, they invariably met a horrid fate at the hands of provincial pretenders to their throne—by assassination, fratricide, or bloody assault. Maintaining stable, central leadership has been a nightmare for successive Chinese rulers, almost for as long as China has existed. The geography of the country, with its steep, mountainous terrain, bisecting river systems, deserts, and language divides are largely to blame for this ancient, national fragmentation.

Most lay observers of the confident, modern Chinese state would be amazed to learn, for example, that it was only in 1913 that Mandarin was made a common language, to be taught in schools. For centuries prior to that, only educated administrators and court officials spoke Mandarin. Indeed, there were seven different language groups with hundreds of sub-dialects, most of which were not mutually intelligible. Paradoxically, it was the emergence of a common, external foe—a Western one—which caused China to mandate one, national language, reinforcing one, national identity and enabling it to come together as one nation.

Against this background, we must grudgingly acknowledge that Xi Jinping has built a strong government, albeit an autocratic one. I sympathise with any leader faced with the challenge of governing a disparate one and a half billion people—the equivalent of five United States' populations. What would any other leader do in Xi's shoes? Even rulers with democratic sensibilities might find it necessary to rule with an iron fist in a velvet glove, to prevent sectional interests from challenging national cohesion or anarchists from working to undermine national unity. In a nation like China, autocracy has a stronger claim in logic to legitimacy. But the confluence of an autocratic government with a new nationalism—a sense of pride and confidence, which is shared by most of the Chinese people—deserves closer analysis.

Humiliation as A Catalyst for Nationalism

As we consider the rise of China, the new nationalism which flowed so evidently in July 2021 from Xi Jinping's address to the world, and the 'wolf warrior' propaganda we hear from China's diplomats, we could be forgiven for feeling a sense of foreboding. These were hauntingly familiar in Germany under the rise of Hitler. And the reasons for a resurgence of nationalism in both nations are similar. Hitler's nationalism was a cry for revenge following the humiliation of Versailles, while China's is likely a cry for revenge following its humiliation by the West, which must linger like a festering sore in the consciousness of every literate Chinese. Any fair analysis of the western penetration of China must condemn the West's naked aggression and its flaunted opulence, so closely juxtaposed to China's desperately poor people, lurking in the streets and laneways outside extravagant western garden walls. No wonder communism was such a charismatic alternative. As Churchill said ... *"Those who fail to learn from history are doomed to repeat it:"*

Equally, any dispassionate analysis of the rise of Nazism will find that the dubious victors of WWI must forever carry a huge burden of responsibility for causing the next World War, which had its genesis in the way they hammered

Germany into ignominy with their brutal reparations. Under the Treaty of Versailles, Germany lost 13 % of its territory and 10 percent of its population. It was forced to concede Eupen-Malmédy to Belgium; the Hultschin district to Czechoslovakia; Poznan, West Prussia, and Upper Silesia to Poland and to return Alsace and Lorraine, annexed in 1871 after the Franco-Prussian War, to France. The Treaty called for demilitarisation and occupation of the Rhineland; special status for the Saarland under French control and referendums to determine the future of areas in northern Schleswig on the Danish-German frontier and parts of Upper Silesia on the border with Poland.

All German overseas colonies were taken from Germany and became *League of Nation Mandates*. Danzig (today's Gdansk), with its large ethnically German population, became a so-called *Free City*. But the most humiliating portion of the treaty for defeated Germany was Article 231, commonly known as the "War Guilt Clause." This clause forced the German nation to accept complete responsibility for starting World War I. As such, Germany was to be held liable for all material damages. That constituted a huge national loss of face—one which made every German rally to any half-reasonable voice promising to return their national pride and to reject outrageous financial reparations, which Germany could never hope to pay.

I cannot help drawing parallels between Germany's humiliation and the humiliation which was visited upon China during and after the Opium Wars, initially by British and European gunboats, and later, by the occupation of Western concessions in Shanghai, Tianjin, Chingdao and other coastal cities, compounded by a barbarous Japanese invasion, when soldiers raped pregnant women, pillaged, bayonetted and buried innocent men, women and children and visited unspeakable atrocities upon the people. In Chinese culture, losing face is much more than just being embarrassed. It is a subtle concept—one which is difficult for westerners to grasp. And Chinese memories are long, calibrated in centuries, not years.

Chinese people spend their entire lives trying to build—or rebuild—face. That is, social prestige and reputation. They also strive to avoid causing others to lose theirs. One does not gain face by individual achievement so much as by promoting social harmony and by being seen as a benevolent person. And there has always been a universal love of motherland—paralleling the German love of fatherland—innate in every Chinese person. We see that in the way overseas Chinese—in countries like Singapore and Australia—still feel a deep sense of attachment to their ancient homeland and culture. That is surely something to admire, but it is also the precondition for strong nationalism. And that national pride is growing stronger as China begins, again, to confidently stride an international stage.

But why, I ask, should China not aspire to global greatness? It has as much right to do so as any other nation …provided it does so peacefully. Considering the rise of China and its growing military might, I am persuaded that our path forward must be based upon agreement to coexist peacefully and with mutual respect. Our western diplomacy must be couched in careful language, not feisty or combative.

Mutual respect

Alas, the pugnacious rhetoric has almost entirely come from the Chinese government, rather than from the West. Consider the repeated efforts in 2020 by Australia's Trade Minister to seek a dialogue with his Chinese counterpart. They were all rebuffed, along with requests to visit, talk and resolve differences. Australia is being 'put in its place' as never before, as China emerges, like a dragon from its den, and projects its fiery breath towards those who dare to question its motives.

As if to confirm the reality of China's unnecessary belligerence towards it, and despite Australia's efforts to normalise relations, the Global Times—a mouthpiece of the Chinese Communist Party—threatened Australia with "retaliatory punishment" involving *"missile strikes on military facilities and relevant key facilities on Australian soil,"* if we send Australian Defence Force troops to assist the US in, participate in or support any war with the People's Liberation Army over Taiwan. This threat was specific. It was made by no less a person than the Global Times editor, Hu Xijin, on 7 May 2021, when he wrote: *"China has a strong production capability, including producing additional long-range missiles with conventional warheads that target military objectives in Australia, when the situation becomes highly tense."* In November 2021, the threat was repeated. In explosive comments published in the same Chinese tabloid, editor-in-chief Hu Xijin was blunt in his analysis of Australia's promise to come to Taiwan's aid should US allied forces get involved in the conflict.

'If Australian troops come to fight in the Taiwan Straits, it is unimaginable that China won't carry out a heavy attack on them and the Australian military facilities that support them,' Mr Xijin tweeted.

It is remarkable that such blatant threats were uttered and received so little attention in the Australian media. They signalled a complete lack of diplomacy and a reckless disregard for the relationship with Australia.

One particular phrase in the Global Times article was *"long-range missiles with conventional warheads."* China could hardly have been more specific about its threat (although even sophisticated intelligence cannot reliably detect the difference between an incoming missile with a conventional warhead and one with a nuclear warhead). This differentiation is made more difficult by the fact that China co-mingles conventional and nuclear warheads in its missile stockpile. Why the emphasis on conventional? Perhaps to reassure the US that China will not attack Australia with nuclear weapons, and thus prevent the US from deploying more nuclear, and conventional, resources into the Asia-Pacific, to honour its defence arrangements with Australia.

Beijing is not only being careless about its language around long-range missile strikes on Australian targets. It has clearly gone too far in describing what it terms *"relevant key facilities on Australian soil."* Understanding that puzzling statement will be critical to understanding the nature of any future conflict with Australia and whether a military escalation could be controlled. For example, taking out the joint US-Australian intelligence facility at Pine Gap might be seen in Washington as an attempt to blind America to actions in the Asia-Pacific theatre, to prevent any early warnings of deliberate nuclear escalation by Beijing.

If those on the left of Australian politics, who criticise Australia's defence of its democratic values, have not yet got the message, I suggest they read China's latest memo. It is contained in the words of Xi Jinping's address in Tiananmen Square and in the accompanying Global Times editorial. Wake up! Appeasement is fool's gold and China's newfound belligerence is not imaginary… it is real!

The US estimates that China will double its strategic nuclear forces in the short term. On 3 July 2021, the Weekend Australian reported that Beijing was building more than 100 new silos for intercontinental ballistic missiles in the northwest of the country. All this suggests movement away from a minimum nuclear deterrent force towards a potent one. By comparison, the US has 1500 deployed strategic nuclear warheads and another 5000 or so stockpiled or retired. (Russia has a similar number of strategic nuclear warheads totalling about 6800.)

However, Beijing has about 2000 theatre missiles capable of targeting much of the Indo-Pacific. Most of these are nuclear-armed but some of its conventionally armed missiles have already, for some time, been targeting the north of Australia.

Unless Australia urgently acquires long-range missiles, it will not be able to interdict, let alone retaliate against, any missile attack upon it by China. In any event, a country of Australia's size and population can neither contemplate retaliating against a large power such as China nor defending itself against a concerted Chinese attack, without US support. In the light of the growing verbal threats and harsh rhetoric directed at it from Beijing, Australia needs much clearer signals from its US ally about its commitment to providing both a nuclear and a conventional umbrella for Australia against China, and its willingness to interdict any Chinese long-range missile strike against Australia during the hiatus while it acquires a missile defence system, which it must.

It is imperative that Australia acquire such a system to defend it against the now public threat of ballistic missile attacks on strategic Australian targets. General Jim Molan said *"we should immediately fit anti-missile capability to our existing air warfare destroyers, but a nationwide capability needs a much more extensive missile defence system."*

In his speech marking the 100th anniversary of the Chinese Communist Party, Xi Jinping made the somewhat bizarre claim that China does not have "*an aggressive gene in its body*." However, a healthy cynic would not rely on those words. They are the words of a communist dictator and of a nation increasingly buoyed by strong nationalism… a nation determined to carve out a space for itself. To dominate and to do so with a swagger. As that swagger develops, Australia must depend more than ever before upon the US, our only superpower ally with the military capacity to deter China from its regional ambitions and to counter its recent threat to use ballistic missiles against us. While British and other early, colonial hegemons must accept responsibility for their abuse of China in the 19th and 20th centuries—a root cause of China's need to reassert itself as a nation, it is disappointing that modern Australians, who identify more closely with Asia and now include many people of Asian ethnicity, are tarred with the same colonial brush. Few Australians identify with earlier, more distant, European roots. Most now have Asian hearts and minds, if not also ethnicity, and are deeply invested in building peaceful relationships in their own region.

Australia and its' Asian neighbours have a right to defend their cultures and value systems, including free and open societies. China must respect that right, which is shared by all nations. But Australia can only defend its culture and values effectively by doing so in concert with its regional neighbours, particularly Japan and India. Treading carefully, ignoring the storm clouds to our north and uttering muted words of appeasement will neither mount an effective deterrence nor a defence.

As the balance of power shifts from West to East and nations calculate how to re-align, it seems possible that a polarity may evolve, such as Orwell's sinister novel portrayed, with Western and Eastern fields of influence. In such a divided world, India remains an enigma. Like China, it embraces 18% of the world's population, is a rising economy and has the potential to be a third sphere of influence. That makes a compelling case for India, the world's largest democracy, to be part of the western compact and a closely aligned friend in the new Indo-Pacific theatre.

Let us hope that democracy can withstand the forces rising against it and remain cognisant of the threat so eloquently defined by Julius Caesar, over two thousand years ago—'Divide and Conquer'—for that strategy still holds true. Its counterpart—'Unite and Defend', will surely serve democracy much better.

Chapter 3
Are We Sleepwalking into Disaster?

Peace is just an armistice in an endless war.
Thucydides 460-400 BC

In December 2020, as regional tensions in South-East. Asia increased, Senator Jim Molan, a former Major General in the Australian Army, expressed concern that Australia's trade war with China could escalate into a military conflict. Australia's relationship with the superpower had deteriorated rapidly following the Prime Minister's quite reasonable call for an inquiry into the origins of the coronavirus. China's response was adjudged by the entire western world to be unnecessarily belligerent, even preposterous. It not only told Australia to mind its own business, in ungraded language, but also demanded that Australia change its position on 14 of its policies, which China considered offensive. Then it slapped tariffs on, or cancelled, Australian exports of wine, barley, beef, coal and timber. Speaking on Australian television at the time, the former Major General said that he thought a war with China was now "more likely than is generally recognised" and urged the federal government to immediately "prepare for the worst-case scenario."

"China has been priming for war for a long time," he said. "It is threatening Taiwan every day of the week and regularly interferes in Japanese airspace. It has stolen the South China Sea, in breach of international rules and laws, and is picking fights with neighbours and others around the world. It now has extraordinary military capability, not just in rockets and aircraft but in overall capability to do things.

"They are primed for war, and America is also primed for war. This is a situation which is changing rapidly, and we have got to be prepared for the worst case. I am not saying it is inevitable, but we have got to be prepared," he added.

This view was branded 'alarmist' by the Australian Labor party and by liberal-socialists who, despite their noble intent, preferred a more passive response—even appeasement—over a straight-forward defence of Australia's right to manage its own affairs. Labor faithful routinely condemned the Prime Minister's firm diplomacy in response to China's belligerence. Indeed, the chorus of leftist sentiment almost rose to a defence of China's ludicrous position. How can China, or any foreign power, demand that a sovereign nation change its domestic policies? It seems axiomatic that a nation which is proud and free must defend its democratic values at any cost, else it betrays them. Vacillation on such naked interference in another nation's affairs is not a viable option but rather, creates a slippery slope from which the vacillator cannot escape. What choice was there? To quiver with indecision, sit on a metaphorical fence, appease, agree to China's log of claims, excuse its trade coercion, signal acquiescence? I think not! The answer was to seek a dialogue about the unlawful trade sanctions, a reasonable request which China rejected.

Prior to this troubling interference by China in Australia's domestic affairs, it is fair to say that fears about China's intentions in the Indo-Pacific were less obvious. It was not until September 2019, when something unexpected happened, that foreign policy experts sat up and took notice. In that month, at a reception in Beijing's Great Hall of the People, Filipino President Duterte surprised a world audience by announcing his country's *separation* from America and proclaimed a *future closer dependence on China*. In return for his switching allegiance, China promised Duterte some $24 billion worth of loans and investments.

High on Duterte's wish-list was a railway connecting Manila to development zones at Subic Bay and Clark Field, the former American air bases abandoned in the 1990s during a previous surge of Filipino nationalism. The long-standing and hitherto reliable post-war agreement between the US and the Philippines—to provide major naval anchorage to the American Pacific fleet—was put at risk, when Duterte fired these first shots, cancelling use of some port facilities by the US navy and offering them, ambiguously, to others, including Russia.

How short Duterte's memory must have been, or dull his recall of his nation's dark history? Had he forgotten the Japanese invasion and the unspeakable atrocities committed by Japanese troops, who threw Filipino babies into the air and caught them on bayonets? Had he forgotten that it was American troops whose rivers of blood rescued his nation from the occupying Japanese? The triumphant return of General MacArthur in 1944 to liberate the Philippines was the wellspring of an abiding affection between Filipinos and Americans. Indeed, seventy years on, the Philippines looks more like a 'little America', having adopted the English language, a US-styled system of government, and a love of fast food and Hollywood.

Duterte must have been aware of Chinese territorial ambitions in Asia and seen that a flashpoint for war lay barely 170 nautical miles from Corregidor—in the Scarborough Shoals (a big fishing ground, and a former bombing range for American and Filipino forces, the shoals were seized by China in 2012). If China were to build a military base there, as it has done in the nearby Spratly Islands, it would become a dagger in the heart of the Philippines. One would have hoped that the Filipino President understood that his nation's security was heavily dependent upon its alliance with the US. But Duterte saw it otherwise, gambling his nation's future and even using offensive language to make his point.

"The Philippines is not a US vassal, you son of a whore," he exclaimed, when questioned by a US journalist about his attacks on the drug trade, which had killed many innocent villagers and destroyed peaceful rural lives.

American use of the term '*Asian Pivot*' had once described movement of one third of its navy to the Philippines, to counter the rise of China. Duterte's use of the term had a more sinister connotation, exposing the soft underbelly of his ASEAN colleagues. Duterte's speech was made during a media frenzy over Trump's actions in the lead-up to the US election and as Boris Johnson's UK wrestled with the fallout from Brexit, so it passed unnoticed by the Australian and international media. It hardly raised an eyebrow.

But for General Jim Molan, it lent new poignancy to his warnings about an encroaching conflict. In his view, Chinese control of Scarborough Shoal, the emergence of a pro-China Filipino government, and the incidence of Chinese naval patrols pushing deeper into antipodean waters were a nasty cocktail (China was directing its spy ships to patrol deep into Australian waters to follow its naval movements and monitor its joint military exercises with US and other troops).

According to other, informed naval reports, while Chinese nuclear subs were 'a bit noisy', thanks to the deal with Duterte, they were now able to slip into the South Pacific, within missile range of both Australia and America. But why were we worried about new Chinese anchorages to Australia's near north? China already had a strong foothold, not just near but literally on Australian shores. It had leased marine ports in Darwin and New Guinea, and an airport, in Western Australia. Moreover, China's fingers of influence reached much more widely than many people realised.

On 15th August 2021, as the Taliban poured back into Kabul and recaptured the Presidential Palace, the world learned that China had, during the protracted conflict, been in negotiation with the Taliban government-in-exile, agreeing to provide assistance with infrastructure and reconstruction should they regain government! Russia was also in dialogue with the Taliban, despite the fact that both nations had appalling records of abuse of Muslims in their own countries. The Chinese overture looked like a clever 'Belt and Road' initiative, but it could have disastrous wider consequences for the West and for democracy in that region, should it succeed.

China's soft diplomacy is not the only chess piece in the global power play. Other, less subtle weapons have emerged in the new-age arsenal which exploit new technology. The digital age, for example, has opened frightening new military frontiers. Russia has elevated *cyber intrusion* to an art form and is using it as a new military and ideological weapon. When cyber intrusion is used to bend truth and shape public sentiment in an opponent's country, or to corrupt an election, that amounts to an insidious but effective act of war. We saw that in the lead up to the 2020 US election and when China posted a 'propaganda image'— a photo-shopped image of an Aussie soldier in Afghanistan, apparently slitting the throat of a child.

China has developed other, new military hardware. Consider these: A drone launcher capable of launching a flock of drones, like a flight of birds, which hovers for 15 minutes above a target before intelligently calculating the best line of attack. Each mini drone can separately enter a structure, through a chimney or window, and regroup inside the building to attack en masse. China is also said by the Indian government to have a military *microwave weapon* that can agitate human cells. In the dispute between India and China over the north Indian frontier, it accused China of having directed its new microwave beam weapon at Indian troops to agitate their human cells—to literally cook them—and force them off a high vantage point. If the report is true, this weapon would certainly be in breach of the Geneva convention.

If those things were not enough to rattle our western cages, what about the coronavirus? What if the conspiracy theorists are right about biological weapons research in Wuhan? On 8th May 2021, the US State Department revealed the contents of a report published in 2015 by People's Liberation Army scientists and Chinese health officials. In it, Chinese military scientists discussed the weaponization of a SARS-type coronaviruses five years before the coronavirus pandemic appeared, outlining their ideas in a document that predicted a third world war would be fought with biological weapons. Then, on 1 July 2021, China showcased its military might during celebrations marking the 100th anniversary of the Chinese Communist Party. This was the straw which broke the camel's back. Together, this display and the development of a new armoury of insidious weapons, combined to create a heightened sense of urgency about the rise of China, and a re-evaluation of the seriousness of the threat. It also prompted some clumsy and precipitous decision making about defence procurement.

On September 15th, 2021, Australia gave its anxiety about China a public face when it suddenly announced a new deal with the UK and the US to acquire nuclear submarines (albeit, subject to their being delivered some 20 years later). The decision was said to be justified by the radically changed threat environment. The news sent defence analysts scurrying back to their desks to see how the Australian decision changed the landscape. The consensus view of most commentators was that the deal was not about submarines or defence spending at all. It was symbolic.

The strategic merit—indeed the genius—of a revitalised US-UK-Australian alliance, under an aptly named AUKUS agreement, was that it drew the US back into the Indo-Pacific. That was a more powerful outcome than the nuclear subs, which will not appear until about 2040, albeit while discussions have started about leasing a couple of nuclear subs in the very near future to put teeth on the deal, provide training of mariners and allow operational integration with the US navy. The Indo-Pacific—a new 'grey-power' theatre which had been neglected by the west and where Australia had languished, naked and afraid, was back on the agenda, and renewed US interest in it must be celebrated.

In the face of these developments, the debate will inevitably return, again, to the size of spending on nuclear subs at a time when *corona-debt* has blown even the most conservative budgets out of the water. But I remain persuaded by the simple, unassailable, logic offered by former Secretary of Defence, Paul Barratt. For him, and for me, the public policy argument is clear, and should not be burdened by sophistry. It turns on the basic obligation of every democratic government to protect its citizens, their freedoms, and their way of life. Those things are not negotiable. In the final analysis, if we close our eyes to real, rather than imagined threats, we will sleep-walk into a disastrous conflict and risk losing our freedom—a price that is much too high to pay, for no one, not even a Treasurer, can place a dollar value on freedom.

Despite that clear public policy position, defence budgets can be quite precisely costed, and they should be, because they tell an important story. In 2016, China's defence spending was $146 billion, up 11% from $131 billion in 2014. That made China's military budget the second largest in the world, just behind the US. One cannot help but draw parallels with another period in history, when another apparently benign regime began ramping up its defence spending. Between 1933 and 1935, Hitler began rebuilding Germany's military. He kept his rearmament program secret because he knew the world would react to his violation of the Treaty of Versailles. China faces no constraint on its militarisation. Indeed, it is proudly publishing propaganda movies about its newfound military ascendancy.

By March 1935, Hitler's rearmament program was no longer secret. That year, he publicly proclaimed his intention to rebuild his air force, reinstate conscription, and to arm Germany to the teeth. At the same time, just as China has done, he assured world leaders that these were not *aggressive* but purely *defensive* measures. In a speech to the Reichstag, he said, "*The principal effect of war is to destroy the flower of a nation. Germany does not want this. It needs peace and desires peace. The German government will agree to any limitation which leads to abolition of the heaviest arms, especially those suited for aggression—the heaviest artillery and the heaviest tanks. Whoever lights the torch of war in Europe can wish for nothing but chaos.*"

Consider these words in the context of Xi Jinping's recent address to a huge rally in Tiananmen Square to mark the centenary of the Chinese Communist Party. "*China has not one aggressive gene in its DNA,*" he said, while simultaneously declaring that *China will not be lectured to by the west.* These words were spoken in front of a display of formidable Dongfeng missiles and other military hardware, as young Chinese in red costumes, reminiscent of 'Hitler Youth', danced and twirled banners featuring stars, hammers and sickles.

The mass rallies, metaphors and symbolism are hauntingly familiar, just as Xi's assurance that China has *not one aggressive gene in its DNA* is hauntingly familiar. It echoes Hitler's specious statement that *the principal effect of war is to destroy the flower of a nation ... and Germany does not want that*. Those words, uttered just before the invasion of Poland, fooled Chamberlain. Let not let Xi's words lull us into a similar, false sense of security and find us sleepwalking into disaster.

Chapter 4
A New World Order

Will a 'Blind Watchmaker' shape our future?
Who wins ... Democracy or Authoritarianism?

Can you guess who wrote these words? ... "If you want a vision for the future, imagine a boot stamping on your face... forever." Brutal words, aren't they? They were written in 1944, by George Orwell, as he began thinking about his next fiction, '1984'. His previous novel, 'Animal Farm', was an allegory of the events of the 1917 Russian Revolution. It dealt with freedom, rebellion and the corrupting nature of power, while '1984' explored a dystopian world, divided into 3 zones of influence. Orwell was inspired to write his 3-zone Sci-Fi by the *Tehran Conference of 1943*, where Churchill, Roosevelt and Stalin discussed the creation of a new world order and the need for a new body—an international policeman—to regulate global behaviour. That new body was the United Nations.

At the conference, the three world leaders effectively carved-up the world, into cake slices, rather than orbs of influence. Orwell's manuscript was originally to be called 'The last man in Europe'. Finally published as '1984', it was calculated to shock a global audience, jaded and disoriented by the horrors of war, into realising that there were real risks of a new world order which would be oppressive, rather than uplifting. Totalitarian, instead of free and democratic.

As we contemplate what the world might look like in 2050, it is easy to imagine three or four, Orwellian orbs, or hubs, constructed around emerging spheres of political influence. If that were to occur, it seems likely there would be a *European hub*, governed by a huge, supra-territorial institution—the European Union perhaps—an *Americas hub*, dominated by the United States, and an *Asian hub,* dominated by the new kid on the block—China. One might add a fourth— an *Islamic hub*—taking in the Middle East and Africa, but that geopolitical sphere is difficult to imagine as a unified geopolitical hub, since it would struggle to meld Islamic influences with dictatorships, corrupt pseudodemocratic entities and Sino-Russian ambitions.

This idea may seem fanciful, but in truth, the world has revolved around political hubs, or axes, since time in memorial. Take the post war period of reconstruction, for example. There is no doubt that the new world order which emerged from the chaos of World War II was shaped by the hands of men, rather than by fate. *'To the victors go the spoils'*, so the saying goes. In this case, those victors were Britain, the US and Russia, only two of whose three statesmen represented democracies. The third statesman, if one were to abuse that term so thoroughly, was a brutal dictator and murderer, whose legacy was the bloody purging of all of his political opponents in the 1930s. Churchill and Roosevelt must have choked on their words as they managed the distasteful task of negotiating with Stalin.

Despite their vastly different ideologies, the three men shared a common goal—that of bringing social order to a war-weary world, returning territories taken by the Nazis to their national owners, and restoring government to them. That, in turn, required agreement about how those nations should be governed. The kindest thing one can say about that process was that it mimicked a cartoon, published in 1801, depicting two buffoons, George III and Napoleon, wearing hats with plumes, carving up a giant turkey which symbolised the globe. For that is essentially how the chips fell for those living in Eastern Europe.

History was repeating itself. In 1937, Churchill had warned: "I cannot recall at any time when the gap between the kind of words which statesmen use and what is actually happening in many countries is so great as it is now. The habit of saying words to 'smooth things over' and uttering pious platitudes and sentiments to gain applause, without any relation to the underlying facts, is more pronounced now than it has ever been in my experience."

I hold that there are strong parallels with today's appeasers, who think China's rise harmless and rail at the Australian government's defence of its different, democratic values. It troubles me that some commentators call this defence of our values an incitement of the Chinese to anger. But let us return to the way Churchill, Roosevelt and Stalin carved up the globe. Even as Churchill continued his strained dialogue with Stalin, he concurrently warned the world that Russia was becoming a monster, when he said; "from Stettin in the Baltic to

Trieste in the Adriatic, an Iron Curtain has descended across a (whole) continent."

I believe we are at a similar crossroads—one like that which Churchill described in 1932. In 2020, as democracies reeled from the impacts of their domestic political dysfunction and a numbing, global coronavirus, making them increasingly introspective, China continued its relentless militarisation and was becoming increasingly assertive. Despite this worrying trend, I have great faith in the capacity of man, through his own agency, to shape a positive future. Under Trump, the US was so distracted that it ignored the geopolitical changes rumbling beneath its feet. However, Trump's successor, Joe Biden, initially surprised many with his assertive re-engagement, on behalf of democracy.

One of Biden's first tasks was to reassure NATO that the US was again in lockstep with it, both in its military commitment to it and in spirit. Then, in July 2021, Biden declared that Cuban communism was *a failed experiment*, after a meeting with German Chancellor Angela Merkel. The US and Europe's most powerful economic leaders had once again agreed to defend international law and democracy and, to signal that intention, had issued a veiled warning to Russia and China.

"Communism is a failed system—a universally failed system. And I don't see socialism as a very useful substitute, but that's another story," said Biden. a remarkable concession for a social democrat and one which seemed to favour not just freedom over authoritarianism, but also free-market capitalism over communism.

On her 23rd trip to the US, Chancellor Merkel signalled the determination of the free world to counter the growing power of an emerging 'authoritarian bloc', which seemed destined to challenge the rule of democracy as a preferred system of government. She did so by signing a *Washington Declaration* which committed the US and Germany, respectively the largest and fourth largest economies in the world, to preventing the emergence of "competing spheres of influence, be it through attempts at territorial annexation, control of digital infrastructure, transnational repression, or by weaponizing energy flows."

The two leaders set aside differences over the Nordstream pipeline, which will pipe Russian gas directly to Germany, and over patents for coronavirus vaccines, which the US would like waived. "We are united … that Russia must not be allowed to use energy as a weapon to coerce or threaten its neighbours," said Biden. Merkle added: "Let me be clear: The Ukraine must remain a (safe) transit country for natural gas." Biden and Merkel also talked about new areas of co-operation to counter and compete with the rise of China ... "be it in the economic area, on climate protection, in the military sector or on security," said Merkel. "And, obviously, there are a lot of challenges ahead." Were Sino-Russian ears listening in? You bet they were! Will those words resonate with them? That seems unlikely.

If, as I suspect, man will be the principal agent of his own, future destiny, we can be confident that the geopolitical events which are presently unfolding rapidly before us will send clear signals to help men and women of good conscience shape a positive new world order. All we need is some clever diplomacy, some clever deterrence, and some clever political scientists, untainted by ideological bias, to tell us what the world will look like in 2050. On the face of it, that sounds like a dawdle, but here is the rub. Where are these men and women of good conscience be found?

Can a new breed of western political leader rise above political vanities to direct a new, golden age of democracy, or will dictators, like Xi and Putin, who truck no dissent and silence their critics, prevail over western dysfunction? History teaches that it is rarely just the hand of man that shapes his destiny. Other forces are silently at work—the omnipotent hands of nature and of good and evil. They exert a parallel, sometimes greater influence and can turn the tide of events, like the metaphorical hands of a clock being set by a blind watchmaker.

Will Our Future Be Determined by A Blind Watchmaker?

'The Blind Watchmaker' is a book by Richard Dawkins which attempts to explain, and argue for, the theory of natural selection and to apply it to the rise and fall of nations. Dawkins presents arguments to refute criticisms of his first book, *The Selfish Gene*. Both books espouse the politically incorrect, gene-centric view of evolution as a catalyst for the strongest conquering the weakest, similar to the view on racial superiority expressed by Hitler. Dawkins' book channels the watchmaker analogy made famous in William Paley's 1802 book, *Natural Theology*, written 50 years before Charles Darwin's *Origin of Species*. Paley held that man could not direct his own destiny without the intervention of a divine power, which he seriously doubted existed, or the hand of nature. Dawkins said that he wrote the book "to persuade the reader, not that Darwin's world happens in practice, but that it is the only theory that adequately explains the mystery of our existence."

Hitler invoked a similar ideology to support his view that German's were a chosen race, with strong genes, and that weaker races, like the Jews, should be eliminated. These 'master race' ideas were abhorrent, but they unfortunately drew upon accepted science—Darwin's theory of natural selection. We should respect and fear the racist abuse of this science whenever it appears in the public discourse, as we might oppose a massive military power stalking a lesser one. Rome was able to impose its law and culture by dint of its superior military strength, and the same phenomenon has recurred throughout history. Potential exists for China to rise to empire. It is already a superpower. Should that rebirth of empire play out, we must hope that its leaders give it a beneficial face—rather than a malign, Orwellian one.

Hitler's rise and the rise of China have one thing in common—both were motivated by a strong, latent nationalism, born of a fervent need to avenge an earlier, national humiliation. In Hitler's case, it was Germany's humiliation at the hands of the Treaty of Versailles, which bankrupted a once proud nation. In China's case, it was the humiliation of a once great empire when, in June 1840, the British sailed up the mouth of the Canton River to fight the Opium Wars—a state-sponsored drug trade which reduced Chinese people to addiction and emaciation in Opium dens and saw the annexation by force of China's port cities along its eastern seaboard. China's capitulation in 1842, after Shanghai fell and Nanking cowered under British guns, was a final, brutal humiliation.

I believe a strong, silent undercurrent of resentment and recrimination still flows in the Chinese psyche; a desperate need, felt by many Chinese people, to restore China's loss of face and rebuild its national prestige. It should not be underestimated and is already manifest. It is the new Chinese nationalism so emphatically displayed by Xi Jinping in his 2021 address to the world, from a pulpit in Tiananmen Square, to mark the centenary of the Chinese Communist Party.

One hopes and expects that our future will see good triumph over evil, open and compassionate societies triumph over malign, autocratic ones, and free and open democracies triumph over closed, tightly controlled regimes. I suspect that those value differences will be the ideological battleground on which we must fight. Like a blind watchmaker, things beyond our control, like the coronavirus pandemic—will also likely have an influence as we navigate a path towards a new world order.

Shape Your Own Future, Or Someone Will Shape It for You!

When my pen reached this point, it seemed to pause and sigh. It had not run out of ink so much as courage. Shadows were now creeping across my page, like storm clouds, bringing a dull, but persistent sense of rising menace. I imagined the muted tones of war drums. Still reeling from the impact of the coronavirus on our lives, I saw families in face masks begging to be released from their living rooms. Their windows now had prison bars to protect them from new pandemics, yet to visit their shores. A new political, rather than medical disease—*Medical authoritarianism*—had infected our lives and dashed our hopes and dreams. Bureaucrats working to save our clinical lives had succeeded in destroying our spiritual ones. Streets and school playgrounds, which once rang with youthful exuberance, were now empty and silent. Where were the kids playing ball? Did they remember how to laugh?

I tried to look forward and imagined that chief medical officers have become camp-commandants, robbing us of freedoms won in ancient battles. That we voters were wringing our hands in frustration, confused about which side of this dysfunctional dichotomy, Labor or the Conservatives, we should vote for. Who, I asked, now represented us? Meanwhile, I saw governments robotically printing more bank notes and building a bonfire of debt which will one day have to be repaid. Nobody in government seemed to be defending our free and open society. In China, Russia and Cuba, however, authoritarian fists are raised in delight, as they watch our democratic dysfunction play out and seize the opportunity to press home any political advantage they have.

Would our grandchildren forgive us for stealing their youth, their school educations, their exuberant pursuit of school sports and their right to rebel? Or could their young, covid-misshapen lives still be rescued and replaced by a new age of hope, freedom and prosperity? I would not be around to find out, but I could not leave these thoughts hanging. They were weighty ones and demanded answers.

As a passionate student of history and one who prefers hard facts to conjecture, I have always tended to look back, not forward, in time. I incline towards history as a reliable source of knowledge, rather than speculate about what the future might hold. So, writing about the future is difficult for a man like me. It is not *informed* writing, nor can it offer *knowledge*. It is *science fiction*. It demands that the writer imagine a false reality, rather than record a truth. Despite these reservations, I decided to plough on, in search of information that might ease my malaise.

The first few paragraphs would be easy, I thought. My rapidly evolving world would either see democracy triumph over authoritarianism, or the reverse; a world in which the freedoms we take for granted—freedom of speech, movement and expression—were restricted. Could I hope for a world in which people still realised their hopes, dreams and aspirations, and were able to maximise their human potential, or would the hopes and dreams of future generations be dashed by state intervention and bureaucratic control. Those seemed like the only two possibilities.

As I reflected upon this, I realised it was too simplistic. There could be a third, darker outcome; a world divided into political zones of influence which competed with one another for domination—like the world George Orwell foresaw, way back in 1943, when he wrote his prescient novel, '1984'.

Chapter 5
'Lebensraum' and Territorial Ambition

Democracy, dignity and decency cannot survive overpopulation. The value of life declines until it doesn't matter...
Isaac Asimov

When one considers the many issues pressing upon mankind, and upon western democracy, it is easy to see individual problems in parenthesis and to overlook the fact that most of our present ills can be sheeted home to two, central issues—the way we have overpopulated our planet and our appetite for consuming everything on it! In June 2021, the global population was 7.9 billion. By 2100 it is forecast to be over 11 billion (although population growth peaked in the 1960s and will fall). Population will be the next, truly global crisis, with reduced fertile, or arable land, fewer temperate areas, insufficient potable water and dwindling or overstretched energy resources.

The 1927 Nobel Peace Prize went to French philosopher Henri Bergson, who warned a war-weary world, after the first world war, that Europe was *"overpopulated, the world will soon be, and if man's reproduction is not contained, we shall be at war again."* He was right. The next war was arguably about *Lebensraum* (room to live).

Overpopulation stretches a nation's resources, giving rise to resource-related territorial ambitions and creating fertile preconditions for war. The contest for control of critical resources, like food and water, and for fertile lands, stretches back to pre-history. This primeval need to access resources and win land (*lebensraum*) remains keen, and raises the possibility that China may, for the first time in its history, be looking with envy beyond its borders. There are reliable indicators of this. In 2016, China abandoned its crazy 'one-child' policy in favour of a 'two-child policy' (achieving zero population growth if the genders are balanced). Then, in 2021 its two-child policy was expanded to allow three children per family, signalling a return to positive population growth in the world's most populous nation (which, however, was short of women of breeding age, as a consequence of its crazy one child policy).

China already houses, feeds and clothes 1.45 billion people—one fifth of the world's total population. The switch to positive population growth now guarantees that it will expand beyond its resources, particularly of energy fuels and water. Commenting on this, Major Amit Bansal, a Defence Strategist with a keen interest in international affairs and maritime security, has warned the democratic world to resist China's claims over the South China Sea. He describes this maritime threat thus:

"Surrounded by 13 countries and deeply impacting dozens more, it is probably the most disputed place on earth today. It is the place which I foresee as the site and origin of the next world war. It is no ordinary waterbody. It is (the site of) a dirty show of Chinese Imperialism and expansionism."

Bansal is Indian, and thus biased against China, which has been disputing territory on his nation's northern border. But he has offered the following startling facts about the South China Sea which all nations, particularly Australia, should note:

- Over 60% of global maritime trade and 22% of total (air, land and sea) trade passes through this body of water. A whopping US$ 5.3 trillion in trade passes through it every year.
- 40% of the global petroleum products trade passes through it.
- 65% of China's total trade and 42% of Japan's passes through it.
- It is the economic lifeline of several major nations, who depend upon it.

The South China Sea stretches from the strait of Malacca to the straits of Taiwan and is now the most disputed area on the planet, after China annexed over 3,200 acres of land on various island groups and constructed five military bases on them, challenging the sovereignty of countries located close by. China's imaginary *Nine Dash line* claims the entire South China Sea, putting it in dispute not only with countries located close by, but with other global powers. According to the UN Convention on the Law of the Sea, the territorial boundaries of a country extend 12 nautical miles from its coast. The next 12 nautical miles is the area of so called contiguous (shared) waters. All nations follow this rule except China, which insists that the entire sea sits above the continental shelf of China and has been under its control for 2000 years. Thus, it says, *'the sea belongs to China'*—a spurious claim.

The ramping up by China of its air and naval capacity, its deployment of marine patrols much further afield, and its investments to secure critical resources (iron ore, coal etc.) for its industrial revolution and water, for intensive food and fibre production, lend further credibility to the sinister possibility that it is in search of space to expand into. Moreover, following a recent formal directive from Beijing, China's investments abroad in ports, power stations and other critical infrastructure facilities must now be *'capable of both military and civilian application'*. Together, these things begin to make credible the case for China's pursuit of a *'Lebensraum'* strategy.

China's access to resources could, of course, be achieved without attendant territorial ambition. After all, foreign investments and trade arrangements are just part of everyday, international affairs. But China has added the phenomenon of economic coercion, as evident from its recent exchanges with Australia, whose foreign policy offended China, resulting in the cancelation of commodity contracts. Moreover, the Chinese navy has begun patrolling the Indo-Pacific with a fleet of so-called *'spy ships'* and recently *'stood off'* to observe allied military exercises in northern Australia. While espionage is an ancient craft, and most nations are more or less guilty of it, China's ventures into extra-territorial waters and across invisible, global cyber boundaries appear to go beyond a benign interest in trade and investment.

In early September 2021, a Chinese Type 815 intelligence vessel, the *Tianwangxing* had to be shadowed by Australia's *HMAS Childers* and by surveillance aircraft as it approached Australian waters to eavesdrop on the 2021 *'Talisman Sabre'* war-games—a large-scale, simulated amphibious assault operation held in the north of Australia, involving the United States, Japan, Canada, South Korea, New Zealand and the United Kingdom. Should China harbour secret territorial ambitions, especially towards Australia, its most important supplier of raw materials, the consequences for the free world are dire and open dark pathways towards conflict.

Stretching Man's Global Resources

It is now abundantly clear, and has been for the past century that, by the unrestrained multiplication of his species, man has destroyed the balance of his own natural environment, infested his planetary nest and is now soiling it beyond comprehension. The consequences of man overpopulating his planet are arguably more dangerous to his survival, and more immediate than even climate change, which is intimately associated with it, and the trigger for a chain reaction of other critical problems. Despite this, man continues to reproduce in plague proportions. Most of our present and emerging global problems, be they climate change, food security, water security, energy security etc., can fairly be sheeted home to this single, causal factor—our having overpopulated our planet. And within our planet's population crucible, a molten flux is threatening to bubble over and burn us all.

Habitable Land

Nations like Bangladesh have already run out of dry, habitable land while other nations, like Australia and Canada, appear to have endless open space (Australia has just 2.2 people per square kilometre, compared with China's and Indonesia's 148 people per square kilometre). This apparently abundant space, however, is a 'Lebensraum' mirage, which has driven desperate people to escape poverty and military conflicts, and to risk life and limb by making illegal forays across mountains, deserts, and swirling river boundaries, and in tiny boats bobbing across boiling oceans, for more human-friendly environments. Who can blame them? As finite borders close in upon densely overpopulated nations, as their water and food resources dwindle and as death and pestilence visit them, we can be confident that the number of illegals, in trucks and on boats, will grow in size and desperation.

These facts make passion about climate change seem trite, since it fails to respect this greater challenge—people. They raise serious questions about our public policy response to nature and the way in which we allow climate politics to corrupt a broader interrogation of science and fact. Population policy is missing in the climate debate. In September 2021, the *World Population Clock* put the human population at 7.9 billion. Population policy must surely be central to all global policy considerations as its consequences impact so many subsidiary areas of policy, making it the largest existential threat to man's future survival, as the following graph makes crystal clear.

World Human Population: 10,000 BC—2021 AD

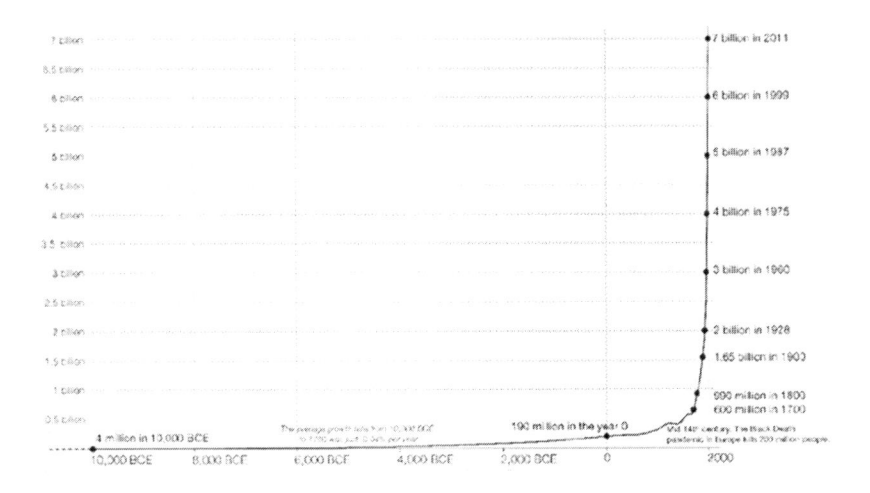

Source: Estimates by HYDE and the UN: Data available at OurWolrdData. org—Total at Sep. 2021 7.9 billion

When seen in this context, climate change is just one blip on our public policy radar amongst a miscellany of rapidly approaching crises we will all have to deal with in the immediate future (indeed, within a geological nanosecond). In Darwinian terms, we will have our hands full very soon, just surviving. How will that affect our geo-political landscape? Well, I suggest the immediate impacts are already evident—unfolding under our noses, as illegal immigrants and boat people crowd borders in the US, Europe and more distant nations, like New Zealand. As desperate people seek Lebensraum (room to live) they will challenge food, water and other resources across the globe. I conjecture that, while democracies will tend to respond to this new challenge with compassion and humanity, authoritarian states, who strictly control their populations, resources and borders, like Russia and China, may not.

Let us explore one example. For almost 20 years, Australia has permitted high immigration, and there has been no serious political challenge to that policy. Over that period, however, immigration has been a hugely political issue throughout the developed world, particularly in the UK and the US. Australia's Dr Bob Birrell thinks that will change. That the conditions which made *Big Australia*, *Big UK* and *Big USA* policies viable will no longer exist in the post-COVID world. Birrell thinks the risk of pandemic-induced recessions is too high and sees heightened political risks around the likelihood that new immigrants will take jobs away from nationals. Even in a post Covid world, the health risks associated with immigration will remain high and may add to a xenophobic resentment of immigrants on the part of those who see immigration as mocking the sacrifices they have made during the pandemic.

As the world begins to nuance its response to the coronavirus, searching for creative, new ways to respond to it, so too will the social contract between people and their rulers change. Indeed, despite its negative health consequences, the virus has already inspired both the best and the worst instincts in man. It has lifted innovation, created new rules around workplace practices, encouraged new business models, induced a preference for more regional and less capital city concentrations of population and reduced the need for expensive, high-rise office blocks.

Our clever western response to the Covid pandemic seems to have ushered in a new dawn of opportunity, for example, for exploiting the vast untapped potential of regional employment and decentralisation in countries like Australia. On the negative side, the retreat to a sort of cyber-autism in our communications, including the wearing of masks, social distancing and other barriers to warm interaction with our fellow citizens, has challenged another side of our nature, causing a generation of youth to adopt new emotional rules for human interaction which lack empathy. And just as overpopulation is set to challenge our democratic institutions, so too are other less obvious challenges.

Spoiling Our Planet—A New Frontier for Conflict

In March 2018, I was invited to join an old friend, Vaughan Wellington, in Fiji whence we would cruise together around the Pacific on his ocean yacht 'Viking'. We were joined by another mate from our university days, Geoff Wallace. Geoff and I were to provide gregarious companionship for Vaughan in his lonely task of measuring nanoparticles of plastic in our oceans and visiting island tourist resorts as a guest speaker, to tell guests about the scourge of ocean plastic. Wellington had been a successful businessman until tragically losing his wife, Jilly and becoming more philosophical about life and the universe. He swapped his business life and Saks suits for flip-flops, shorts and tee-shirts, undergoing a personal transformation to become an 'Attenborough of the oceans', trawling over the five 'Gyres', plastic vortexes, which swirl out of control in our five major oceans. These five 'Gyres' are islands of swirling plastic debris, almost the size of their neighbouring continents.

While I had always been a lover of nature, having spent time on a family farm, one could never call me a 'greenie' or even an environmentalist, desperate to save my planet. But my experiences on board 'Viking' with its Master, Vaughan Wellington, had an indelible impact on my social conscience and converted me, too, into something of an environmental warrior.

Invigorated by this experience, I persuaded Vaughan to fly back to Melbourne and be my guest speaker at our next public policy debate—to be entitled '*Ocean Plastics—the Tip of the Iceberg*'. The debate was held at the Royal Automobile Club, so Vaughan had to discard his shorts and tee-shirt and climb into a suit and tie, but his articulate address was riveting, alarming and a desperate call to action.

Vaughan explained that the plastic we produce every year weighs more than the combined weight of people on our planet. By 2050, in terms of its weight, there will be more plastic in the oceans than fish. Moreover, 80% of marine litter is plastic, with five trillion pieces of it floating about. Between 8 and 12 million tonnes of plastic enter our oceans every year, killing over 100,000 marine mammals and one million sea birds. Forty-six percent of this is comprised of plastic fishing nets and lines. A plastic drink bottle takes 450 years to break down and a fishing line 600 years. China is the worst offender, throwing five million tonnes per annum into its rivers, followed by the Philippines, Indonesia, Vietnam and Malaysia. No-one is responsible for cleaning it up, no one knows how to, and no nation regulates this environmental time bomb.

Wellington's audience was mesmerised by his disturbing presentation of these facts and by the enormity of the global challenge he outlined, which confronts all nations. It is already 5 seconds past midnight! Following his presentation, our Quaffers debaters explored a range of possible answers, and endorsed the following, global public policy initiatives:

- A bold, international policy response, shared by all nations, is required, right now.
- Governments must introduce laws which reduce or eliminate the use of plastic whenever other organic materials, like paper and cardboard, can replace them.

- Practical efforts should be focussed upon (dam-like) physical barriers and other engineering solutions to stop plastics getting from rivers into our oceans, and ...
- There must be a global push to identify smarter ways to collect and reuse plastic.

Germany is a world leader in this area, with clever solutions. They have positioned public collection cubicles strategically, into which plastic bottles and other plastic items may be deposited to earn a financial reward, via a coin return function. Street people, drug addicts etc. are thus recruited to the cause, collecting waste plastic from streets and gutters to claim their reward. We all agreed that the fastest pathway towards a solution was to make plastic collection and recycling more profitable, by this or other creative devices. Indeed, researchers now focus on this. Plastics can be combined with other aggregates to make brilliant road surfaces, cart paths for golf clubs and used in many other applications. '*Plasrock*', a New Zealand company, uses granulated plastic as a substitute for sand in concrete mixers. Other businesses are developing technologies to generate diesel and other fuels from plastics.

At the conclusion of Wellington's address, 'Quaffers' members called upon Governments around the world to seek global accord on recognising and responding to this huge challenge. They noted that political and legislative leadership was lacking. Global leadership could turn this threat to economic advantage whilst also removing this scourge from our oceans and from the marine food chain.

For most people, Wellington's address was about overpopulation and global pollution. For me, it was about '*Lebensraum*'. It evoked a sense of foreboding when I considered it in the context of the following words, written in 1925 by Adolf Hitler in his book Mein Kampf:

"Germany must find the courage to gather our people and their strength for an advance along the road that will lead the German people from their present restricted living space to new land and soil, and hence also free Germany from the danger of vanishing from the earth or of serving others as a slave nation. It is ... in the acquisition of a territory for settlement, which will enhance the area of the mother country, and hence not only keep the new settlers in the most intimate

community with the land, but secure for the total area those advantages which lie in its unified magnitude."

It was this logic—Lebensraum—which Hitler used to plan for and justify his invasion of Poland and other territorial ambitions, laced with a generous dose of racism—a belief that his Germanic stock deserved better than other, lesser races.

In the final analysis, my prize for the largest existential threat goes to overpopulating our planet, not to climate change or environmental pollution. These threats are subsidiary to the ultimate and likely event that territorial ambitions will spark wars over essential raw materials and resources. Western democracies will respect the sovereignty of other nations and the voices of young climate warriors, like Greta Thunberg, will continue to be heard in them. But in nations like China, which recently endorsed a new, 'three-child policy', returning it to positive population growth, those voices will likely be muted, as China hunts for new resources and *Lebensraum* to accommodate its bourgeoning population.

Chapter 6
War and Peace

In peace, sons bury their fathers. In war, fathers bury their sons.
Herodotus, 400 BC

When one talks about threats to democracy and the rise of authoritarian regimes, like China, one is inevitably drawn into two strategic discussion—one about defence and the other, about military alliances. These are central to the ability of democracies to defend themselves and the life and liberty of their people. As Churchill famously pointed out, and as those who trembled before Napoleon's and Hitler's forces soon learned, preparing for war is costly but being unprepared is much costlier. It is playing Russian Roulette with the lives of your citizens and robbing them, their children and their grandchildren of their futures.

The rise and fall of nations, even Hitler's short-lived 3rd Reich, demonstrates that nations which become powerful first acquire substantial military might to wrest that power from others and then require a sustained military superiority to hold onto that power. History also teaches that even great empires can be overthrown when opposing forces are able to combine their military capacity, through military alliances, to raise a superior opposing force. The rise of China, controversy surrounding Australia's continuing reliance upon an outdated ANZUS alliance and decisions around defence spending, including the French submarine contract, persuaded the Melbourne-based policy forum—*Quaffers*—to explore the challenge democracies face in determining appropriate levels of defence spending, and the role strategic alliances play in defending democracy.

How Much Should We Spend Defending Democracy?

The fist Quaffers policy forum into Australia's defence spending was held in 2015. At that time, Australia's relationship with China was becoming more fragile, but was still civilised and not nearly as fragile as it has become. The forum explored the appropriate level and direction of defence spending for Australia and was led by former Secretary of Defence, Paul Barratt, who addressed three simple questions:

- Is defence spending essential?
- What is the appropriate level of spending for Australia?
- What is the opportunity cost to a nation of a defence budget (i.e., what benefits might taxpayers receive if defence spending went to other portfolios)?

Barratt opened by observing that … "Wars are expensive but losing them is not an option, because a government's first responsibility is to preserve its national sovereignty and the life, well-being and freedom of its people. That makes alternative spending options an exercise in futility.

"Secondly," he said, "spending should be needs-based, not driven by artificial benchmarks, like 2% of GDP." To determine levels of spending we should first decide what we want to achieve. For example, if it is to control the sea and air space to Australia's north, one might argue that our defence spending should be wholly directed at that single outcome, not on adventures in the Middle East.

"Thirdly," said Barratt, "a nation should never go to war without the imprimatur of a Parliament. The simple exercise of executive privilege by a Prime Minister, as is presently the case in Australia, lacks moral authority."

If we concede that politicians can exploit xenophobia as an electoral lever, we must also make war decisions transparent to avoid blatant politicisation of threats, (as in General MacArthur's *Reds under the Bed* and Menzies' *Yellow Peril* campaigns of the mid-twentieth century). Colonel Jock Burns, a Vietnam veteran, made a very fine point. He questioned why we use confected terms, like 'Ministry of Defence', when we really mean 'Ministry of War'. He raised the controversial idea of a 'Ministry of Peace', mandated to focus first upon non-combative solutions to global problems. He also thought women would make better generals than men, since they are not given to testosterone-fed machismo or macho flights of fancy. But we agreed that no democratic government should ever abrogate the contract between itself and its citizens that requires it to guarantee their liberty and national sovereignty. The forum observed that neither hardware salesmen (defence manufacturers or contractors, with a pecuniary interest), nor politicians with an electoral conflict (as some assert Defence Minister Christopher Pine had when he decided to place the submarine contract and supporting industry in South Australia), could be trusted to get the settings right. Defence spending requires an independent, impartial assessment. Moreover, spending decisions should be prescient and timely, not made after the horse has bolted. Such decisions are already complicated by the lead times required to acquire and commission new hardware, and to retrofit aging hardware. Time lags and technical advances conspire to make new hardware redundant, even before it is delivered.

The decisions to buy IFVs (infantry fighting vehicles) for Middle Eastern theatres and nuclear subs, which will not be delivered until 2040, are examples of *rear-window* rather than *prescient* defence procurement. The same, massive budgets might have financed 'just-in-time' military assets, to be deployed now, and closer to home. Drones or missile defence systems. Australia's decision to build nuclear submarines, while it had symbolic merit, was highly controversial and begged the question what that A$ 90 billion might have purchased in *off-the-shelf* hardware; for example, missile defence systems which could be deployed right now, to meet current, rather than future threats.

Moreover, defence technology is fast-moving and has lots of moving parts. The Melbourne forum noted that Putin claimed to have "*a new, super weapon, making all conventional weapons redundant.*" (An electro-magnetic pulse weapon perhaps?). The US has established a '*Space Force*', creating a new battle front and sparking a military space-race. Cyber threats have added another complexity. A cyber-attack on US financial and capital markets would wreak global havoc, making it a new battle front. 'Soft diplomacy', used by China to coerce or build economic dependence, is another battle front, and has the free world wondering how to counter this clever strategy.

The forum observed that, since the time of legendary Chinese General Sun Tzu (554-496 BC), alliances have been central to every nation's defence. But Australia's reliance on the US has become problematic in this new age, as it puts Australia uncomfortably at odds with China and gives them ground to assert that we are simply US lapdogs. Compared with spending on military hardware, the cost of negotiating more contemporary alliances is small, since it is covered by existing diplomacy / international relations budgets. Diplomacy must thus be a first line strategy and spending decisions guided by inputs from foreign affairs, defence, and treasury, so that geopolitical and economic considerations moderate a purely militaristic assessment.

The forum identified growing tension in balancing Australia's relationships with China and the US and observed that the new, geo-political landscape had altered the nature of the ANZUS pact. In the brave new Indo-Pacific theatre in which Australia now has to live and operate, miles from the *Anglosphere* and *Eurosphere*, I suggested it was time that we buttressed ANZUS with more contemporary treaties. I recommended a JAPINDA Pact (Japan, India and Indonesia), to rebalance Australia's interests and counter growing Chinese military and economic influence in our region. The government has since accepted that logic and is now building those additional alliances.

There is compelling logic in having India in the tent, not only to expand Australia's defence alliance with a nation having one of the largest peace-time armies in the world, but also to diversify our trade relationship. It also makes huge sense to align with another parliamentary democracy with an English language heritage, and a nation with a love of cricket, cultural and immigration ties with Australia and one which shares Australia's concern about the Chinese threat.

At its conclusion, the Melbourne forum on defence agreed that, even with ambitious defence spending, Australia would be a minnow in any serious stoush. It also found that 'those who dance with elephants get trampled'. Australia would prefer to have China as a friend, but at what cost to its sovereignty and to its democratic freedoms?

By September 2021 the debate had shifted again. It now raged around Australia's deal with the US and the UK to acquire nuclear subs and had barely digested an incredible public announcement by China, in August 2021, that it had targeted its ICBMs at key strategic sites in Australia. This had made urgent the need for rapid development and deployment of early warning and missile defence systems. On the positive side, as Chinese spy vessels patrolled Australian waters to monitor war games in Australia's north, it was reassuring that those war games included, for the first time, the firing of US Patriot missiles, costing over $1 million each. These are fired sparingly but were fired on this occasion to demonstrate to China the potency of the patriot's defence capability. (Australia is negotiating a missile cooperation arrangement with the US, with a view to ramping up this critical, missing element in Australia's defence capability).

How quickly the Indo-Pacific theatre is changing! How subtle the sands are shifting beneath out feet! How quickly the distance between Australia, a remote island continent, and China has closed and how much more likely it is that Australia may soon hear the rumbling sounds of war drums over its northern horizon!

Sleepwalking into that disaster is not an option. Instead, Australia and its western allies need to make a sober reassessment of the rapidly emerging risks and commit to ramping up both their alliances and their defence readiness.

The New 'Grey Zone'

Three quarters of a century have elapsed since the last global conflict. We are fortunate that, over that time, a coalition of western democracies, led by the US, has kept us safe. However, all that may be about to change. It is now clear that we are witnessing a fundamental shift in global power—one which is diluting the combined power of western democracies, as China and other autocracies increase their power and re-align their forces. Russia recently signed an agreement with China aligning the nations militarily in any regional conflict. An important third player, India, also entered the fray, rebalancing its global alliances by seeking new alignments in the Indo-Pacific, including with Japan and Australia. This reflected China's incursions on its northern border and ambiguity about future US leadership of the free world. The last major global conflict demonstrated that a coalition of democracies (the Allies) can prevail against a rogue power (Hitler's Germany) or a coalition of malign forces (the Axis powers). NATO is based upon that strategy and remains critical to the deterrence of aggression and defence of democracy. But, in the face of America's messy withdrawal from Afghanistan and its earlier criticisms of NATO, new questions arise about who should lead, who should do the heavy military lifting, and who should pay the hefty bills for a western defence pf democracy?

Australia stills considers a strong alliance with the US essential to counter the rise of China. There is no other viable policy setting for Australia, since there is no other nation with a sufficient military deterrence to counter any regional ambitions threatening the isolated island continent. Informed observers agree that the ANZUS alliance remains critical, and that view is daily reinforced by

China's recent, crude diplomacy, its growing military expansion and its use of economic coercion as a tool of geo-political influence, now being referred to by experts as *'grey zone influence'*.

The term *'grey-zone'* is a new term and is defined by the *'US Operations Command'* as *"competitive interactions among and within state and nonstate actors that fall between the traditional duality of war and peace."* The *'Centre for Strategic and International Studies'* defines the grey-zone better, as *"the contested arena between routine statecraft and open warfare."*

The rise of China and, more generally, of the command economies, is transparently reshaping our world. Despite this, the defence and security postures of the West, over the past decade, have been stumbling at best, uncertain at worst, and have favoured appeasement, rather than the resolve needed to deter a rising threat to democracy. Domestic political distractions, particularly in the US and Europe, over the 2018-2020 period may be partly to blame, but the West's slow response also reflects the relatively rapid emergence of China as a major new global player, uncertainty on the part of the free world about China's true intentions, and confused thinking how the West should respond if China's intentions are malign.

Many on the left of Australian politics, albeit with noble sentiments, since they prefer pacific language to war-like vitriol, have been strident critics of the conservative Morrison government's management of our relationship with China, largely because of its unswerving defence of our democratic values. The Morrison government describes these as *non-negotiable*. Apart from calm Australian rhetoric around respecting each other's different values, it seems to me that most of the vitriol has come from China. Indeed, some of China's most undiplomatic language has come from its Deputy Head of Mission in Canberra who, as a senior diplomat, is supposed to smooth things with soothing, not confronting language.

If there were any doubt about who was doing the abusing, a cartoon published on 15th June 2021 removed any doubt. In it, China used language and symbols which pilloried Australia and arguably ushered in not just a new cold front, but a chill in the relationship, as China condemned Australia's association with the G7. Just as western leaders prepared to meet at the G7, and thereafter, at a NATO summit a controversial cartoon appeared in the Chinese media. It reflected China's disdain for the G7 (and the broader western alliance) because they had demanded transparency from Beijing about, and a fresh investigation into, the origins of the coronavirus pandemic. *The Global Times*, the mouthpiece of the Chinese Communist Party, published and promoted the cartoon, which depicted G7 leaders, as well as Japan, South Korea and Australia, as animals seated at a biblical *'Last supper'*.

The cartoon was insensitive to western Judeo-Christian values, since it mimicked da Vinci's *'Last Supper'* image, replacing Jesus' and his disciples with animals representing the US, the UK, Italy, Canada, Japan, Germany, France, Australia and India. Australia was represented by a kangaroo, the US by a bald eagle, the UK by a lion, Canada by a beaver, France by a rooster, India by an elephant, Italy by a wolf, Japan by a Shiba Innu dog and Germany by a black hawk. Other elements of the cartoon included US dollars being printed on a roll of toilet paper, a cake printed with a map of China and Japan's dog pouring green liquid into everyone's cups from a kettle marked with a radioactive warning symbol. But it was not so much the brilliantly executed cartoon that offended. We in the West love cartoons and appreciate their use as satirical devices, to make a political point. They are a treasured part of our free speech. No, it was not so much the cartoon as the words which supported it. *"Sitting next to the dog is a kangaroo, which is stretching its left hand to the bank notes the US is printing, while grasping a bag in its right hand,"* the Global Times explained. *"The kangaroo symbolises the double-faced Australia which actively cooperates with the US in containing China, but is also eager to earn money from China, its largest trading partner."*

The article also quoted a Chinese *vlogger* saying that the eagle depicts the US *"trapped in its growing debt crisis and racial conflicts, but still pointing fingers at China."* It went on to claim that the wolf waving its hands showed Italy's reluctance to collaborate with the US against China and the green drink being poured by Japan was the *"contaminated water the country planned to release into the Pacific from the destroyed Fukushima nuclear plant."* Since they appeared in an official publication, these slurs were brazened, and they breached all standards of diplomatic protocol.

China was also unhappy that newly elected US President, Jo Biden, had assured NATO that the US 'was back in town' and would return the relationship to one of close cooperation with it. NATO Secretary General, Jens Stoltenberg, also boosted morale by welcoming America's new commitment. He cited China's growing military presence everywhere from the Baltics to Africa as an indication that NATO had to be prepared to defend Western security and democratic values, warning *"China is coming closer to us. We see them in cyber space. We see China in Africa, and we see China investing heavily in our own critical infrastructure,"*—a reference to China's investments in ports and telecoms. *"We need to respond together."*

Since that encouraging remark from Stoltenberg, however, France's Emanuel Macron has backed away from anti-China rhetoric saying "NATO is a North Atlantic organisation. Nothing to do with China. Germany's Angela Merkel has said Europe needs to tread carefully with China, because while there are important ideological differences with China there are also important trade and economic dependencies.

One must applaud those who genuinely desire peace and thus adopt an appeasement approach towards China—but in my view, they are naïve at best, or apologists who place economic self-interest above principle. They underestimate the threat—ideological and military—that China poses to democracy. That ideological difference was showcased in the insensitive cartoon depicting the western alliance as a last supper. The fact that NATO is a remote observer and is focussed upon the North Atlantic, leaves Australia feeling truly isolated. Australia's proximity to the threat lends urgency to its need for new alliances to buttress its geopolitical isolation and for new technology to meet China's new regional missile and naval mobility.

On 15th September 2021, in answer to that need, Australia made an historic decision to invest in US nuclear-powered submarines and dump its contract with France for diesel-electric submarines. Prime Minister Scott Morrison said this was because of a radically changed strategic environment. Informed defence experts agreed with him. US President Joe Biden confirmed the announced and added that, under a new US security alliance with Australia and Britain, the three would develop an Australian nuclear-powered submarine fleet. Australia had already spent A$ 2.4 billion on the French sub project since 2016, but costs had blown out from $50 billion to $90 billion and delivery delays were becoming intolerable.

Morrison explained that the US nuclear submarine wasn't previously an option for Australia because the US had only shared the technology with Britain. That had changed (inferring *'because of China'*). Conventional submarine capability would no longer address Australia's strategic security needs in the Indo-Pacific. Conventional subs have to spend time on the surface, where they are vulnerable.

Zhao Lijian, from China's Ministry of Foreign Affairs, immediately labelled the deal an "irresponsible act" which raised questions about Australia's commitment to the non-proliferation. He said it "severely damaged regional peace and stability, intensified the arms race, and jeopardised efforts to promote non-proliferation." China said the AUKUS alliance was part of a "Cold War mentality by the UK and its allies."

These statements were a bit rich coming from the fastest proliferator of weapons on the planet. Indeed, it was China's bellicose language and actions which precipitated the change in the strategic environment in the Indo-Pacific. Predictably, while Labor used careful language in support of the deal (under bipartisan arrangements around foreign policy), it was critical of lots of elements, like cost and timing. One satirical article said… 'The Chinese must be terrified by this deal, but they will all be grey when it is realised, in 38 years' time!'. But that comment completely missed the point. The type of sub was not really important. What mattered was the symbolism of the US-UK-Australia alliance, which drew the US and the UK more forcefully into alignment with Australia and more, importantly, drew them into the Indo-Pacific theatre, which had been largely overlook by western powers.

Despite this necessarily negative analysis, I remain hopeful that China's leaders, with the help of its gentle people, can find a pathway to enlightened détente with democracy and replace the angst in our presently troubled relationship with new hope. That may be a bridge too far. However, I remain deeply philosophical about China, having made it such a large part of my life. My children, my grandchildren, and many of my readers will find it hard to believe that there was a time, which I recall with great fondness, when the relationship with China rang with laughter and was based upon hope, friendship and cooperation. Let me tell you about that time.

Chapter 7
What Happened to Lao Pengyou?

True friends stab you in the front.
Oscar Wilde

The term *Lao Pengyou* (*old friends*) was once exchanged with undisguised sincerity and exaggerated zeal following Australian Prime Minister Gough Whitlam visited China in 1971, ending China's diplomatic isolation. It gained wider use in 1978, when Deng Xiaoping announced his '*Open Door*' policy, a strategy for re-engagement with the west. But the term was arguably first directed at Australians, and their business, sporting and cultural associates before it was used more liberally with other foreigners slower to enter the fray. Whitlam's friendship visit to China in 1971 had signalled to an incredulous world that Australia planned to be the first western nation to break from the pack and recognise mainland China—to close its Taipei embassy and move it to Beijing. America's then Secretary of State Kissinger was wrongfooted by Australia's daring move, and was soon hot on Whitlam's trail, negotiating recognition on behalf of the US, which Nixon later announced.

Australia was the global pathfinding in commencing a new, western dialogue with China, after its many years of diplomatic isolation, and the principal catalyst for China's acceptance back into the global community. Back then, we became great mates! In 1980, I flew into a very drab Beijing airport to take up my posting as Trade Commissioner to China. As I walked through the terminal, Chinese service personal—Mao-suited functionaries unaccustomed to either *wei guo mo gui* (foreign devils) or any concept of service delivery—were picking their teeth or asleep. Despite the drab indifference of these comrades, I was soon greeted with much enthusiasm by officials, who used the terms Youyi (friendship) and *Lao Pengyou* (old friend) liberally, as Australia and China began a new journey of close partnership.

Since the elevation of Xi Jinping, however, the term *Lao Pengyou* has almost vanished from China's vernacular, not just in its exchanges with Australia, but with other western nations, too, including the US, UK, Canada and others. Tensions with Australia have scaled new heights and this deterioration signals a massive, unimaginable change in attitude, compared with the special standing Australia once enjoyed. Indeed, shortly after my arrival in Beijing, Australia, Canada and New Zealand were declared *'category 1 western friends'*. Those of us who pioneered that close relationship are bemused by the extraordinary change in the relationship that has since occurred. I am lost for answers. It seems that superpower tensions and a silly virus—rather than strong ideology differences—are to blame. How can that be?

Most rational people would accept that major global disasters demand a global response. When, in early 2020, the coronavirus swept the globe, voices around the world began asking *'how could this happen'*? *'Was it inevitable in an over-populated world ...was it just another chapter in our planetary fate?'* Whether it was accidental or man-made, it was a global calamity, like an earthquake or a tsunami, and it was important to ask: *'Where did this come from?'* The world deserved answers if it were to prevent such a calamity happening again.

Most of us responded with humanity and compassion, rather than looking to apportion blame, but the pandemic had brought the world to its knees, causing economic and social havoc, so it was natural that some wanted answers. Instead of finding answers, Australian Prime Minister, Scott Morrison was rebuked when he called for an inquiry to establish how and whence the virus had appeared, so that the world might understand what steps to take to ensure that it never happened again.

Morrison simply articulated what every western leader was thinking. In his free and open society, and in most others, his suggestion was simply good public policy, not based upon any malice. China saw it differently. It began sharpening its sword of revenge, hissing a loud public rebuke and cancelling or delaying shipments of Australian commodities to China. This was just the start, as the rhetoric from Beijing and its ambassadors ramped up, becoming cruder, more strident, and flying in the face of the genteel, cautiously worded language normally employed in diplomatic exchanges. China's language mimicked Trump's, rising to abuse.

As the Chinese caravan of retribution rolled on, it was suddenly accompanied by a '*log of claims*' from China, for want of a better term, outlining 14 Australian policies which it did not like and … *'which would need to be corrected if Australia hoped to normalise relations between the countries'*. These extraordinary demands were handed to *Channel 9 News,* who reported the matter thus:

"The toxic state of the relationship between Canberra and Beijing has been laid bare in a list of 14 grievances Chinese officials have handed to 9 News. At the top of the list are Australia's decision to ban Huawei from the rollout of the 5G network, laws against foreign interference, and Australia's call for an inquiry into the origins of the coronavirus. One Chinese official said to 9 News "Why should China care about Australia? China is angry," the official said. "If you make China the enemy, China will be the enemy." It is the bluntest assessment of the relationship ever delivered by a Chinese government official and the list is the clearest indication of how deep the fracture in the relationship runs."

What on earth had happened to Chinese civility? China's history was redolent with pacific, Confucian culture, a culture in tune with nature and obsessively polite in its interaction with others. Did the terse, uncivilised language now used by China signal a new form of diplomatic suasion, or coercion, bordering upon bullying? If so, how should Australia, and the free world, react to this new phenomenon?

In December 2020, I was asked to deliver an address about China, touching upon our deteriorating relationship. In my speech, I asked my countrymen not to conflate the gentle people of China with its leadership or to allow political ideology to taint the warm interaction between our business communities. I explained that only 90 million Chinese, just 6% of the population, belonged to the Chinese communist party or were fervent about its ideology. Chinese businesspeople are mercantile, not political, I explained, and hold strong Confucian values that parallel our Judeo-Christian ones—around the importance of family, honesty, personal loyalty, and polite social discourse. The ties between our business communities have evolved over time and are based upon a huge personal investment, on both sides, in building business trust. In business, bottom lines matter. People are pragmatic. Political differences are a nuisance, and our common humanity has always been more important than politics. China's socialism—one with market characteristics—supports an open business dialogue.

That description of Chinese communism—'A communism with market characteristics'—is probably the only surviving legacy of China's former leader, Deng Xiao Ping who famously said, *"It doesn't matter if the cat is black or white, as long as it catches the mice."* It is tragic that Deng's gentle plan for re-engagement with the world has been so brutally distorted. Businesspeople in both countries understood Deng's pragmatic approach and allowed for it. They traded professionally ... not politically ...as all businesses should in a highly competitive, global marketplace.

It is troubling that China's central regime has tainted business partnerships with a toxic, political overlay, which sometimes rises to a restraint of trade. It seems that, whenever a political action by Australia causes China an unintended offence, Australia is made to pay a heavy business price. Cancellation of its barley, wine and timber contracts, deregistration of its meat works and the detention of fifty vessels loaded with Australian coal pointed to a spectacular break-down in the relationship. Businesses in both countries were disappointed that their sincere trade and commercial efforts—and close, personal networks—were dismissed in this way.

As political tensions mounted, threatening our commercial arrangements, I thought it important to remind China's leaders of the days when we were close friends. I wrote to China's Ambassador, recounting that history and explaining how much Australia had helped China to re-engage with the world. I received no reply. I now share my letter which demonstrates how much the relationship has regressed:

Your Excellency,

In 1980, Deng Xiao Ping was opening China's doors. I arrived in Beijing as a bitter Gobi wind hunted through its icy streets. There were no western shops, no cars, and Beijing's streets sang to a timpani of rattling bicycle chains and bells, as a million Mao-suited cyclists pedalled down Chang An. I rejoiced in Australia's decision to recognise China and the adventure I would face working with new Chinese friends. Our first Ambassador, Dr Stephen Fitzgerald, and his team of fluent mandarin speakers had made my work easy. They had already forged intimate ties with their counterparts. Australia was a 'Category 1 Western Friend'! Our diplomats could travel out of Beijing. Back then, only Australia,

Canada and New Zealand enjoyed that privilege. Three phrases were repeated, as both sides worked to establish trust. Youyi (Friendship), He Zuo (Cooperation) and Lao Penyou (Old Friend).

I was told that Australia had been singled out for this special treatment because we were a modern, middle ranking, non-threatening nation, ideally placed to assist China's modernisation and re-engagement with the West. Our joint venture with Syme Media (The Melbourne Age) delivered China's first English language newspaper. And Australia was chosen as a testing ground for China's first foreign investments, in our minerals sector, because we were trusted not to take advantage of it. We rewarded that trust, gently guiding China's investment (in the bauxite sector) to ensure a safe outcome. A second soon followed.

In 1983, I was privileged to roll out Trade Minister Lionel Bowen's 'China Action Plan', an initiative aimed at doubling trade between us over five years. With a roving commission to deliver deals as a special trade emissary, I was delighted that we achieved that goal in just three years. The program was breathtaking in its simplicity. We simply asked China's peak bodies, in each sector, to join with their Australian counterparts in building commercial bridges of friendship and removing roadblocks. In the early phases, since trade was weighted heavily in Australia's favour, China asked that we start by balancing our trade. We could only do so by importing Chinese oil. So, we met with Caltex, in Sydney, to discuss that option.

"Not that bloody Daching crude!" said the Caltex executives.

"Too much paraffin wax! Costs the earth to remove! No profit at $28 a barrel!" they replied.

"What about $22 a barrel?" I asked.

"Bloody beautiful crude!" they exclaimed, in the familiar Australian vernacular, and the deal was done. Both sides had seized the moment, and the rest is an extraordinary tale of explosive trade growth.

Mr Ambassador, I urge China to reflect on the many trade missions we sent to help your nation to engage with the West. Our lawyers helped you draft western trade, commercial and dispute settlement laws. We helped you meet western standards for your electrical, medical, food, manufacturing and other products and services, opening new markets for China. You still use our three-pin electrical plug.

Our Ag scientists helped China to modernise its food and fibre sectors, and to move beyond small communes onto larger production plots. Our intellectual property, both professional and commercial, was liberally transferred to assist China's rapid evolution into a modern nation-state. Many other partnerships followed, in the arts and sciences, education, tourism, and in sporting exchanges. These were equally important in building bridges between us.

As a cricket enthusiast, I enjoyed establishing the 'Beijing Cricket Association'. I recall a wonderful exchange with your Ministry of Sports, where it was agreed that China would send one of its Olympic athletes to Australia to play with the Waverly Cricket Club in Sydney for a season, so that he could learn the game, return to China and grow this sport in China. Sport celebrates our common humanity.

Our nascent partnership with China was built upon good humour, real friendship, and genuine trust. The legacy of our goodwill was, in no small part, the emergence of a modern Chinese state, which now strides the globe so confidently. It saddens me that China seems to have forgotten that shared journey with Australia.

Our two nations enjoy a unique balance of comparative advantage in trade. Both have much to lose if either one diminishes that relationship.

Insensitive words, and trade penalties imposed as a political retort, will only encourage our exporters to diversify their trade away from China. That would be tragic for both sides.

In a recent public (radio) address on the subject, I asked the leaders of both nations, as I now ask you, Mr Ambassador, to work with me—and other people of good conscience—to restore trust, reject bellicose language, and replace it instead with soothing words which respect each other's sovereignty and see business partnerships as aloof from our political differences. And above all, by repeating three simple words that once meant so much to both sides: Youyi, He Zou and Lao Penyou (Friendship, cooperation and 'old mates').

After some weeks, having received no reply, I repeated this message in a speech I delivered on Australia-China relations. Damn it, I thought! Australians have either forgotten, or do not know about our splendid investment of people and funds in helping China open its doors and begin its long march to prosperity. Like a biblical disciple, charged with spreading the Gospel, I made it a personal crusade to reacquaint Australian and Chinese officials with that history, and spread that gospel.

However, as I prepared to launch my crusade, news flashed across the globe about an image posted on Chinese social media—a doctored image. Australian military insignias and our national flag had been photo-shopped onto a gruesome image of a soldier slitting the throat of an Afghan child. This followed an investigation into alleged war crimes by 18 troops in Afghanistan—0.001% of Australia's tiny army of 17,350 troops. Outraged by this demeaning of our moral action in pursuing these men, because their actions were anathema to our values and they needed to be held to account, our Prime Minister expressed disappointment that China could allow such an evil image to circulate, along with the disgusting commentary which accompanied it. He asked that the post be taken down. It was still circulating when Prime Minister Morrison posted a more genteel account of the incident, directed at the decent, general Chinese population. The PM's post was immediately taken down.

In his message, posted on *WeChat*, our Prime Minister said that '*Australia was dealing with allegations of war crimes in an honest and transparent way, the way a free, democratic and enlightened nation would.* He followed that commentary with the words '*I give* (the Chinese people) *a promise that the diplomatic spat with Beijing will not diminish the respect and appreciation Australia has for the Chinese people*'.

China's crude response, delivered through diplomatic channels and in their Communist party controlled national newspapers, was a preposterous assertion that the doctored image had exposed Australian barbarism and that we deserved global condemnation. When leaders around the free world condemned China's response, a revised explanation was finally delivered by the Chinese Embassy's Deputy Head of Mission, holding that *'the image was a work of art by a young Chinese man... what was all the fuss about?'* As these events unfolded, tributes of support for Australia poured in, making China's malign action against Australia a foreign policy blunder.

Global sentiment about China's bullying gathered momentum, beginning with a British statement of support and culminating in wine makers around the world—American, British, Italian and many others, condemning China's summary action against Australian wine exporters and urging consumer around the world to '*buy some Aussie wine, and support the Aussies'*. This was a magnificent, free world gesture and accompanied a growing chorus of sentiment that western consumers should stop buying Chinese products, in protest. As global alarm grew at China's brutish diplomacy, this sentiment found political expression in another forum, reported in the British media (an article in the *'Times'*) and later, in the *'Australian'* and other international media, which I summarise below:

"The British government proposes reforms to the G7, established in 1975 to coordinate policy between the world's largest, most advanced market economies. The UK proposes a new coalition of democracies, based on the G7, but adding Australia, India and South Korea, to be known as the 'Democratic 10', or 'D10'."

The G7 was seen as too *'North Atlantic-orientated'* while the G20 was a purely economic grouping that didn't care about the politics of its members. While there is a high correlation between language and institutions, it was not just the English-speaking world that valued freedom, democracy and free markets. The D10 achieved a nice geographic balance between the economic heft of North America, Europe and Asia while focusing on important commonalities, creating a new global leadership group—an anti-authoritarian, democratic, liberal bloc. The D10 could be a magnet for second and third tier countries who subscribe to or aspire to these values, and a useful delineation in a forum like the United Nations, which is based upon the principle of equivalence, regardless of national orientation and interests.

The media went on to report that a major objective of the D10 was to achieve a decoupling from China and a balancing of values not shared by this nation, which could now muster a coalition of between 50 and 60 states. These were either fiscal vassals, 'bought' by China's resource and infrastructure grants (its neo-colonialism) or attracted by China's anti-Western, antidemocratic, anti-liberal disposition. The D10 could also contain other ideological threats to western democracy, from countries like Russia or from Islamist states. This British view was supported by journalists Erik Brattberg, a member of the *Transatlantic Democracy Working Group*, and Ben Judah, the British author of *Fragile Empire*, who described the D10 thus:

It is the right size and shape: neither too big, nor too small. It is not an anti-China alliance but rather focusses on two critical issues which all democracies agree upon but cannot solve alone—5G and critical supply chains. Moreover, it is attractive to both foreign policy "restrainers" and "competitors" alike, as it will address and reduce these two strategic vulnerabilities and lessen future tensions with Beijing.

I believe that a new, democratic alliance like the D10 was overdue. Events over the calamitous 2020 and 2021 years, have galvanised thinking about threats to democracy and what we once called *'the free world'*. Freedom is not free, nor can it be taken for granted. There are opposing forces who are not fans of democracy and who, in pursuing their own agendas, are ready to provide alternatives. Let us hope that the D10 goes from strength to strength, and along with it, the fortunes of a proud alliance of democracies who make up its membership.

So, how should we react to the rise of China and its current, aggressive rhetoric? I believe that we must accept, pragmatically, that China has as much right as the West to global ascendancy—to a golden age and to expanding its power and influence. Great western powers—like Britain and the US—have all enjoyed their place in the sun as great powers. However, while respect for the sovereignty and values of other nations should be axiomatic, it rarely is, when nations rise.

Here's the rub: The West's own track record in respecting the sovereignty of others is appalling! As the West rails against suppression of the pro-democracy movement in Hong Kong, for example, it seems to gloss over the historical fact that British and other European gunboats extorted Hong Kong, the New Territories and other coastal cities from China at the end of their canons, disrespecting China's sovereignty over those territories. Britain also fostered a state-sponsored drug trade—the Opium Wars—which stupefied Chinese people in dark alleyways and opium dens. Who are we Westerners to lecture China on global morality?

We should take care to avoid sanctimonious rhetoric and hope that China's ascendancy works to unite, rather than divide the West. There is certainly a momentum for western democracies to work more closely, to build a countervailing balance as global power gradually shifts to the East. Above all, Western democracies must work to restore a rules-based world order, requiring that China respects—and that the West can enforce with sanctions—the following non-negotiable aspects:

- Each nation's independent sovereignty
- Each nation's right to pursue its own values and system of government (and to find its own pathway to delivering happiness and prosperity to its people)
- Respect for international laws and for the institutions which enforce them
- Respect for rules which protect fair trading and penalise trade abuses, and
  ...
- Respect for institutions which guarantee and protect universal human rights

Protecting those values and holding strong against the subtle shifts in global power and influence that are tugging at them, will require not just brave western diplomacy but some funding of new western initiatives, particularly in portfolios like defence, foreign relations, trade and investment.

Chapter 8
China's 'Belt and Road'—a Roman idea

Build your own dreams, or someone else may hire you to build theirs.
Farrah Gray

The magic ingredient in Rome's building of a vast territorial empire, extending, by AD 117 as far north as Scotland—stretching down through Europe and east into Asia, as far as modern-day Iraq and Iran, and reaching into north Africa—was its network of roads, sea lanes and fortifications, its control of key resources, like fresh water, and its military cantonments. At its height, Rome had a leg in the territories of 48 modern-day countries. Its' control of infrastructure, in particular of roads, rivers and key ports, enabled the efficient movement of its troops at short notice and gave it the ability to trade in a wide range of goods and services to support its Roman subjects, when Rome was the most populous city in the world.

When the Colosseum was built, Rome had a population of one million citizens (and slaves) and was the capital of an astonishing empire. The first fully paved Roman road was laid out in 312 BC during the consulate of Appius Claudius, for whom it was named (the Appian Way). Appius Claudius' was also responsible for the first aqueduct, the Appian Aqueduct, which channelled water from the volcanic hills eight miles to the south of Rome into the city centre, using only gravity. Over the next 5 centuries, fourteen new aqueducts were built, giving Rome the highest per capita water supply of any city before or since. It is estimated that 250 gallons of water entered the city per person, per day, enabling its population to grow as fast as it did. Rome's roads, aqueducts and viaducts were world wonders, and remain a testament to their engineering genius.

Perhaps this is a long bow to draw, but I see similarities in some of the heroic new structures which are the creative genius of modern Chinese engineers, financed and built as nation-building initiatives, or as empire-building statements—in China and other countries which China has persuaded to participate in its strategy, at a cost which western nations might struggle to justify to their taxpayers. The Hong Kong-Zhuhai-Macau Bridge, for example, is a 55-kilometre bridge and tunnel system combining cable-stayed bridges, and an undersea tunnel, anchored across four artificial islands. It is the longest sea crossing and the longest open-sea fixed link bridge ever built. The bridge spans the Lingding and Jiuzhou channels, connecting Hong Kong, Macau, and Zhuhai—three major cities on the Pearl River Delta.

China has also inspired, or financed, similar heroic projects abroad, as the Romans did, but it is the manner in which they have been undertaken and funded that is increasingly concerning a wary global community. Not only do China's foreign 'Belt and Road' projects come at a cost which makes their lesser developed, host country partners 'fiscal vassals', they are not always benevolent in their outcomes.

In 2018, as part of its 'Belt and Road' initiative, China financed a largescale, hydroelectric dam in north-eastern Cambodia which not only bound this very poor nation to repay a crippling debt but, according to 'Human Rights Watch', *'undermined the lives and livelihoods of thousands of indigenous and ethnic minority people'*. The Lower Sesan II dam, one of Asia's widest dams, flooded large areas upstream of the confluence of two tributaries of the Mekong River, displacing nearly 5,000 people whose families had lived in the area for generations, and impacting the livelihoods of tens of thousands of others, both upstream and for miles and miles downstream.

It is alleged that corrupt Cambodian authorities and company officials, who stood to gain personal financial advantage, barely consulted with affected communities before the project's start and largely ignored their concerns. And the deal also involved downstream agreements with Vietnamese energy authorities, whose officials also stood to benefit. Many poor people were coerced into accepting inadequate compensation for lost property and income, provided with poor housing and services at resettlement sites, and given no training or assistance to secure new jobs or livelihoods. Other affected communities upstream and downstream of the dam received no compensation or assistance at all.

While human rights activists were focussed on the impact this project had on directly affected communities, they failed to see its more significant symbolism—the fact that it gave China a stake in controlling the flow of the mighty Mekong River—thus compromising the economic arterial 'blood' supply to the parochial economies of all downstream nations and giving China a coercive lever which it could tweak at any future time should issues arise in the relationship with affected downstream nations.

According to reports,

> *the Lower Sesan II dam has also had a major impact on fishing income. By preventing numerous types of fish from completing migrations vital to their reproduction process, it has resulted in steep decreases in fishery yields... on which tens of millions of people in Cambodia, Vietnam, Thailand, and Laos rely for food and income. Now fish are so scarce," said one man living near the dam, "we sometimes don't even have enough to eat."*

Resettled villagers said their crops had decreased due to the less fertile, rocky soil at resettlement sites, and they had lost income from fruit and nut trees in their old villages. The government provided no compensation for loss of income from mushrooms, medicinal plants, and other products gathered from communal forests. Compensation did not address losses of indigenous culture and livelihood. Water from wells at most of the resettlement sites was contaminated and undrinkable.

China Huaneng power corporation has repeatedly claimed that the dam can produce 1,998 gigawatt hours per year, about one-sixth of Cambodia's entire annual electricity production, but the dam's actual production is less than half of that, based on available reports. As a result, *Human Rights Watch* has called for the Chinese government to drastically reform its Belt and Road project assessment and development financing, to prevent similar abuses in other projects undertaken in countries like Cambodia, where financial naivety and corruption lead to exploitation and inadequate assessment of human and environmental impacts.

In Roman times, the world's population was somewhere between 200 and 300 million. Roman infrastructure works invariably enhanced, rather than degraded or impacted in any negative way the communities on whose lands Roman civic works were undertaken. There was not the same need for environmental impact studies and, in a conquered nation, for much community consultation, although Roman conquerors were extraordinarily sensitive to these issues and often recruited local managers to their projects so that local sensibilities were properly respected.

In today's different circumstances, however, and in a more fragile world, China's Belt and Road initiatives must respect the proper rules of governance expected of responsible global citizens, which are largely prescribed by various global institutions, like the UNDP, the WTO, the International Court of Justice and others, constituting our rules-based world order. The Cambodian, and other insensitive projects, move me to question whether China's largess in financing its Belt and Road projects is genuinely motivated or serves a more sinister purpose.

In December 2020, Australia expressed grave concerns at China's intention to build a $204 million fishery complex in Papua New Guinea, in an area where there was no commercial fishing. Moreover, the complex was to be just 200 kilometres from mainland Australia. The Fujian Zhong Hong Fishery Company, controlled by the Chinese government, had just signed a deal to build the fishery complex at Daru, in Papua New Guinea, sparking fears China had secret plans to turn it into a naval base on Australia's doorstep, since it offered a deep-water anchorage.

Former adviser on PNG affairs, Jeff Wall, said the seas around Daru were not known to have fishery resources of commercial scale, leading him to question why China had spent $200m on a facility there. He said Daru was only 200 km from the Australian mainland, closer to the Torres Strait islands within Australia's northern border, and *strategically as close to Australia as you can get.* Given the rising tensions between Australia and China in recent times, he reflected the views of many Australians that there was cause for real concern.

This development added to concerns over China's leasing of the Port of Darwin, whose new Chinese operator, Ye Cheng, recently made a surprising admission in what appeared to be an offhand remark. In his capacity as founder and chairman of the *Shandong Landbridge Group,* Cheng linked his newly acquired port with China's global soft diplomacy, debt dependence and infrastructure strategy. "*Landbridge* has a port in Rizhao (China) and now we also have a port in Darwin," he bragged, when interviewed by state-owned news agency Xinhua in November 2015. "This is part of our involvement in One Belt, One Road," he added.

It was a curious statement since Australia was not considered part of what the Communist Party calls the Belt and Road Initiative. You can't get closer than

Darwin! And a recent edict from Beijing, requiring that all major foreign infrastructure investments demonstrate both a commercial and a military capability, is a particularly worrying development. What on earth prompted such an incendiary requirement? What ulterior motive might there be, apart from the undisguised statement about future military utility, presumably to be made available to a Chinese military force?

As one who has lived and worked in China, I have grown to admire China's gentle people, and yearn for a closer, more empathetic relationship between our two countries. However, these and other actions of its present leadership trouble me greatly, as they do many other Australians and a growing number of international observers. It is naïve to view China's rapid militarisation as benign or to downgrade Australia's security alignment with the US, simply because of a passing phase of US political dysfunction. Both of our nations now face the same, real threat, one which grows daily as China's military capacity grows. One question hangs like a sword of Damocles over our heads: *"Is China's Belt and Road a wolf in sheep's clothing?"*

Chapter 9
Democratic Dysfunction—A New Malaise

A friend is someone who has the same enemies as you have.
Abraham Lincoln

Dysfunction in Trump's America and in Boris Johnson's once *Great,* but now Brexit-plagued *Britain,* and the rise of China, India and other players, provide strong evidence that global power is rapidly shifting. So too are the alliances which emerged from the smoking ruins of World War II and gave birth to new institutions designed to police rules of fair play and universal justice and to ensure that the terror of global conflict never happened again. These institutions—like the UN and related agencies protecting human rights; the WTO, underpinning trade and economic justice, and NATO, underpinning military security, have maintained peace and global stability for nearly a century. However, their authority seems to be waning.

On the positive side, Japan and Germany, once mortal enemies, are now allies in the defence of democracy. However, Japan is facing down the largest emerging threat, from China, across a small body of water separating the two nations and now dominated by Chinese maritime influence. Moreover, Japan's anxiety must be heightened by the heavy burden of guilt it carries from its blood-thirsty invasion of China in the 1930s. That previous world order has changed beyond words!

The ANZUS Treaty, written in a bygone age to address a bygone threat, tied Australasian security to an alliance with the US, but that alliance, too, is outdated. For 75 years, ANZUS has been the cornerstone of Australia's defence policy, but the alignment of our respective interests is now less clear. New threats are emerging in an Indo-Pacific, rather than an American or European geo-political context. Despite this, ANZUS has continued to require that Australians engage in military adventures important to the US, in distant theatres, far from and extraneous to Australian interests, like Iraq and Afghanistan. This has skewed Australia's defence spending in a perverse direction. It is my strong view that Australia thus needs to assert greater independence from US foreign policy and that this area of public policy needs urgent recalibration in the face of changing geopolitical circumstances. For this reason, in 2016 I proposed that our defence be the subject of a policy forum in Melbourne.

The late Secretary of Defence, Paul Barratt, whose wisdom and judgement I had always respected, opened the forum as my guest speaker. Paul made the point that we must understand the shifting sands of military threats and recognise the new geopolitical realities we, alone, now face. Any dispassionate analysis would suggest the need for Australia to refocus defence spending on its northern waters, and to align its interests with those of closer neighbours who share a common anxiety about the rise of China, rather than on distant, extraneous threats.

The consensus from that debate was that, while ANZUS and our close relationship with the US remain critical, a new defence alliance is needed—a JAPINDA Pact—aligning Australasia with India and Japan to rebalance the strength of our military and geo-political deterrence. This logic may be lost on three generations of Australians, who have experienced great prosperity and never experienced the terror of global conflict. They could be forgiven for their complacency and for a failure to see an encroaching new threat. For change is insidious. It creeps towards us across a new, much closer battlefield, indifferent to our political system.

We seem to be approaching a critical phase in which appeasement argues with prescient warnings, like Churchill's, that a new threat is emerging. In Australia, the left brands those who ask that China respect our values as alarmists; accusing them of 'poking the tiger', while the right demands that China back off and respect our values. The common ground, if we can find it, is agreeing that democracy must be vigilant. Was Churchill right when he said that '*democracy is the worst form of government, except for the others that have been tried*'? or when he said: '*the best argument against democracy is a 5-minute chat with a voter*'. Instead, I ask this: '*Is modern democracy, as a system of government, at risk?' Is personal freedom negotiable? Can we defend it?* If the answer to those questions is 'no', beware, lest we trade our personal freedom for a much darker fate.

We have seen that, in the United States, democracy has been struggling. Indeed, towards the end of the Trump administration, the US appeared to be rushing towards ignominy, floundering under the weight of political toxicity and administrative dysfunction. As observed earlier, whatever your view of his politics, while Trump had some good ideas, he delivered them badly. We must hope that the US, once the world's leading democracy, regains a charismatic leadership role. Biden's election has not changed that prognosis. While he initially appeared to be charting a more dignified course, taking advice from his advisors and leading a return to a more familiar status quo, his Afghanistan debacle was disappointing. Meanwhile, US news services continue to bombard us with images of American democratic dysfunction.

While America struggles to contain its democratic dysfunction, even after Trump has left the stage, China continues its relentless march forward, advantaged, rather than disadvantaged, by its strong, autocratic system of government and the strict public discipline it imposes. While China forges ahead, economically and militarily, a clear vacuum has emerged in global leadership where once strong leadership existed. If leadership is wanting, and if democracy is about the lofty ideals of individual freedom and dignity, it is failing both tests. If this persists, the very survival of democracy, and the freedoms we all take for granted, may be at risk.

Indeed, as they witness the transition to a new global balance of power, several difficult questions arise for Western leaders: Is democracy—particularly the Westminster version, but also the variations which govern some 96 countries—still fit for purpose? Does democracy need an urgent makeover? Do the 96 nations which embrace democracy have the moral courage, political will and military capacity to save democracy and a rules-based world order? And can they act in unison?

In Australia, a new fog is clouding my democratic landscape—a new phenomenon, described in an article by journalist Janet Albrechtsen as *Political Homelessness*. It sums up the way many Australians feel. Since the post-war years, Australia's political landscape has been loosely described as a *2-Party System*, neatly fitting a left-of-centre or a right-of-centre narrative, a business versus the unions tilt, and allowing most Australians to find a comfortable fit for their own political sentiment. But those neat party lines have become blurred, complicating our tribal need to belong, to one side or the other.

Conservative Treasurer Josh Frydenberg's May 2021 budget was so profligate in its spending and so redolent of a Labor social conscience, that we might be excused for confusing it with an earlier, reformist Whitlam budget in

1972, which resulted in supply being blocked and got Whitlam the sack. One must concede however, that Frydenberg, a fiscally conservative Treasurer, was spending in response to a global pandemic … a catastrophe for which there was no government manual to turn to and no sure-fire formula for keeping people and jobs alive. What looked like a social justice budget was, instead, the child of economic necessity.

The same incongruity appeared in May 2021, when a trade union—the CMFEU—congratulated the conservatives on rescuing the coal and gas industries in the Hunter Valley, remarking that '*Labor has forgotten the workers it is supposed to represent*'. It looked like the Liberal Conservatives had changed sides, stolen the middle ground of Australian politics and left Labor with nowhere else to go … while marginal parties, like the Greens, were delighted and mopped up any new, orphan voters, who felt that they no longer belonged to a party saving the environment.

Albrechtsen's article was succinct and articulate, so I have taken the liberty of quoting from it, with grateful thanks to, and acknowledgement of its authorship:

I feel like a political orphan. More and more, I am coming across political orphans like me. Not quite akin to AA meetings, there is nonetheless a sense of group solidarity. We're not trying to give up something that's bad for us.

Instead, we are sharing the loss of having to give up something good. It's a case of: 'Hi, my name is Janet and I'm a liberal'. Or 'My name's Don and I'm homeless because I … used to be a Labor Party true believer'.

Social psychologist Jonathan Haidt says that the worst number of political parties in a country is one (1)—and the second worst number is two (2). I disagree. Having just two, serious political parties was just fine by me when one of those was a decent fit for voters on the left or the right. More often than not, many of our core values—social, economic and cultural—coincided with the party we vote for. Now, with an election on the horizon, the politically homeless will suspend our senses and hold their noses.

I'm talking about people across the left and right spectrum. One very smart woman, who describes herself as centre-left, told me she is feeling increasingly politically homeless over the issue of trans rights: 'I can't vote for a progressive party that tramples over women's rights', she said and implored me to start a political lobby group. I'm not interested in 'raising awareness' but I am keen to ensure that the laws don't eradicate the concept of women.

Another political orphan, a former chief executive of a top company, told me he couldn't vote for Shorten (Labor) in 2019 because he knew him too well. Now he is ashamed of voting for Scott Morrison (conservative). 'Oh well', he said, 'liberals don't have a home anymore. We have to choose between fascists on the right and the religious zealots of the woke left'.

I share their pain. It's not easy having Liberal (conservative) tendencies today. Prime Minister Morrison famously said he wasn't interested in talking about free speech because it didn't create a single job. That is sad. It doesn't cost anything to defend values that underpin a liberal democratic nation; you might even earn political capital by showing genuine conviction. But it will surely cost us, when and if prime ministers stop defending those values.

While these are just the views of one journo, each of us will, from time to time, struggle with the same demons, as we determine our policy allegiance, sifting good public policy from the swirling fog of political toxicity and media spin. But there is a bigger issue than the petty issue of partisan alignment ... it is the hope and wish that a stronger, more unified democracy can evolve from our present democratic dysfunction and rebalance the absence of strong western leadership. That bigger cause—the victory of democracy over the forces of autocracy that oppose it—should unite, rather than divide us. Alas, that desirable outcome may be a pipe dream, given the wide language, cultural and other chasms which seem to be plaguing democracy and dividing us, rather than uniting us.

Do You Trust Your Government?

We in the West like to think that people living under the hands of authoritarian governments will lust after freedom and eventually rebel. Some China watchers and political observers even hold that the greatest threat faced by Xi Jinping is an internal one—a sub-terranean pro-democracy movement, silently pervading the intelligentsia, who believe Xi's authoritarian rule must end and he must be brought to heel. But guess what? Recent research bears out the unassailable truth that most people, whether living under democratic or authoritarian rule, just want strong leadership and a government that just 'gets on with business', rather than one that procrastinates.

Who are we to arrogantly assert that only democracy can answer that need in people? China's resurgent nationalism belies the claim that the Chinese people want change and thirst after democracy. The flames of that resurgent nationalism were recently kindled into a bonfire at the massive rally in 2021, in Tiananmen Square, where Xi Jinping put the west on notice that China would not be lectured by the West on any subject. Xi outlined his so called three phases of China's march towards empire. Phase one, he said, had been successfully completed and phases two and three were now underway. Many of China's citizens have bought into this dream.

The dilemma for the West is this: If, by its standards, China's system of government is so oppressive, how come its people seem so happy with their present government? If the success of a system of government is measured as a function of *public trust in it*, the West is falling way behind, with a 'trust index' of around 38%, while China, with a trust index of 84%, has 'hit it out of the park'. Results of a 2019 survey by the Edelman organisation, which measured *trust in government*, were shocking. They revealed that China topped the list, while trust in government by the citizens of OECD countries languished in the low percentile range. Why was that so?

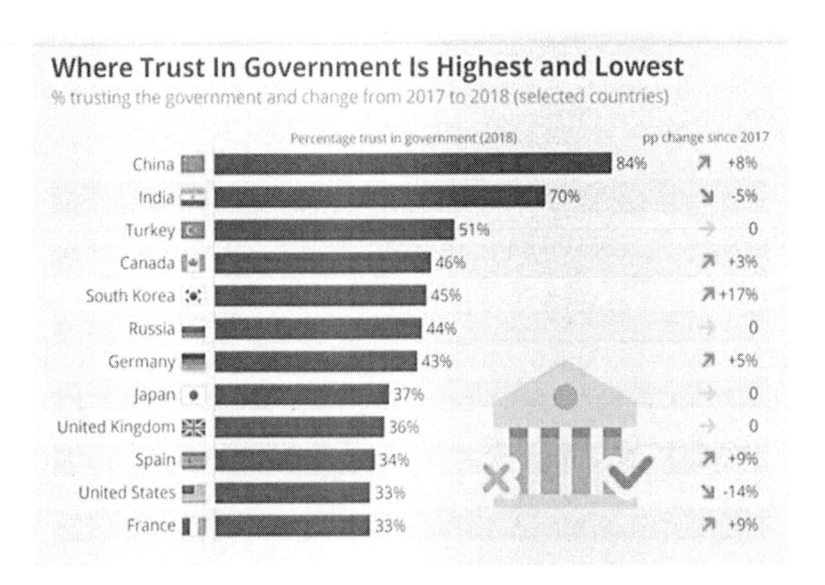

Where Trust In Government Is Highest and Lowest
% trusting the government and change from 2017 to 2018 (selected countries)

Country	Percentage trust in government (2018)	pp change since 2017
China	84%	+8%
India	70%	-5%
Turkey	51%	0
Canada	46%	+3%
South Korea	45%	+17%
Russia	44%	0
Germany	43%	+5%
Japan	37%	0
United Kingdom	36%	0
Spain	34%	+9%
United States	33%	-14%
France	33%	+9%

Source: Edelman 'Trust in Government' Barometer—2018-19

Is Democracy Divisive or Does It Ultimately Unite?

Democracy has become its own worst enemy. Contemporary democratic voices seem determined to accentuate our *differences* rather than our *shared values*—our cultural, racial, gender, sexual, ethnic and other differences. And a new toxin, *political correctness,* wants to silence free speech, rather than defend it as a democratic sacred cow. Defenders of democratic values and freedoms should strive to bring people together, not divide them; and defend our sacred democratic values against the forces that oppose them, not criticise them. Those who espouse political correctness are enemies of democracy, not its friends. They want to destroy it.

In seeking to explain this divisiveness, I turn again to history for answers, for the urge to rise above ignorance and become civilised is an ancient one. It is innate in man. It manifests as a thirst to make order out of chaos and to seek peace, instead of conflict. It gave birth to a science of 'public policy' and, along the way, unlocked some mysteries about democracy, about us and about social cohesion. It is important, therefore, that we understand how public policy has shaped systems of government and enabled democracy to rise above or fall below them.

Chapter 10
Is Democracy Dying?

When people fear government there is tyranny; when government fears people, there is liberty.
Thomas Jefferson

As I pause to consider the impact a fast-rising China is having on our comfortable western world, the question *'is democracy at risk'* nags at my consciousness. Surely no other system can challenge democracy in its universal respect for freedom, dignity, and the human condition. A thirst for democracy seems to be innate in mankind. It usually springs from oppression, which feeds a cry for change and is only sated by the granting of freedom and individual dignity. But what drives that urge in man, and what constitutes genuine democracy? Does our modern version of it measure up? And can it stand against the threats posed by authoritarian regimes, who rule with a heartless, central fist or grow fat on the proceeds of corruption? For me, the answer to these questions is simple. It is found in the words of John Stuart Mill, a father of modern democracy, who explained it thus: *'A true democracy is one which derives its moral and legal authority from the will of its people'*.

I turn my mind to my country, Australia, a middle ranking power with a democracy which is generally considered functional and stable. Does it pass John Stuart Mills test? I baulk at that question, for there is a logical inconsistency in the notion that its government, although it is elected by a national plebiscite, is unable to govern freely. In the notion that its actions are thwarted by an upper house, or directed by a pervasive media cycle, or by populism, rather than by carefully crafted policies answering the needs of its people.

When compared to the clinical efficiency of autocratic regimes, like China's, there is folly in the notion that democracy is a more efficient system of government. It is clearly not, particularly when it is asked to address long term, structural issues requiring vision, political courage and decisions reaching beyond a term of office. These things never plague dictators or autocrats, but they operate perversely within our modern democracies to stymie progress.

Several recent papers, in particular the *Economist's* heroic 2021 essay entitled *'The Democratic Distemper'*, suggest that democratic institutions around the world are showing similar cracks, and those cracks are widening as the world order rapidly changes. At a policy forum I chaired in Melbourne, in 2015, these sentiments were echoed and resulted in a debate which identified several major issues plaguing modern democracy.

Declining Moral Authority

The first issue plaguing it is the dilution of 'moral authority'. Nowadays, the 'will of the people' is routinely over-ridden by trans-national pressures, which transcend the national 'will' of the people and pull democracy out of shape. This occurred, for example, when the *'Coalition of the willing'* invaded Iraq, disrespecting that nation's sovereignty and the plight of its people, to go after Saddam Hussein. There is now abundant evidence that individual member states comprising the *'Coalition of the willing'* were very uncomfortable with that decision, and with US pressure to support a military adventure which, it emerged, was justified on fabricated, not real evidence of weapons of mass destruction (WMDs).

The United States had always been a beacon-light for liberty and justice, but that light dimmed when US indignation about the 9-11 attack became a Trojan horse for revenge. That light dimmed again when Donald Rumsfeld and his CIA goons displayed a fabricated cartoon to the UN Security Council to explain how Saddam Hussein hid his weapons of mass destruction in delivery vans, to justify the invasion of Iraq, while the real culprit, Osama Bin Laden, sat in his mountain retreat in a completely different nation—Afghanistan.

Later, when prisoners were taken, America's allies watched in disbelief as the horror of illegal detentions unfolded in Guantanamo Bay, breaching every concept of universal justice. Finally, when the US eventually decided to go after the real culprit, Osama Bin Laden, and his Al-Qaida band in Afghanistan, its actions arguably spurred a new wave of global terrorism, rather than dampening it. The Afghanistan campaign, brutal and deceitful in its rules of war, also dehumanised troops, making them 'murderers', not warriors. The doctored photo, which China released, of an Aussie soldier slitting a child's throat was extremely unhelpful. Where was the will of voters and their moral authority in evidence? Certainly not in many of the allied nations who constituted the *coalition of the willing*—nations like Denmark, Britain and Australia, which felt compelled to say, 'yes' when many of their people would have said 'no'. And when Biden abandoned Afghanistan his betrayal of the promise of democracy for that struggling nation, and for its downtrodden female population, was gut wrenching, particularly dishonouring the fallen troops.

In Australia, the decision to go to war is still an executive decision, made by a PM on the advice of his security council. Incredibly, it does not come after a public debate or even with the imprimatur of a Parliamentary vote. It can hardly be said to be made with moral authority, since Australian voters have no say in such decisions and are not consulted about their views on a particular war. In defence of the current procedure, a decision to go to war which is not backed by popular sentiment or on strong moral grounds, will likely bring that government down. To that extent there is an invisible hand of justice guiding our democracy. Moreover, there is clearly a policy middle ground, where the emergency use of executive power is justified, when missiles or bombers are airborne, violating our air space and an attack is imminent, but not when there is time for a parliament to consider its options.

Global alliances, too, can impose obligations beyond our borders, which do not reflect the national will of a people. Democracy now routinely bends to ill-defined, international winds and to the obligations it has under international treaties. External forces—like the UN, the WTO, the Paris Accord on climate change, the rise of the military ascendancy of China—now shape domestic politics beyond a nation's borders or the will of its citizens and another force, cyber-citizens, or netizens, now exert a strong, international pull upon national sentiment, bending it out of shape.

Government by Media Proxy

Another problem identified at the Melbourne forum was the fact that democracy was increasingly becoming *government by media proxy*, with policy being shaped by the relentless pursuit of a good news story. Public policy is sacrificed on the bonfire of political expedience, as governments shrink from unpopular decisions which the media then exploit, and from hard decisions—

about things like spending cuts or tax increases—which they fear will excite negative media coverage or have negative electoral consequences. Modern media and communications technology have conspired to create a new, cyber-electorate.

Economic Coercion

A new phenomenon, which I will call *economic coercion*, but which might equally be called *Trojan diplomacy,* exemplified by China's *soft diplomacy*, is also troubling. Let me share with you an example of how this works to distort national policy. Philippines President Duterte recently redefined the term *'Asian Pivot',* coined by the US Navy, when he declared that he would review US use of naval bases there and, instead, pivot towards China and Russia. This followed China's offer to fund significant infrastructure works in his nation. Duterte's acquiescence may have been good for domestic political consumption, as it significantly improved his nation's economic fortunes, but it was an irrational response to the rise of China, and disastrous foreign policy. It was the product of economic coercion.

When Australia suggested the world look into the origins of the coronavirus, China was so incensed that it cancelled a number of commodity contracts, in breach of WTO rules, and lodged a log of claims, demanding that Australia change 14 of its policy settings. This, too, was economic coercion dressed up as diplomacy and left the relationship in tatters.

Death by Indecision

These failings are compounded by another democratic dysfunction, *death by indecision*, a malaise which has spread through western democracies like a virus. When both houses are not controlled by one elected party, the upper houses (e.g., the Australian Senate, the US Senate and the British House of Lords) routinely exchange pugnacious words or filibuster, paralysing the decision process. In Europe, member states cower before the might of a transnational, bureaucratic monster of their own making, the European Union. Upper houses are also distorted by minorities—Keating's *'unrepresentative swill'*.

Death by indecision is now a metaphor for Australian politics. Its Senate routinely abuses its intended role as a house of review, governing instead by negative proxy and making an ass of the House of Representatives, the only truly representative chamber, which holds the only legitimate mandate to govern—the authority of a national plebiscite.

The exercise of a parallel, *executive power* to challenge and sometimes override the mandate of elected houses, such as we see in the office of the US President, also raises questions about how to achieve more decisive democratic government while retaining the necessary, democratic checks and balances which are sacred to it. Compared with the Westminster system, where authority resides almost exclusively with the Parliament, rather than an external power, the U.S. presidential power seems to rival, rather than support, the power of the two elected houses. Should Australia become a Republic, which seems inevitable, a strong case can be made for avoiding parallel (executive presidential) powers.

Should Australia choose a pathway to republic, I believe it should retain its Westminster model, with a PM remaining unambiguously the national leader and a President serving as a symbolic head of state, with constrained, ceremonial powers (as is presently the case with the Crown, its agents and State and Federal Governors-General). This would prevent a fifth column of power developing around a President and competing with an elected Prime Minister or a Parliament. We saw this 5th column phenomenon when Trump lost his last campaign and encouraged a strident 5th column to march on the Capitol building. Polling has suggested that some 50 million had voted for him and that he retained millions of supporters, many of whom would join him should he form a new political party.

The Culture of Entitlement

The culture of entitlement is another growing democratic dysfunction. The global financial crisis and the coronavirus provide stark examples of that. When an economy stalls, or employment is threatened, demands upon government for greater subsidy or welfare multiply. We have seen explosive examples of this around the world in answer to the coronavirus pandemic. The *culture of entitlement* which Plato warned us about in 500BC—dubbed *The Greek Disease* during the global financial crisis—has become democracy's new *Achilles Heel*. As debt mounts, and budgets are stressed, this unrelenting culture feeds the political beast, pulling public policy in one direction, then another, requiring that it meet a growing sense of *citizen entitlement*, even when doing so is bad public policy or fiscal folly.

Policy Myopia

Policy myopia (political short-sightedness) is another persistent weakness. Across the political divide, politicians now lack both the appetite and the resolve for addressing difficult, long-term structural issues. Decisions with consequences beyond a term of office are considered too risky ... or electorally toxic. Brave leadership—risking one's own political survival to put the national interest above one's own self-interest—is needed but always found wanting. Not so in Putin's and Xi Jinping's autocracies, where there are no electoral consequences, since poll results are pre-determined. *Policy myopia* joins hands with *policy paralysis* in sowing the seeds of democracy's own demise, as decisions critical to economic and social cohesion are routinely deferred to the next electoral cycle.

The Rise of Politocracy

My list of flaws in democracy would be incomplete if it failed to include the rise of a new political class, which I have dubbed the *Politocracy*. In the 18th and 19th centuries, the Westminster system was arguably more dignified. Parliamentary discourse was genteel, politicians were generally respected, and their careers considered high public office. Back then, candidates were chosen differently. With few exceptions, only men and women with mature judgement and life experience were considered. To be chosen as a candidate, a candidate had first to rise to prominence in another career or profession before asking citizens to elect him or her as their representative. A person's candidacy was thus buttressed by their legacy of achievement or excellence in another calling. Nowadays, young men and women are simply 'groomed' for a future in politics, *'prepared'*, as it were, by attachments to the offices of partisan or allied organisations or as political staffers, until they are *preferred* for pre-selection and parachuted into office (often, with little or no life experience).

If democracy is about the will of the people, an open preselection process must be the front line of any democratic contest to choose our leaders. Conversely, insider deals, or nepotism, corrupt that process and tear at the very fabric of democracy. It is a pity, therefore, that in contemporary Australia, in the US and in other Western democracies, the major parties now routinely groom 'internal' candidates for preselection, creating a career path for a privileged few. Young partisans are identified and prepared in young party movements—which operate like Hitler's youth, to nurture and direct thinking. The chosen few are then given party apparatchik jobs and injected into closed preselection, on both sides of politics.

In Australia, Labor and the Liberals do it through the union movement or conservative-leaning institutions, like the Institute of Public Affairs. Without disparaging the many excellent exceptions who mature into great politicians, it remains a fact that many young people with no business acumen and little life experience are attached as 'staffers' to politicians, with an expectation of safe passage into a seat in Parliament and mentoring through their political careers. They contemplate long careers, ending in retirement and an attractive pension. In this way the once patriotic call to public service has become a bureaucratic pathway for those I have described as *Politocrats*. They emerge from the loins of political parties, rather than as *community heroes* who enter public life to give back to society and are chosen on the basis of their hard-won reputations.

When distinguished Australian General, Jim Molan, failed to gain pre-selection for the Senate, this distortion of the process was made transparent. His military contemporaries regarded him as one of the most skilful tacticians of his generation. Despite his exemplary reputation, he was widely regarded by the Liberal Party' as an outsider. They tolerated him because of his reputation, but that tolerance did not extend to sitting beside him in the Senate. Even so, with little effort, General Molan garnered 10,000 below the line votes, the highest for that election. When, in December 2017, the High Court ruled that another senator was ineligible to sit, the way was cleared for Jim Molan to replace her in the upper house. Despite his splendid performance in the House and his excellent media skills, at the next election, Molan was again relegated to an unwinnable spot on the ticket. There are similar examples, at home and abroad and on both sides of the political divide, of factional interference to ensure internal candidates are chosen over charismatic community leaders.

Has Social Media Changed Democracy?

A public policy forum I was privileged to chair in Melbourne in 2013 explored constructive ideas for reforming our electoral processes. That forum pre-dated the advent of *Trumpian dysfunction*—his 'Sleepy Joe' name-calling, swamp-draining, and Twitter loud-hailing. It preceded the present political toxicity and undignified language which has since crept into high public office and arguably lowered the standards of the public discourse. Since then, seismic changes in technology and culture have changed both political messaging and its delivery. Whether you like him or not, Trump was an innovator. He took the gloves off, broke all the rules of statesmanship and changed the model for future election campaigns. His often-reckless comments found an audience and in Twitter, Trump found an effective, low-cost medium for communicating with voters. He changed the game.

Trump is an interesting case study. He provides new insights into what happens when a candidate from outside the political establishment—an interloper—enters the fray, with little or no regard for convention. I explored this phenomenon in an article contributed to John Menadue's public policy journal—*Pearls and Irritations*—in the following piece, which I was moved to write after watching an interview on CNN. The presenter interviewed a prominent US psychologist who asserted that Trump exhibited all the signs of '*grandiose, malignant narcissism*', a fascinating diagnosis. While I agreed that Trump had lowered standards of statesmanship and civil discourse, I had not considered that condition and found the diagnosis disturbing. How could we grant a man with that psychological profile access to the nuclear codes? So, on 15th November 2020, I offered the following piece:

The US Election—A Tragic Comedy

Historians may define the seminal moment when a once great nation began its decline, as the moment when a grandiose narcissist, with a fondness for crude invective, ascended to the US Presidency. For over a century, America had been the world's leading democracy—a shining beacon of hope for the dispossessed and oppressed. An ascendant American superpower had led the west through times of war, peace, prosperity and moments of great political tension. In four short years, however, America's symbolic role as a global democratic exemplar, reassuring an anxious world that democracy was the most durable and secure system of government, may have been irrevocably damaged.

Trump's tweets about vote-rigging, though incendiary and redolent with his usual hyperbole, have arguably achieved two important things: They have exposed extraordinary dysfunction in the US electoral system and bolstered a universal passion for a more dignified political discourse. It is incomprehensible that a nation which pioneered space exploration...

- *Has no national body, like the Australian or British Electoral Commissions, to manage national elections fairly and independently.*
- *Has no uniform, national election procedures; permitting instead a hotchpotch of different electoral rules which vary—often quite radically—from state to state.*
- *Has no uniform counting and scrutineering procedures to ensure an identical, nation-wide count and a timely, nation-wide delivery of an election result.*

These flaws are incongruous in a democracy which draws great moral authority from the lofty words of Jefferson and Lincoln in texts like the Declaration of Rights, the Declaration of Independence and the Gettysburg address—documents which share a place in the pantheon of great democratic scriptures, alongside Magna Carta and others. The heroic democratic principles they espouse stand strangely juxtaposed to the deeply flawed electoral machinery upon which American democracy presently depends.

Beyond this electoral dysfunction, a more concerning legacy of the Trump years has been his disdain for global institutions and lack of moral leadership in a world dislocated by tectonic events; the coronavirus, Britain's withdrawal from the EU, the rise of China and the appearance of worrying cracks in the rules-based world order. Trump's America has thus fallen from grace just when we needed it most—and so precipitously that it has caught us by surprise. As America licks the wounds of its deeply divided society in search of its own, lost identity, the free world is floundering in search of a new, charismatic leader to fill the void created by US political malaise.

As this tragic comedy unfolded, a more insidious event was playing out in the East. Unobserved by a world hooked on the addictive daily coverage of the

US election, Putin was quietly proposing a new axis—a military alliance with China. His proposal was welcomed by Xi Jinping, who agreed to work swiftly towards it. The development shifted the balance of power a little further towards two, arguably malign, eastern autocratic regimes, whose combined nuclear and military power presented new risk for the free world. The event was barely noticed and hardly reported.

The free world seemed indifferent to this development, as if in a trance, as these enemies of freedom moved quietly to fill the void created by America's new democratic dysfunction. If the free world continues to look with such indifference upon events like these, the freedoms we take for granted will be sorely tested. We must try to understand what these developments mean for democracy and be nimble in recalibrating our diplomacy. As old friends of democracy, we must surely stand with America as it seeks to rebuild its credibility and resume a global leadership role.

Shortly after his election, Joe Biden seemed to have returned a measure of dignity to the office of President. He seemed to be listening to advisers and taking advice from experts. Alas, this honeymoon was short lived. His withdrawal from Afghanistan was a debacle which undoubtedly damaged America's leadership of the free world and its standing as a defender of democracy. Siding with the US on global policy had, once again, become difficult for its allies. But despite this debacle and differences with some conservative leaders, Biden's calmer, more predictable administration has been generally welcomed by the West. One hopes that he can manage a new geo-political frontier which grows more complex every day.

Biden's foreign policy achievements are a work in progress and will become clearer over time. There is a risk that a more assertive US foreign policy might be muted by continued, domestic political distractions, and by forces within his own Democratic party, whose far left faction troubles some observers. Moreover, a Democrat President may occupy the White House, but his Republican opponents still have significant clout in the Senate. For the time being, the passing of legislation will rely upon the casting vote of his unpredictable Vice President, who does not sit in the Senate and is strongly influenced by the extreme left of her party. Senate elections may also see another change in the domestic political balance, further destabilising the US at a time when its global leadership is sorely needed.

A New Ideological Battlefront

As the winds of change blow across an increasingly troubled political landscape, two pivotal questions arise: Is democracy losing ground? If it is, where is the new battlefront? I suggest it is the Indo-Pacific, and I fear that US policy settings which fail to refocus on that region, will fail to defend democracy. For that is where the greatest risks to it are emerging, and where the most exposed western democracies are located—Australia, a loyal US ally, Japan the third largest economy in the world, with a GDP of $US 5 trillion and Taiwan, where a democratic David faces a Chinese Goliath and will need to find a bullseye with its miniscule military slingshot if it hopes to defend itself. Taiwan is probably the line in the sand which must not be crossed, else democracy loses whatever moral authority it has, and Japan finds itself the next steppingstone on China's road to regional territorial domination. Since Taiwan and Japan are tucked beneath China's chin, just a short distance from it across a stretch of water controlled by China, the forces of democracy must now gather further south, in a closely allied staging place, the Indo-Pacific. Any strident defence of democracy will need to focus on the Indo-Pacific, not on a tired European or Middle Eastern theatre, and the diplomacy needed to contain China must be voiced by the US—not by Australia, Japan or Taiwan, nations which China dismisses as *'US lap dogs.'* A strong US presence in the Indo-Pacific has demonstrably been lacking and has not been backed-up by commensurate regional military deployments.

In that context, despite the clumsy handling or the politics around it, one must applaud the Australian decision to joint venture with the US and the UK to develop, acquire and deploy nuclear submarines, if for no other reason than because it draws the US into the Indo-Pacific region, where we need it, and gives it new skin in the game. How else can the West hope to contain the rise of China?

Instead of asking whether democracy is winning or losing, we must begin to ask new questions of it ... What will the future look like if the US and other free societies fail to rescue democracy? Can US leadership of the free world be replaced by new democratic alliances (a new direction which a worried West now seems to be pursuing)? Will a realignment of that sort create new axis powers and lead to a more complex balance of power, such as the one we saw leading up to World War 1, which became a dangerous powder keg? Do we truly understand what China is up to, or just imagine that we do? And finally, can those of us who live in democracies contain and shape the rise of China, or will China shape us?

Chapter 11
Democracy Versus Autocracy

Continuous improvement is better than delayed perfection.
Mark Twain

There is little doubt that democracy is under attack, that other political systems are testing its architecture, and that China's autocracy is outmanoeuvring western democracy in the present, global contest. However, autocracies like China's can only deliver their economic gains with such breath-taking speed and efficiency because they don't anguish over democratic processes which respect people's freedoms, human rights or things like fair-trading conventions. Disrespecting those things removes bureaucratic roadblocks but does not make autocracy an intrinsically better system of government. Autocracies, dictatorships and plutocracies don't waste time on community consultation or environmental impact studies before bulldozing apartments for a freeway, or pander to demonstrators on street corners before introducing rules restricting public gatherings or freedom of movement.

Like it or not, China's hybrid system of government—*'communism with market characteristics'*—has, over the past two decades, significantly outperformed many western free market economies. It has lifted over 400 million people out of poverty, delivered consistent growth in GDP, dominated global markets, and achieved an alarming resurgence in military capacity. Its strict, authoritarian rule has provided stability for China's disparate population of almost 1 ½ billion subjects and given many a renewed sense of nation, as China reasserts its global leadership.

There has been another worrying development—one which has passed unnoticed because it has happened so quietly. In 2019, the command economies, led by China, overtook the world's free-market economies to control more than 58% of world trade. Command (rather than free market) economies include

China, Russia, Brazil, Cuba and India (while India is a huge democracy, it *canalises* its trade through state trading enterprises, and thus qualifies as a command economy). Moreover, some command economies, most notably China, routinely ignore or skirt around WTO rules which the world trade body now seems unwilling, or unable, to enforce. When governance of trade breaks down, there is fertile ground for theft of intellectual property, passing off, dumping, hidden subsidies, tariff and non-tariff barriers to trade and other subtle mechanisms which tilt the playing field in a nation's favour.

If command economies now control more trade than market determined ones, one must conclude that democracy is not just coming second because of its administrative dysfunction, but also because of its economic dysfunction—making it less nimble in the global economic footrace. And democratic dysfunction has spread beyond the public administration and trade and economic affairs, seeping into other, governance agencies once genuinely able to enforce a rules-based world order. They have become impotent because they have been infiltrated by undemocratic members with alternative agendas.

Take, for example, UNESCO and its World Heritage Committee, which recently blindsided Australia when it suddenly threatened to list the Great Barrier Reef as 'endangered'. This move, a consequence of China's desire to punish Australia for seeking an inquiry into the coronavirus pandemic, had significant implications for Australia's multi-billion-dollar tourism industry. China was able to pull this stunt because it chaired the heritage committee and because 15 of the 21 members of the committee were partners in its Belt and Road initiative and thus economically beholden to China.

We have seen the same perversion of other bodies, most notably the Human Rights Commission, on whose committees China and other nations with atrocious human rights records sit, smugly condemning other nations while remaining themselves immune from condemnation. These are troubling realities. They presage the rise of a sinister world order, and they raise uncomfortable new questions.

Is democracy losing its effectiveness as a system of government? Could it be in retreat? And if so, is its' retreat happening under the indifferent noses of western nations, unable to react in unison or paralysed by new forms of democratic dysfunction? If the pillars of western democracy are crumbling under a battery of new assaults upon them, we had better hasten to shore them up.

But before we leap to the conclusion that democracy is in decline, we should ask whether, instead, it is a work in progress and simply needs time to adjust. Whether these challenging times for democracy could stimulate new shoots, to refresh and reinvigorate it. Democracy took time to evolve, and it may need time to adjust. Let's face it, we are witnessing a revolution in the way we communicate… one which now enables us to reach new audiences; ubiquitously, across hallways, across vast ocean spaces and even across ideological divides— in a nanosecond. And we can do so in full, living colour. That new freedom to communicate can enhance free speech, which is good for democracy or be abused, to assault and corrupt our democratic rights by giving too many people too much voice, so that genuine democratic voices are drowned-out by a new chorus of cyber-babble.

If democracy is in trouble and we hope to save it, we must begin by accepting an awful truth; that democracy is not a preordained, natural order but rather, a hard-won privilege. If you need persuading of this fact, consider the historic lessons of great conquests which first shaped the ancient world, and continue to shape our contemporary world. None of them are pretty. All of them have been bloody. And none of them have been very democratic.

Consider the fall of Babylon, the sweeping conquests of Alexander the Great, the swashbuckling Islamic caliphate created under Mohammed, which is often forgotten. The bloody incursions of the Christian Crusaders into foreign Islamic lands, justified by a belief that their faith was more correct than the faith of their adversaries and demonstrating how religion can tear nations apart. Consider the tensions between King John and his Barons, and the blood-soaked turf of Culloden Moor. The French revolution, with its baskets full of guillotined heads. History reminds us that democracy has always had its genesis in a bitter struggle, most often to rise above oppression, and has always demanded a bloody price.

The forces which now shape our government are more subtle than they have ever been. They don't come galloping through our lives on horseback, brandishing a sabre or a crossbow, as they did in the Middle Ages. Their attack upon our senses is less visible; almost inaudible. It comes stealthily through the lenses and speakers of a thousand public and private, fixed and hand-held devices. Their electronic voices, rather than warm, personal voices we can trust, now control the flow of information to our brains and shape our views. Their electronic voices laugh at us, instruct us and even abuse us, through earpieces or via images projected on shiny screens held in our hands. They deliver the information we use to judge the world around us and to elect our leaders. These pseudo-cyborgs instruct us, rather than the orators of old—real people standing for public office, addressing us, in parks and on street corners, in warm, personal terms. Persuading us that we should elect them to public office.

Smart phones, iPads and TV screens have replaced people's faces, and social media, like Twitter and Facebook, have replaced people's voices, in our just-in-time cyberworld. The word *demos*—meaning the common people—gave birth to the word *democracy*. Should we now call it by another stem, *cybos for cybocracy*?

Can democracy be a beneficiary in this brave new world or is it seriously at risk because of it? Is the architecture of western democracy in need of urgent review, to establish that it is still fit for purpose? Or should we, as mediaeval English barons and French peasants once did, rise up to rescue democracy from its emerging dysfunction? If we hope to defend democracy's hallowed ground as a system of government, one thing seems clear. We must demonstrate, unambiguously, that it places a higher value on life and dignity and on freedom of thought and expression than other systems of government. The cancel culture and political correctness betray that cause. Above all, democracy must demonstrate that it is the best system for elevating the human condition, delivering happiness and opposing oppression.

When western democracies joined forces to defeat the Nazis and marauding Japanese, it was not only because they feared losing their sovereignty, but also because they risked losing a system of government which empowered people to challenge political leaders and gave people individual value and dignity. Dark forces threatened those values and created a huge psychological incentive to defend them vigorously. The post-war years put these opposing ideologies into parenthesis. In the post-war era, they sharpened the divide between democracy, which flourished, the brutal east bloc, which oppressed, Mao's sterile communism, which robbed people of their individuality, and the regimes of petty dictators and others masquerading as democracies.

The choice for clear-thinking people was easy. Democracy was a vastly more attractive system of government. But over the last three decades, with the stunning achievements of China, that distinction has been blurred, muting the attraction of democracy while making transparent a new, creeping disease—democratic dysfunction. Democratic dysfunction is everywhere to behold—in the Woke movement, in political correctness, in gender assignment, in academic institutions which teach kids to be ashamed of white privilege, instead of teaching maths and science, and in other attacks upon our democratic senses. These are threatening democracy and should be ringing alarm bells across a sleepy, complacent free world.

As one who is alarmed by this creeping dysfunction, I recently turned to 'Freedom House', a champion of democracy, albeit one which some hold is leftist in its views, for answers about where the new trends in our western discourse are taking us and whether they presage a decline in democracy. Freedom House is not-for-profit American organisation which tracks trends in democracy, political freedom, and human rights. It measures the ascendancy or decline of democracy according to indices, which they summarise in a *'sensitivity wheel diagram'*. In its 2018 report, this sensitivity diagram recorded the 13th consecutive year of decline in global freedom across countries in every region of the globe, including in long-standing democracies like the United States and in authoritarian regimes like China and Russia.

Recent *'declines in freedoms'* were smaller than the *'gains in freedoms'* recorded through most of the 20th century, but research indicated that a pattern of decline had emerged and that the trend was ominous. If the analysis is correct, democracy *is* in retreat. I respect the important work of this agency, despite its sometimes-biased orientation, and share with you excerpts from its findings, extracted from an excellent piece published by its President, Michael Abramowitz.

Those states which behave in an authoritarian way, but hide behind a thin façade of democracy, are now banning opposition groups or jailing their leaders, dispensing with limited terms of office, and censuring independent media. Many countries that democratised after the Cold War have regressed in the face of rampant corruption, antiliberal populism, and a breakdown in the rule of law. Some so-called democracies now ignore basic democratic principles, like the separation of powers, and are targeting minority groups for discriminatory treatment.

On the positive side, Freedom House has identified ... *'improvements in some countries, including Malaysia, Armenia, Ethiopia, Angola, and Ecuador'*, suggesting that democracy still has appeal as a means of holding leaders accountable and demanding conditions for a better life. *'In Europe and North America, some democratic institutions are under pressure. But citizens action groups demanding justice and inclusion continue to expand, informing citizens what they should expect from democracy'.*

So, the promise and allure of democracy as a means of delivering personal freedom, happiness and prosperity remains powerful. The fall of the Berlin Wall in 1989 and the Soviet Union's collapse in 1991 cleared the way for the formation of liberal democracies in Eastern Europe, the Americas, sub-Saharan Africa, and Asia. For a moment in time, under Gorbachev, it looked like the Soviet Union might move towards a free and open society. The fact that the freedom movement in Russia stalled is arguably one of the most tragic moments in modern history. However, demonstrations in support of the Russian dissident, Alexei Navalny, show that democracy still breathes beneath the surface of Putin's autocracy.

On balance, other gains during the late 20th Century have compensated. Between 1988 and 2005, the percentage of countries ranked *Not Free* dropped from 37% to 23%, while *Free* countries grew from 36% to 46%. Alas, *Freedom House* says these late 20th Century gains have begun to retreat. Between 2005 and 2018, the share of *Not Free* countries rose to 26%, while the share of *Free* countries declined to 44%. (In 2019, the Pew Research Centre found that, of 167 sovereign nations on earth, 96 (57%) were democracies of a sort, with parliamentary systems, 21 (14%) were autocracies and the remaining 46 (29%) had a mix of these systems.

However, I fear that the prognosis for democracy has been radically altered—indeed, stalled again—by one, hugely symbolic event which trumpeted to a disbelieving world that the once confident American leadership of the free world can no longer be trusted. If I am right about this, democracy is in deep trouble.

Afghanistan: The Graveyard of Empire

Whatever pretensions the US may have had to being a guardian of democracy, they were dashed on the rocks of incompetence when the US withdrew from Afghanistan. It was more than just a logistical debacle; it was a democratic debacle which signalled to the free world that the US was more focussed upon its own internal political dysfunction than upon critical foreign policy. That precipitous action was callously indifferent to trusted relationships, built over decades, with allies.

US media coverage confirmed this. It focussed upon domestic political concerns over the betrayal of America's sons and daughters who had lost their lives there, and whose families now sought answers to the question: '*What were they fighting for in that God forsaken, distant battle?*' They failed to mention the lives lost by allied troops standing shoulder to shoulder with the US in that dusty foreign war zone. US media also questioned the Biden administration's mismanagement of a military-logistical debacle, and the President's apparent indifferent to the advice of generals and allied strategic commanders. There was little or no US media coverage of what countries like Britain and Australia saw as a betrayal of the free world, and of the many allies who had stood beside the US for over 20 years, to liberate Afghanis from the oppression of their Islamic fundamentalist rulers.

The war had its genesis in an American need to avenge the 9-11 attacks that brought down the World Trade Centre. That event, too, precipitated a hurried decision to deploy forces to that God-forsaken war zone. A decision justified by rhetoric around running Bin Laden to ground and shutting down his breeding ground for Islamic terrorism. However, no clear objective was ever stated, or agreed, and scant regard was given to the facts that wars cost billions, are easily started, are much more difficult to end and leave lasting social and political scars.

Some in the media have observed that the speed with which the Pakistani-backed Taliban was able to reclaim control of Afghanistan is evidence that the entire conflict was essentially futile—a waste of both lives and military resources—and will likely see a return to Islamic fundamentalism of the worst kind—the kind which abuses women and denies people democratic freedoms. It may also have reignited fundamentalist hatred of America. Moreover, the sudden, clumsy withdrawal gifted US military machinery to the Taliban, which they reclaimed as they rushed in to fill the void. The US exodus from Afghanistan will undoubtedly leave behind a new, fertile breeding ground for Islamic terrorism and a safe haven for global terrorists.

But the real issue, which the shallow US media seemed to have ignored, was the absolute betrayal by the US of its allies, and the damage that act inflicted upon its leadership of the free world. Afghanistan has sent western allies scuttling in search of a new leader, or a coalition of leaders, willing to defend democracy. America's allies observed the debacle with incredulity. Some fifty countries had participated with America in the Afghan conflict, including all 19 NATO members and more distant allies, like Australia. At its peak, 130,000 troops were deployed there. Every one of those who served in support of America must now feel betrayed, while those aligned against democracy are rubbing their hands together with glee.

In 2020, *Freedom House* declared that *'the United States is critical to the survival of world democracy'*. It made this statement when Trumpian dysfunction was at its height and arguably damaging US leadership of the free world. When Biden was elected and appeared to recast his administration in a more conventional light, suggesting a return to a more dignified status quo, Western allies heaved a sigh of relief. Biden also seemed to be taking advice, not giving it. However, the Afghanistan debacle has reversed that feeling and is troubling. We must hope that Biden learns from the event. The US remains the most potent military force on the planet, but China is closing the gap, so western nations are desperate for signs that the United States can shore up its military leadership and expand its alliances, to deepen, not lessen, its commitment to democracy. As Freedom House puts it …

Only a united front among the world's leading democracies and a defence of democracy—as a universal right rather than an historical inheritance by a few Western societies—can roll back the world's authoritarian and antiliberal trends.

If the Afghanistan debacle is an indication of foreign policy priorities, these words have fallen on deaf ears within the Biden administration. The withdrawal of the United States from a policing role on behalf of democracy will accelerate its decline.

As if to confirm this fear, Joe Biden chose the 70th anniversary of ANZUS, the Australia-US defence alliance, to signal a fundamental reset of America's global priorities, saying Washington would no longer seek to '*remake*' other countries such as Afghanistan. His comments will be interpreted as a sign of a broad, US global retreat, fuelling anxiety in Australia and the Indo-Pacific about America's willingness to play a leading role in the region in the face of an increasingly aggressive China.

We may look back on the Afghanistan debacle as the moment America fell from grace … and as a confirmation of Australian General Jim Molan's prophetic words that… '*Afghanistan is the graveyard of empire'*. Has America's rise to greatness turned a corner? Is it now in decline, and is democracy at risk?' In searching for answers to those questions, we may find that defending democracy is not just about defending an ideology. With China's penetration of world markets, it must also include a defence of economic self-interests. In our brave new world, we must consider these competing influences upon democracy.

Chapter 12
Re-Aligning a Troubled World

Woe betide the leaders who cast away at the conference table what soldiers have won on a hundred blood-soaked battlefields.
Winston Churchill

The rapidly changing world order is making people nervous. Old alliances established in a different era, which were Euro-Pacific-centric—are rapidly becoming outdated and do not reflect the new reality. The Quadrilateral Security Dialogue (also known as the *QUAD* or colloquially, as the *Asian NATO*) is an example of that realignment, as is AUKUS, which evolved from the recent nuclear submarine deal with Australia. The QUAD is a seismic shift in alignment for Australia, an informal, strategic alliance between the Unites States, Japan, Australia and India. It holds semiregular summits, exchanges information and conducts joint military drills and is significant for the way it pulls the security focus back into the Indo-Pacific theatre.

It is the latest example of how nations, alarmed by the rapid rise of China and an attendant seismic shift in the balance of power, are seeking new alliances to strengthen security in emerging new areas of threat. While the Quad is transparently a democratic alliance, others outside of the democratic community are also realigning, alarmed by the shifts in global economic and geopolitical influence. Most of these new alliances have one purpose—to build a countervailing force against the rise of China. Many partners, particularly those co-located down the South-East Asian archipelago, have been frustrated in their attempts to reach consensus within their newfound alliances because of their very different systems of government, ranging from monarchies to pseudo-democracies and military regimes.

And the building of new alliances is not just confined to those agreed between like-minded governments, concerned about common geo-political threats. A new, cyber phenomenon has emerged—'online political alliances' which have allowed groups of individuals—not just governments—to form citizens' alliances spanning oceans to express democratic passion and join hands in opposing emerging threats.

In April 2020, as the Myanmar coup unfolded, young pro-democracy activists in Asia began displaying solidarity with their counterparts in Myanmar under a loose, trans-national, online network called the '*Milk Tea Alliance*'. Thai TV star, Vachirawit Chivaaree (whose pop-culture-name is 'Bright'), could never have imagined that his careless tweet, which included a description of Hong Kong as a democracy and attracted the ire of pro-Beijing protagonists, would spark a firestorm, galvanising youths across borders to protest in cyberspace and on real-world streets against authoritarianism. Soon thereafter, thousands more—in countries like Malaysia and Indonesia—joined in, holding online protests in answer to a call from the Myanmar pro-democracy campaigners. Many posted pictures of themselves holding signs and flags bearing *#MilkTeaAlliance*—the hashtag linked to Bright's April 2020 Twitter.

As liberal democratic values in many Asian countries take a hammering from military coups, security crackdowns ordered by Communist party authorities or monarchical lèse-majesté guardians… explained Dorain Malkovic, author of several books on China and Asia, and editor of French daily, *La Croix*… '*citizens across the region are braving bullets, arrests and harassment to fight'*. Protesters in countries around the world which recognised civil liberties and fundamental rights, joined forces to share information, campaign strategies or simply to keep the message alive. They built an online movement which transcended authoritarian controls.

Malkovic relates how this accidental movement began:

Paradoxically, credit for the #MilkTeaAlliance must go to China and its legions of Chinese Communist Party supporters who are granted access to Twitter, which is 'banned' but accessible to 'loyal citizens trusted to police the social media site'. Instead of accepting Bright's apology back in April 2020, Beijing's trolls adopted an online 'Wolf Warrior' strategy, (named after a 3D blockbuster starring a muscled Chinese commando). Digging around the Internet, pro-Beijing trolls stoked the outrage, uncovering an Instagram by Bright's girlfriend, Weeraya "Nnevvy" Sukaram, that appeared to suggest support for Taiwan, a democracy that China considers part of its territory.

The pro-Beijing Chinese trolls criticised Thai authorities, pointing to past atrocities in Thailand, including a 1970s crackdown on leftist students protesting at a Bangkok university. That was a big mistake! The effect was electric for Thai protesters, who still wanted democratic reforms and a loosening of the iron-clad alliance between the country's military and the monarchy. The irony of Chinese trolls attacking Thais sparked hilarious memes and messages that were picked up by Hong Kong and Taiwanese '*netizens*', who were also being harassed by Beijing.

I was particularly moved by the beautiful new term *'Netizen'* which this online movement evolved. It includes all of us, liberating us whatever our nationality, and enabling us to defend democracy across cold ideological borders, like those between China and Hong Kong, Russia and Norway and across rigid borders between distant authoritarian regimes and democracies. The *#MilkTeaAlliance* enabled protesters in Myanmar to access manuals on Hong Kong protest tactics—including umbrella protests, use of flash bombs etc., and gave rise to other fast-changing hashtags that were translated into Burmese and posted online, to keep the Chinese authorities guessing what was coming next and wrong-foot them. But while the original *Milk Tea Alliance* was a united alliance against nationalist Chinese *netizens*, it has since broadened into a display of solidarity against authoritarianism around the world.

Economic Alliances

This story of emerging new alliances would be incomplete if it only covered geo-political alliances and failed to include those which seek to address an equivalent, or greater threat in the way China is manipulating global markets. The speed at which markets are changing under the influence of unorthodox Chinese economic strategies has nations scrambling to find answers. China may be the new kid on the block, but it seems to be rewriting the rules, thumbing its nose at regulators, like the World Trade Organisation (WTO) and, instead, enforcing rules of its own, which are blindsiding slow respondents. For example, to control markets, it is vertically integrating its investments in critical raw materials, natural resources and commodities, and in strategic infrastructure, like ports and power stations.

Examples are Chinalco's plan to investment in iron ore mines like the Simandou resource in Guinea, West Africa, described as a 'Pilbara breaker' project—to discipline Australian iron ore producers, and projects like the Cubby Cotton station which, on closer analysis, was not about cotton production so much as about controlling water rights, since China's is running out. And in agriculture, not only is China using the cancellation of barley and wine contracts to coerce Australia to change unrelated policies, but it has also created a reverse dependence, since many of Australia's key agricultural inputs—things like chemicals and fertilisers—are now imported from China, who also control that supply chain dependence.

In this new frontier of global strategic realignment, the OECD has an increasingly important role to play on behalf of the developed, free-market economies, so its choice of Mathias Cormann as its new Secretary General was clever. He was an ideal candidate. An Australian of European (Belgian) birth, he speaks four languages (French, German, Dutch and English) and has served as Australia's Finance Minister. He will thus make an ideal economic diplomat, and hopefully be able to strengthen western economic alliances, not only against China's new economic stratagems but in answer to the coronavirus pandemic which is also pulling markets in new directions and reorganising supply chain dependencies. The following excerpts from his inaugural speech give an insight into his thinking on how to preserve a rules-based world order:

"The core purpose of the OECD is to preserve individual liberty and increase the economic and social wellbeing of people. The organisation's members share a commitment to democracy, human rights, the rule of law, market-based economic principles, a global level playing field and a rules-based order as the best way to maximise sustainable growth, prosperity and general wellbeing."

"Many countries around the world face serious challenges as a result of the most significant pandemic in a century. Our mission—to promote stronger, cleaner, fairer economic growth and to raise employment and living standards—thus remains critically important for the future. We need to … remember what made us strong in the past. Market-based economic principles. Global competition at its best is a powerful engine for progress, innovation and an improvement in living standards."

"We need effective rules to protect our values and ensure a level playing field. Expansion of world trade and investment is one of the most important drivers of economic development. Core to our economic mission, and that of all governments, is the preservation, restoration and creation of as many new jobs as possible—creating opportunities for people to get ahead. We need to ensure our policy settings facilitate, encourage and incentivise post-Covid recovery and investment."

"More countries are committing to net-zero emissions by 2050. The challenge is to turn those commitments into outcomes in a cost-effective, economically responsible and publicly supported way that will not leave people behind."

"The digital economy has grown during the pandemic. Risks and challenges will need to be well managed—from transitional supports and skills development requirements related to the future of work, to cyber security, privacy and tax policy implications of the digitalisation of an increasingly globalised economy."

"Great power competition will shape the world order in the coming decades. The OECD must demonstrate how democratic, market-based economic values make us politically, socially and economically stronger. Our strategy must include a focus on engagement with the Asia-Pacific, including ASEAN countries and China. Together, we can be stronger than the sum of our separate parts."

Cormann has sent a clear signal that the OECD will develop new settings to counter the rise of China and ensure that markets remain free, open and subject to universally accepted rules, failing which sanctions will be applied to constrain abuses. These things will be critical to shaping the emerging balance of power, which will be as much about economic as it is about military power. Will democracy meet these new challenges? Let us see. That is a work in progress. Before I end this analysis of the challenges faced by the West, if it hopes to defend democracy as a system of government, permit me to share some prophetic words of wisdom about the rise and fall of nations from no less a man than the founder of Dubai, Sheikh Rashid. When asked about the future of his country, and he replied:

"My grandfather rode a camel. My father rode a camel; I ride a Mercedes. My son now rides a Land Rover. My grandson is probably going to ride a Land Rover too…but my great-grandson is going to have to learn to ride a camel again."

When asked why that was so, he said… "Hard times create strong men. Strong men succeed and create easy times. Easy times create weak men. Weak men create difficult times. Many will not understand it, but you have to raise warriors, not parasites."

As I consider this Arabian wisdom, I am reminded that great empires—whether Egyptian, Greek, Roman, British or Dubaian—rose to greatness and then declined—within a span of just 240 years. Moreover, the decline of empire has rarely been at the hands of an external conqueror, but invariably because of internal decadence or dysfunction.

The great democratic experiment that has been the United States of America has passed Rome's 240-year benchmark and the first signs of moral decay are arguably visible within its institutions—in the invasion of Iraq to bring down one ruler, in the injustices surrounding Guantanamo Bay, in the storming of the Capitol building by enraged voters, in the betrayal of the Afghani people when Biden summarily pulled his troops out, and in the increasing toxicity of its domestic politics. Is American dysfunction accelerating? Has the US passed the Mercedes and Land Rover stages and now has camels on its horizon?" Let us hope not, for America is crucial to the defence of global democracy and we must strive to keep it strong.

Chapter 13
Free Speech

Whoever would overthrow the liberty of a nation must first begin by subduing the freeness of speech.
Benjamin Franklin

Voltaire's plea that we should respect each other's right to a view has been a philosophical cornerstone in the building of democracy. But when he said: "I may not agree with you, but I will defend to the death your right to a different view," was he implying that free speech was a human right? In the 17th century world in which he lived, it was not. The ability to speak out, for example against a King or a provincial ruler, was the sole province of the privileged elite. Most modern democracies protect free speech in their constitutions, but speech has never been truly free. Words matter. They have consequences. You can't just throw them around. And in today's world, speech is no longer just spoken, whispered or perhaps shouted. It travels silently, at light-speed, like a ghost, over a network of invisible ethereal highways.

Before the innovations of Alexander Bell, Guglielmo Marconi and Thomas Edison, we spoke to each other. But *speech*, as it is defined in modern laws, can now also written, printed, emailed, Tweeted, SMSed, Facebooked, blogged, Instagram-ed or even Zoomed. Speech has therefore never been so free because we have never had so many ways to communicate with each another. But that newfound freedom does not save us from the consequences of our speech (though politicians, under Parliamentary privilege, still enjoy freedoms that the rest of us are denied). However, agreeing legally on what we should be free to say, or not say, is becoming a tangled web, as new phenomena—like political correctness—invades our lives.

For thousands of years, no-one thought much about free speech or for that matter, free thought and expression. These things were not regulated. A stone-age man simply grunted, looked angry, clubbed his opponent or dragged his quarry into his cave. Over time, tribal cultures developed traditions and lore regulating behaviour, often based upon religious, moral or ethical ideas. These then evolved to regulate thought, speech and action. Disrespecting those tribal boundaries could attract punishment—a spearing or clubbing perhaps, or even banishment from the tribe—but public condemnation and punishment were arbitrary, not codified or informed by a bill of rights or by laws defining breaches and prescribing penalties.

Speech was free *precisely because* it was unregulated. Indeed, humans have always used a rich lexicon of words to display a wide range of emotions in their daily interaction—benign indifference, brutality, tenderness, happiness, sadness, anger and elation—and reflected those thoughts and emotions in their speech. Over the centuries, speech has rallied troops in battle, inspired revolutions, torn down institutions and attracted reprisals, when it incurred the wrath of a ruler. We have been clubbed, speared, arrowed, hung-drawn-and-quartered, guillotined and shot for views which challenged the status quo, threatened a ruler or offended someone.

Nowadays, when we speak freely, we take legal risks, as our speech can be lethal and can travel much further than we intended. Have you ever sent an email in error to an unintended recipient? Embarrassing, isn't it? Moreover, modern speech is rarely dismissed as a passing comment. It is routinely captured for eternity in a cyber vault, to come back and haunt us later. When we add passion and personal animus to our discourse, our outbursts can offend, vilify, defame, bully and assault. But while resolving such verbal conflicts in the past was an intensely personal matter—by clubbing a fellow cave dweller, throwing down a gauntlet or drawing pistols at 30 yards—our modern abuse seeps into the public domain, and when it offends, defames or vilifies, becomes punishable at law. Verbal expression is now a small part—perhaps the smallest—of our modern discourse. The range of communication platforms we use would astound a cave man, a mediaeval serf or a baron.

Clearly, *free speech* did not happen by accident. Nor was it tolerated because it was a human right. The term *free speech* had to evolve as a legal construct, as we did, over time into a civilised, regulated form. Its' progress towards a legal recognition was slow but gained sudden bursts of momentum whenever it exploded from the loins of injustice—for example, when English barons rebelled against King John's taxes, when people rebelled against those who bullied them into submission, as in the Spanish Inquisition, or when innocent people were unjustly oppressed. Justice and free speech are bedfellows, working hand in glove to shape our civil discourse.

Freedom of speech is one thing, but what about *freedom of thought*? Surely *thought*, too, must be free since we think before we utter words or act. And what about *free expression*? Should that not also be free? Where do these three democratic articles of faith—*freedom of thought, freedom of speech* and *freedom of expression*—sit in the constellation of human rights? One can understand why *free thought and free speech* might be protected in an open, democratic society, but *expression* can never be *protected*. An artist might *think* creatively, then express that thought in a beautiful painting, but here is the rub: a terrorist might *express* his thoughts by planting a bomb. It is this moral conundrum which has made *free speech* so difficult to define. *Free* is a relative term, since the exercise of freedoms in a democracy can have both good and bad consequences. So, what led to the idea that speech should be free, if making it so could also have negative consequences?

In the 6th Century BC, the Athenians first discussed a concept of free speech, but the granting of it by a nascent Greek government, about the size of a modern shire council, was only to a privileged few. Commoners and slaves had little or no say in things. It was not until 1166 that the '*Assize of Clarendon*' provided the right to a trial by jury, allowing an accused to *speak out* in his or her own defence to a bench of peers. This was a justice measure, but it was also an early step towards codifying a right of free speech. In 1215, *Magna Carta* built upon that tentative first step, stating that '*no free man should be imprisoned, dispossessed, exiled or destroyed except by the judgement of his peers*'. In elevating and defending the dignity of the individual, Magna Carta emboldened men to speak out against injustice and unwittingly provided new political momentum towards free speech.

The concept of *habeas corpus* first appeared in 1305. It flowed from Magna Carta and required that anyone arrested must be brought before a judge and not unlawfully detained. (It was not until 1679 that *habeas corpus, let's have the person*, became law). In 1688 the *English Bill of Rights* was a landmark document. It shaped British Constitutional Law, and later, the constitutions of emerging democracies. While its focus was on the prevention of cruel and unjust punishment, its practical effect was to give the downtrodden and other victims a *voice*—a right to speak out.

In 1789, just one year after British Governor Arthur Phillip stepped onto the sand at Sydney Cove, in the then Terra Australis, two things finally cemented free speech as a 'right', albeit subject to caveats. The French *'Declaration of the Rights of Men and Citizens'* brought together and better defined many vaguely expressed ideas, including free speech. And on the heels of that document—when the fledgling United States was framing its new republic and drawing upon the English Bill of Rights and the French revolution as sources of constitutional inspiration—America's founding fathers began drafting the *'US Bill of Rights'*. That task took nine years and was finally contained in ten amendments to the US Constitution (the initial document had been framed in such haste that it had required many political compromises and later, heavy editing, cleaning-up and correction).

The US Bill of Rights was a seminal document because it specifically protected freedom of speech as a human right, along with freedom of religion, freedom of assembly, the right to keep and bear arms, due process, a just trial etc. It also prohibited self-incrimination and, in a bold tour de force, guaranteed press freedom, enshrined the right to vote and abolished slavery.

Although free speech is protected in the US constitution, it is not specifically protected in most other democracies. It must compete with other human rights. John Stuart Mill defended free speech, but he said that a struggle always took place between… *'authority and liberty. One could not have the latter without the former'*.

In today's diverse, geo-political landscape, it is impossible to imagine a uniform, globally regulated right of free speech. Russia and China would have to be dragged kicking to the negotiating table, and that won't happen soon. Instead, nation states must seek shelter under their own, national legislation protecting free speech, rather than looking to international law. For sadly, free speech has no international champion—none with any teeth, not even the United Nations.

In 1948, the UN General Assembly passed the *'Universal Declaration of Human Rights'*. In retrospect, it has been a huge disappointment. It is not binding on any nation, is couched in very general language and is not specific on free speech. (It tells of the right to be born free and equal, to live in dignity whatever one's nationality, gender, ethnicity, colour, religion, language or culture etc.) But freeing speech is a political bridge too far. In June 2020, the Australian Council of Jewry said this …

"The UN Human Rights Council has surpassed its discredited and disbanded predecessor, the UN Commission on Human Rights, in its hypocrisy. It has allowed countries with the worst human rights records in the world, like China, Russia, Cuba and the Arab states, to preside over and sit in judgment upon countries with far superior human rights records, including Israel, the only genuine, rule-of-law democracy in the Middle East. Instead of fulfilling its purpose of being a beacon for human rights, it has made a mockery of that sacred cause with its cynical, politically motivated agenda, especially concerning Israel."

At the time of that statement, the Jews had very just cause for that view. Since its creation in 2006, the UN Human Rights Council had passed more resolutions condemning Israel than against all other nations on earth (68 against Israel out of 130 globally). In 2020, the U.S. Ambassador to the UN, Nikki Haley, called the Council *"a protector of human rights abusers; a cesspool of political bias."*

Over the past decade, reports on the Israeli-Palestinian clashes have been biased towards one side's version of events, or the others, using incendiary language to escalate tension rather than calm arbitration to deescalate. In May 2021, rocket attacks by the Palestinian Hamas group, defined as a terrorist group under Australian law, were launched from densely populated areas, using Palestinians as human shields to prevent retaliatory action by Israel. While many disagree with Israeli incursions into Palestinian territory and its creeping occupation of lands, both sides shape their versions of the narrative to better fit their political motives. *'Open Democracy'*, a UK-based political website, described clashes between Israel and Palestinian Hamas forces thus:

The most striking aspect of... BBC coverage of Israel and the Palestinians is that both 'sides'—supporters of Israel and supporters of the Palestinians—argue that the broadcaster tends to favour the other side. (The same is said of Australia's ABC).

Pro-Palestinians cite the BBC's failure to mention the crippling blockade of Gaza, as a vital context for the violence. The 2006 Thomas report noted the "asymmetry of power between the two sides" and stated that "given this asymmetry, the BBC's concern with balance gave an impression of equality between the two sides which was fundamentally, if unintentionally, misleading." Meanwhile, supporters of Israel say, conversely, that the BBC over-emphasises the suffering of Gaza's population and neglects to highlight the cause of the Israeli civilians, now living in fear and in reach of rocket attacks from Gaza, which Hamas, a Palestinian terrorist group, often deliver. Both sides can't be right, can they? Reporting must be biased.

Media analyses from both camps focus upon a single article, radio broadcast, or TV report that is ... held up as an instance of chronic bias. This will always be possible from whichever perspective one approaches the news because journalists are human beings and journalism is not an exact science. However, the mere fact that supporters of both sides find much to complain about does not mean that the coverage is fair, accurate, or 'good' journalism. They are mutually exclusive accounts of history and of present-day reality that could only co-exist in a parallel universe.

In a perfect world, one hopes that truth might lie somewhere between two biased accounts. If the mission of journalism is to find truth, it should surely strive to reflect reality, not pander to one side or the other in some weird 'contest of truth' as if 'truth' were a World Cup Final or a US Superbowl.

There must be an objective reality comprising material facts that can't be disputed. But truth in reporting is scarce these days. Judgements made on the facts vary greatly, since the facts must still be interpreted subjectively, along with the relative importance we ascribe to them.

Both sides of the political spectrum realise that news is, ultimately, a story presented to a target audience, and the story can be 'spun' to better fit the appetite of the target audience, be it a leftist or a rightist one. In that way the stories told by the BBC, Sky, CNN and by Fox, are influenced by the cohort being targeted. Just as news reporting seems to divide into leftist or rightist camps, so too geopolitical views and policy interpretations around issues like human rights fall into two camps—democratic or authoritarian. According to the Australian Institute of International Affairs ...

Western democracies have been locked in a bitter struggle with authoritarian powers at the United Nations since 2009. Russia and China have waged a systematic campaign to dismantle international human rights. They have sought to undermine the UN's human rights machinery in order to stifle international criticism of their own, poor human rights records and repressive domestic regimes.

Since it was re-elected to the UN's Human Rights Council in 2013, China has stepped up its attacks on UN human rights. Its re-election was regarded by western leaders as a sham and totally at odds with UN human rights values. (In

2016, Russia failed in its bid for re-election and is now forced to agitate behind the scenes).

The present Chinese Government has reflected Xi Jinping's antipathy towards human rights, including free speech. Xi has displayed a growing hostility towards human rights since taking control of the Chinese Communist Party in November 2012. Since then, by obstructing civilised debate and discourse in the UN, both China and Russia have sought to dampen criticism of their own human rights abuses. And by collaborating with other repressive regimes, they have been able to thwart country-specific scrutiny by the UNHRC. China also uses its position on the *UN Economic and Social Council Committee* to block or delay applications by human rights organisations for accreditation to the UN. China has exploited the committee's rules by repeatedly asking applicants to formally respond to new questions during committee sessions. Any questioning by committee members defers accreditation by a further six months, when the applicant organisation is asked to return and resubmit its proposal. By this clever obfuscation, China has managed to obstruct the applications of several groups for years. As a result, many human rights groups have been unable to participate in UN forums, sponsor events, or even gain access to UN venues.

China also harasses and intimidates human rights campaigners during UN forums. In 2014, Anna Wang, the daughter of a jailed Chinese dissident, was conspicuously photographed by a Chinese official during a session of the UNHRC. In March 2015, Golog Jigme, a Buddhist monk and rights activist, was photographed by a Chinese diplomat as he prepared to address the UNHRC on Chinese human rights abuses. For human rights activists, many of whom have suffered years of surveillance and repression at the hands of the CCP, these actions were meant to intimidate and prevent them from speaking out on China's rights violations.

No authoritarian regime wants a universal right of free speech. Whether as an international construct, or as an essential plank in each nation's own, distinctive democracy. At the heart of the matter is one, burning philosophical question:

Is free speech so fundamental to our human existence that it transcends all other rights, even when it offends, or causes harm to others?

In Australia, the conservative-leaning *Institute of Public Affairs* holds that free speech, even when it offends, should be *inalienable.* On the other side of this debate, liberal socialists, including Labor and the former Human Rights

Commissioner, Prof. Gillian Triggs, say that speech *must be limited*, to prevent it harming others.

I disagree with Triggs. Paradoxically, the same liberal socialists who would limit free speech defend the Wikileaks founder, Julian Assange, calling him a hero of free speech because he laid bare confidential government secrets. Surely Assange failed to meet their own test that free speech may not harm others. Their logic is malleable ... able to be adjusted to fit a cause, rather than rigid in its legal shape. In revealing military secrets, the US asserts that Assange put many military and civilian lives at risk, so the issue, and the swirling politics which shape it, are complex.

As Voltaire would say, I try to understand both views. However, I find four compelling reasons why speech must be absolutely free, even when it rises to offence. The first is this: For over 100,000 years, without the protection of laws or regulations, man has had to face many life-threatening challenges. In addition to the obvious ones, like Sabre-tooth tigers, wars etc, these have always included verbal abuse. Consider, for example, the *Maori Haka*—a native war chant meant to intimidate tribal enemies. This marvellous cultural spectacle is performed by New Zealand's *'All Blacks'* before international rugby matches. Similar rituals with abusive language are as old as time itself and simply part of the fabric of life, and of diverse cultures. It would be tragic if political correctness operated to censure them.

Clearly, verbal abuse has always shaped man's psychological toughness, in a Darwinian sense, and ought to be the least of man's Darwinian problems. '*Sticks and stones may break my bones* ... etc.' But today, if someone sulks, feels offended by a word or says ... "*Suck it up*" ... as one politician did ... one could pay a heavy price.

There is a second, more compelling reason why I hold that we should make free speech an *unconditional right* and it is powerful in its logic. It is this: If I am in the company of a bigot, a racist, or a cyber bully, I want to know who he is ... and equally, where he is. To discover that, I must first let him speak. When he speaks, he identifies himself and condemns himself with his own tongue. Speaking freely, he exposes his true nature. If I gag him, he hides in plain sight, walks silently amongst us, is undetected, and is still the same bigot, racist or cyber bully, free to continue.

A third reason is this: While protecting free speech may come at the cost of allowing bad people to abuse that privilege and cause harm, most democracies provide legal remedies which penalise offensive speech whenever and wherever it occurs. The breadth and scale of legal remedies varies across western jurisdictions, but remedies are available in all of those which embrace a British or US system of law and justice.

Most jurisdictions provide remedies to victims of defamation, discrimination, vilification, or verbal assault (though grounds differ slightly from jurisdiction to jurisdiction). All Australian jurisdictions provide redress when a person is victimised on account of race, ethnicity or religion. They also give redress when a person is victimised on account of disability, gender identity, health status or sexual orientation. And new laws are being added almost daily to provide protection against new forms of expression that cause harm. Online pornography and cyber bullying for example. So, even when it harms, I prefer that speech is free. That exposes those who abuse their free speech, so that we can prosecute them.

My fourth reason is simply this: How beige and colourless would life be without free speech? Coarse language is used liberally on the stage, for example in plays, in movies and in stand-up comedy. It was used liberally by Chaucer and Shakespeare to reflect real life. When it is employed creatively, to portray irony, comedy or farce, it delights many audiences. For me, free speech is thus a fundamental plank in democracy, and must give everyone a free voice.

Are 'Tech Giants' Undermining Free Speech?

Protecting the right to speak freely, within acceptable boundaries, is becoming increasingly complex. Even as you read this, our world is hurtling towards an uncertain, un-edited cyber future in which speech is taking many new, complex forms and becoming so pervasive in its reach that none of us can run from it, or hide from its new, lethal tongue. Instead of reinforcing democracy, some people think that, by providing media reach which exceeds the spoken word, and the reach of the print press and television media, tech giants are, directly or indirectly, exploiting unregulated free speech and infecting our democratic process. But is that so?

In late 2020, the Australian government unveiled the world's first draft law to force Tech-giants—like Google and Facebook—to pay traditional news media for the right to publish their material. The move immediately encountered resistance, not only from the tech behemoths, but from the US Government, whose ambassador called upon Australia to withdraw its legislation.

The US Government was clearly an interested party because the largest tech giants are all US corporations, generating massive advertising revenues and employing lots of people.

But was this a 'free speech' issue or simply protecting media companies from theft of their intellectual property—their media content? Defending the proposed legislation, Australian Treasurer Josh Frydenberg explained that a "mandatory code of conduct" would govern relations between the news industry, social media and search firms. This came after 18 months of negotiations failed to bring the sides together. The proposed code also covered access to user data, transparency of algorithms and ranking of content in the platforms' news feeds and search results.

"It's about a fair go for Australian news media businesses," Frydenberg told a media conference. *"It's about ensuring that we have increased competition, increased consumer protection, and a sustainable media landscape."* It is to be a market regulatory measure.

Google and Facebook, the world's biggest sellers of online ads, have for years, rejected demands by news media around the world that they be given a share of the tech giant's advertising revenue, since the Tech-giants freely use their content. The tech giants are an oligopoly, they say, and uniquely placed to multiply their advertising revenues by holding the public to ransom and controlling access to news content—other people's news content. The revenue sums at stake are enormous.

The pioneering code, drawn up by the *Australian Competition and Consumer Commission,* was still being debated at the time of writing and was to be introduced to parliament after consultation with industry. It will include penalties that could cost the tech giants hundreds of millions of dollars. Other national jurisdictions have expressed similar concerns and are following Australia's lead closely, with a view to enacting similar legislation. On closer inspection, the draft Australian measures are not about restricting speech, controlling speech or undermining democracy. In public policy terms, they are simply about 'protecting intellectual property'.

On that basis, I conclude that, by better informing the public, Google and Facebook are supporting rather than undermining democracy. They broaden our research, help us to inform ourselves as voters and allow us to communicate our views more freely. But there is a sting in the tail. On the positive side, when tech giants are politically benign—that is to say, when they simply provide a search platform, or a platform for individuals to express personal views, as Twitter, Instagram and similar platforms do—they give everybody an equal voice, better inform us and amplify free speech. This is an argument very much in their favour, and one I subscribe to, for free and open discourse is the lifeblood of democracy.

However, when rich and powerful forces—like the owners of these cyber platforms, intervene to censure or control their content, they cross a line. They become *editors* whenever they express a partisan view of restrict content from any source which they don't like, as was the case when Trump's tweets were shut down. When they do that, even in response to Trump's crazy rantings, they immediately inhibit free speech and cease being a neutral information highway.

There is a simple way to test whether a line has been crossed. If we think of cyber platforms as a sophisticated telephone system, the distinction becomes clearer. When Alexander Bell rolled out telephones, he provided an efficient, new communications highway. Communications travelled along a telegraph wire, just as a train might travel down iron rails. But Bell didn't listen in on personal conversations or judge their political correctness. In preferring any one user of an information highway over another, communication carriers, be they a Bell telephone company or a cyber medium, like Google, Facebook, Twitter, Instagram and others, are intervening politically, to limit, rather than support, free speech. They are editing, rather than simply conveying speech, and manipulating the public discourse.

The struggling Australian news industry, which precipitated this pioneering legislation, had been assailed by the dominance of tech giants and was being further hammered by the economic impact of the coronavirus pandemic. In Australia, dozens of newspapers had closed, and hundreds of journalists had been sacked, both because of dwindling demand for print copy and because of covid concerns about handling newsprint. But in stark contrast to this negative impact of the virus, tech giants continued to prosper, as online demand soared. And while face to face discourse was limited, online solutions exploded. In 2020, Facebook reported a net profit of $5.2 billion for the 3 months ended June. Ad sales on its platform rose by 10% to $18.3 billion. Google, which makes money through advertising on search sites and through sites such as YouTube, said online ad sales were recovering strongly after a brief pause and were rising on YouTube. Its second quarter profit was above expectations, at nearly $7 billion.

This supports the view that the Australian Treasurer had strong anti-trust grounds when he warned that a code was needed to prohibit discrimination against local media by US tech giants. "Today's draft legislation will draw the attention of many regulatory agencies and many governments around the world," he said, calling the proposed law *world-leading*. "Nothing less than the future of the Australian media landscape is at stake with these changes," he said.

The challenge is not just to control oligopoly advertising but also to ensure that tech giants remain benign, neutral carriers of content. If these two aspects can be controlled through legislation, albeit across a broad democratic landscape, that legislation will facilitate, not hinder, free speech.

Is Media Bias Undermining Democracy?

While the owners of cyber platforms have been largely neutral information carriers, print and TV media have been serial offenders—clearly aligning themselves politically, as an invisible hand of the market forces them to maximise their circulation and viewership by choosing political sides, to target a leftist or rightist market segment. This is most obvious in the counterpoise of the Fox and CNN channels and is mimicked in similar print and TV alignments around the free world. But does this alignment, which results in news and current affairs being skewed to feed a particular leftists or rightist narrative, have any impact upon democracy? We should answer this question, not just because these significant communications media speak loudly and with global reach, but because they are not elected or representative voices.

In the US, there are thousands of media outlets—newspapers, radio stations, network and cable TV channels, blogs, websites and social media—offering a range of perspectives on any given issue. If you want to find a conservative news site, or a liberal one, it is easy to do so. The American Constitution's First Amendment says:

Congress shall make no law limiting the freedom of the press. It does not say that the media must be neutral or unbiased. Moreover, media bias is as old as the Gutenberg press, invented in 1450. In 1789, Jefferson described the *Gazette of the United States* as a '*paper of pure Toryism*' *disseminating the doctrines of monarchy, aristocracy and the exclusion of people.*

Recent research in the US has shown that party affiliation remains the main predictor of attitudes about media bias. 67% percent of Republicans but fewer

Democrats (20%) and Independents (48%) have an unfavourable opinion of the news media. Across all measures, Republicans express more negative sentiments about the media than do Democrats and Independents. Communications scholars have found that if, using scientific polling methods, you ask any group of people, in any community, whether their local media are biased, you will find that about half say yes. But of that half, about 28% say that their local media are biased against conservatives, and about 22% say the same media are biased against liberal or socialist voters. The two tend to roughly equate and balance each other out.

The same US research also shows that Republicans and Democrats only spot bias in articles which clearly favour the other party. If an article tilts in favour of their own party, they tend to see it as unbiased. So, we can define 'bias' as being *'any view that does not agree with mine'.* That should not surprise us. Clearly, each one of us is our own arbiter of bias. One US commentator noted that *'American party politics has become increasingly polarised. Republicans have become more consistently conservative, and Democrats have become more consistently liberal (socialist)'*. The same trend holds true in other democracies. The political toxicity of media commentary is another matter, and it appears to be increasing.

In its summary, the researchers concluded that having lots of media to turn to, even when their content is biased towards a liberal or a conservative audience, is *not* damaging democracy but, rather, operates like comfort food to reinforce existing prejudices. The research also shows that bias is in the eye of the beholder. And finally, it shows that, if we are troubled by an issue, we have lots of alternative media comfort food to turn to, to better inform us and even sway us to become swing voters.

Altered Truth and Political Spin

While researchers have found that media bias is an equivalent force and thus a benign influence, *altered truth* and *disinformation* are truly troubling to democracy. If untruths are unchecked by experts, or not corrected by honest, professional journalists, they distort reality and thus our logical perception of political issues. Politicians are the best at altering truth. They have developed it into an art form.

Former Australian Prime Minister Kevin Rudd is said to share a common ancestry with Remus Rudd, a horse thief who was captured by police and jailed in Melbourne in 1885. Remus escaped in 1887 and went on to rob the Melbourne-Geelong train six times. I cannot vouch for the truth of this account, which appeared in a comedic social column and was redolent with political satire, but the journo who carried the story reported that, upon discovering this fact, an interested genealogist e-mailed the former Prime Minister seeking more information about his great-great uncle. Kevin Rudd's staff are said to have sent the following reply, making Rudd's great-great Uncle look rather more saintly than he was, as follows:

"Thank you for your inquiry. Remus Rudd was famous in Victoria during the mid to late 1800s. His business empire grew to include acquisition of valuable equestrian assets (his stolen horses?) and intimate dealings with the Melbourne-Geelong Railroad (the enterprise he frequently robbed?). Beginning in 1883, he devoted several years of his life to government service (in prison?), finally taking leave to resume his dealings with the railroad. In 1887, he was a key player in a vital investigation run by the Victoria Police (into his own crime?) In 1889, Remus passed away during a civic function held in his honour when the platform he was standing on collapsed.

Apparently, the platform which collapsed was the gallows!

In October 2020, the New York Times reported that '*a bipartisan group of academics, journalists, pollsters, former government officials and campaigners convened for an initiative called the 'Transition Integrity Project'. They met to 'game' hypothetical threats to the November 2020 election and their likely impact on a peaceful transfer of power if Democrat Joe Biden were to win*'. The idea was to test the robustness of American democracy.

At the same time, a former national security adviser to President Trump published an article about the *Transition Integrity Project,* calling it '*The Coming Coup*', which accused Democrats of laying the groundwork for revolution. By mid-September, while the bipartisan research project was largely ignored by the media, the *coup* scenario was '*shared*' more than 100,000 times on Facebook, generating millions of interactions and video views in the lead-up to the November US election. While its research purpose and sentiment were almost laudable, this seeding of the political atmosphere with a fantasy scenario, not a real one, infected the public discourse in a way which made a fair and democratic election almost impossible.

"The United States may be in the middle of a coronavirus public-health crisis," said one commentator, "but it is also in the middle of an information crisis caused by ... viral scenarios, disinformation and falsehoods, to achieve political outcomes."

There is an old saying in the newspaper business—*If it bleeds, it leads.* This often results in sensational journalism, which lies somewhere between fantasy and fact but uses rich language, imagery and hyperbole to make stories irresistible. Readers, and viewers, don't want to read a story headlined 'Dog bites man'. They want 'Man bites dog'. Alas, sensational stories sell more papers and attract more viewers, so they tend to crowd out more sober coverage of issues important to democratic function—important public policy issues, like education, health care, national defence and others. Issues like these are vital to all of us as voters, but not nearly as much fun to read. Writer Dave Barry demonstrated this aspect of creative media license in favour of drama in a 1998 column, where he wrote:

Consider two headlines. 'Federal Reserve Ponders Reversal of Postponement decision on Deferral of Policy Reconsiderations.'... and ... 'Fed Reserve Member Caught in Motel with Underage Sheep.' Which would you read?

He went on to explain that, by focusing on the content equivalent of the underage sheep, the media can, if they choose to, direct our attention in a particular way, not only *towards* but also *away* from important issues. That isn't the media's fault; we are the audience whose attention they want to attract. So long as we think of news in terms of its entertainment, rather than its instructive value, and of media bias in terms of our Republican or Democratic political prejudice, we will continue to be less informed than we need to be. That, he says, is the real impact of media bias.

Is Academic Freedom the Same as Free Speech?

If we agree that freedom of speech is a fundamental right, even when it rises to offense, does that include a scientist taking exception to another scientist's view, when there are differences of scientific opinion. When Galileo disagreed with the scientific dogma of his time, he did so on pain of death. How else might he have advanced planetary science. How can we expect contemporary scientists to advance science, if we silence questioning minds? Despite this obvious logic, it seems that, in modern scientific and academic circles, some people will silence those who challenge their peer science or speak inconvenient truths. In this context, the recent controversy surrounding an Australia Professor, Peter Ridd, deserve examination.

Professor Ridd was awarded compensation after an unfair dismissal case against his former employer, James Cook University. The media had described the case as being about academic freedom—about Professor Ridd's right to a dissenting view about the health of the Great Barrier Reef. The judge—Judge Vasta—disagreed.

"Some have thought that this trial was about freedom of speech and intellectual freedom," he said. *"Media reports have suggested that this trial was about silencing persons with controversial or unpopular [scientific or academic] views. Rather, this trial was purely about the proper construction of a clause in an enterprise bargaining (employment) agreement."*

Vasta's ruling required him to determine the extent of the economic loss suffered by Ridd, because of his censure and dismissal. The scientist, who had endeared himself to some in the agricultural sector by arguing against the consensus view that farm fertilisers were damaging the reef, argued that, after his dismissal, academic institutions would not hire him. During the hearing, it was put to Ridd that he had received widespread acclaim and promotion because of the case, and that this had helped, not hindered his ability to maintain his reputation.

"Quite the opposite!" said Ridd. *"In terms of companies hiring scientists, all the fame of being in the national press or of being a hero of the right-leaning Institute of Public Affairs doesn't help one iota. It's bad for me. Maybe it will produce a different career outcome but ... most big institutions don't want a bar of somebody who has been through my sort of controversy."*

Judge Vasta finally agreed. He conceded that Ridd was "*damaged goods*" and that the University's action had '*poisoned the well*' for Ridd's future employment.

"The fact that the University had not removed either of their press statements (despite my judgment) is tantamount to an attempt to ensure that Professor Ridd does not obtain employment in his field," said Judge Vasta.

Despite the judge's earlier comments that it was not, Ridd insisted that the case "was always about academic freedom." However, the so called 'Expert Panel' said—"We have seen the sowing of doubt play out over the years: in tobacco use, in lead in petrol, anti-vaccination, climate change and now, in the Great Barrier Reef case. In all these cases, scientific evidence was disputed ... but often for obvious reasons—usually money."

At issue was an academic's right to express a different view. But if that view is for financial benefit (e.g. to finance personal research projects) and is supported by science which is skewed to achieve that end, is that still a right, even if it misleads? Differences persist, and have always done so, across science and academia, about climate change and across other fields of scientific endeavour. Climate scientists, for example, are dining out on a research grant bonanza as world leaders try to find answers to that existential threat, but research funding in other areas has probably become a casualty. So, is academic freedom the same as free speech? Or is academic freedom only as good as the quality of the academic assertion?

Simply being an academic does not confer a right to bend science or mislead and there seemed to be reasonable scientific consensus that the Great Barrier Reef *was* being damaged by fertilisers flushed into reef waters. That made the academic case not just weak, but wrong. But Professor Ridd, and his supporters appealed, insisting it was about academic freedom—the freedom to think outside the square.

The debate about controversial science and academic freedom is not new. It is as old as history itself, and it is not about free speech versus academic freedom. It is about questioning minds triumphing over accepted dogma, which can sterilise science. The Ridd case ran out of steam when, on 14th October 2021, his appeal was rejected. He had spent $300,000 of his own money and an estimated $1.3 million in funds donated by the public, in a passionate defence of academic freedom. But the judges had found the original verdict in order—that is, that the matter was about an employment contract, not free speech.

This was a terrible outcome and a blow for academic freedom. Are our universities and schools so constricted by academic egos, marketing of student places and political correctness they have forgotten they were supposed to be Centres of Learningl The Ridd case verdict will create a dangerous legal precedent, preventing the extension of the principles of free speech to scientific and academic freedom. In public policy terms, the Ridd case pits two freedoms against each other.

I share the view that the right to disagree scientifically, as a construct of freedom of speech, is critical to advancing science. If controversial science is unacceptable, how can we apologise for Galileo's triumph over a religiously biased world, to lift it above its biblical prejudice and scientific ignorance, when he asserted that the earth revolved around the sun, not the sun around the earth—or in Darwin's case, how would we otherwise have overcome the blasphemous assertion that man descended from the apes? These two examples changed science forever.

On 11 February 2021, Ridd told *The Australian* that the court's decision to grant special leave and hear his case showed why codes of conduct restricting speech should be rewritten, to combine the right of free speech with a new right of academic freedom. In the case of scientific disagreement about climate change, that right could be crucial to a balanced debate, since the science continues to evolve while religious fervour runs ahead of it. I am disappointed, for example, that the word 'sceptic' has become a derogatory term, used to discredit scientists who disagree with some aspects of climate science. Scepticism, and questioning minds are essential to advancing science and knowledge. Shutting them down sterilises science. Let the scientific debate be robust … and let the truth prevail!

"The way academic codes of conduct are written," says Ridd, "means you can't say 'Universities are Orwellian'. If saying that sort of thing amounts to serious misconduct, and if that's the state we've got to, it's an absolute disaster."

"The court should be troubled by this," said Stuart Wood QC. "The commitment from the university to protect academic freedom was denied Dr Ridd. He was punished for doing what he should be doing. The purpose of the clause … (in his employment contract)…" he said, "was to allow academics to robustly exchange ideas without being censured, as long as they don't harass, bully, vilify or intimidate."

Ridd held that the Australian Institute of Marine Science could "no longer be trusted" and accused colleagues of "doom science about the Great Barrier Reef." After his initial trial, Dr Ridd said if he were to lose his appeal, Australian academics would be deterred from engaging in controversial science and free debate. "It means that academics are going to be fearful of saying anything robust on any matter," he said, and added "the left wing and the right wing now both agree on this," he said.

I return to the word 'sceptic', which has now developed a negative connotation. If good policy is informed by good science, we must welcome scepticism and a scientific contest of ideas, just as democracy demands a social, political of cultural contest of ideas. Only by this device can democracy—the power of people to decide whether a policy is serving them—reach a public consensus and guide the actions of our leaders. We should welcome ideological and scientific differences, for they are the crucible in which we smelt democratic metal. That process is unique to democracy and not permitted in closed, autocratic regimes, like China and Russia. However, China and Russia have no aversion to acquiring new scientific knowledge. They will pounce on it, steal it if they can, and use it against us. We must make heroes of our sceptical scientists, not condemn them for questioning dogma.

'Neuro Rights'—The Next Frontier for Ethics in A Democracy

The emerging ability of artificial intelligence and other new technologies to tinker with our brains, or even compete with them—including robots which 'learn from their mistakes and gain experience', is a frightening new frontier of science, with both positive and negative potential for mankind. We must watch its potential impact upon free thought and expression. I was heartened to read that Chile, of all places, is a global leader in this debate and aims to be the first country to protect people from mind control, as the ability to tinker with our brains edges closer to reality.

Chilean Senator Guido Girardi is leading moves to ensure Chileans' "neuro-rights" are enshrined by law and that the constitution is reformed to recognise the need to protect "fundamental human autonomy". In a prediction that echoes the plots of Hollywood films, Senator Girardi has said that the science, if unregulated, could threaten "the essence of humans, their autonomy, their freedom and their free will. If this technology manages to read your mind, before you're aware of what you're thinking, it could write emotions into your brain: life stories that aren't yours," he said.

In 2020, Senator Girardi's proposal was supported in Chile's parliament and is being considered in a constitutional revamp. Rapid advances in neuroscience to beat disorders such as Parkinson's disease, motor neurone disease and epilepsy have raised this legal-ethical dilemma, as researchers test ways to access and manipulate electrical and chemical activity in our brains. Where might this lead us? This science will require new laws, policies and human ethical settings, to chart a middle course which encourages the science which works in humanity's best interests while banning its sinister applications, adding another layer of challenge for democracy if it is to remain competitive in safeguarding people and their happiness.

Chapter 14
Political Correctness — "I Feel, So I Must Be Right"

Political correctness does not legislate tolerance; it only organises hatred.
Jacques Barzun

When I reflect upon my joyous interaction with other young men and women as an irreverent young rugby player and *'hash house harrier'*... when I recall my masterful leadership of bawdy limericks and rugby songs that brought spontaneous mirth to our post-match gatherings ... indeed, when I think upon the generally laconic nature of Australians, a trait which is much admired in our national psyche, I find it difficult to understand what is driving the toxic phenomenon of political correctness. It is infecting our discourse like a cancer. How can any society allow this constraint upon freedom of thought, speech and expression to develop, unchecked by the majority? It is damaging our democracy and inhibiting productive public discourse.

Those who defend political correctness hold that its purpose is to respect the sensibilities of others—those whose racial, sexual, gender or other sensibilities might be offended by particular words, or actions. On the face of it, that seems a noble cause. But social and moral environments change subtly over time. Historically, public morality has ranged from the promiscuity of early Rome to the prudence of Victorian England, and from the sexual revolution of the 60s to present day sensitivities about things like gender reassignment and sexual harassment.

Is it fair to allege offence when someone speaks to you in plain English, particularly if what they say is essentially true? If freedom of speech and expression are essential in a free and open society, and if political correctness is constraining our free speech, political correctness must surely be a creeping blight upon democracy. Let me share some examples of how absurd this has become.

On a sparkling morning in 2021, I wandered to a beachside café for a morning coffee and to read the daily newspapers. There were serious issues I wanted to read about, including the federal budget, which would chart the nation's recovery from the coronavirus. Alas, my newspapers contained multiple reports of what I considered insane, alternative language, and about the indignation of a politically correct few about the way words were used ... words which I had always considered mundane, and which had, for centuries, been considered *plain English*. Consider the following example, lifted from that day's *Australian* newspaper:

"People who 'chest-feed' are the beneficiaries of a new, transgender guide from the Australian Breastfeeding Association. The booklet, the result of a two-year, project costing $20,000 undertaken in consultation with the 'LGBTQ + Rainbow' community, details how biological males who identify as females can chemically induce human milk. So, we should now use the term 'chest feed' not 'breast feed'."

I consider myself a broadminded, tolerant fellow. I despise those who intrude into or judge the private lives of others. I sympathise with the idea that one's sexuality is an intensely personal matter, and that people should be free to explore theirs, as long as they don't offend others. That tolerance extends to all variations covered by the epithet 'LGBTIQ'. But I was astounded by this arrant male lactation nonsense and the tragic misuse of both the English language and the valuable public research funds expended in the name of this social dyslexia. Those funds might have been spent on research which benefitted the whole community, not just lactating males!

Reflecting further on this, I turned to my laptop and *Googled* information about just how representative *the views of the LGBTIQ + rainbow* community were. I typed into the search field *"Heterosexuals as percentage of general population,"* thinking it must be a significant cohort—around 10% or 12%—since it now commands tremendous sway in the way our society thinks, speaks and behaves.

According to a study conducted in 2021, 96.5% of those sampled (96.8% of men and 96.3% of women) identified as heterosexual, slightly fewer than the 2003 finding of 97.5%. Leaving aside issues affecting women, which are mainstream because they impact 50% of the population, one is moved to ask why our public discourse is so greatly impacted by the LGBTIQ cohort? It occurred to me that the term *'LGBTIQ'* did not indicate much about our collective humanity, because it omitted the letters HN—*hetero-normal*—96% of us. Let us have *'LGBTIQHN + Rainbow'* to fairly represent all gender preferences. Or will that take up too many lines in a press release or too much time when speaking from a bully-pulpit?

Straight people constitute an overwhelming majority of us but are the group most directly targeted by the LGBTIQ community with their notions of political correctness, so that the majority is instructed by the minority to mind their language. If non-straight people make up just 3.2% of the male population and 3.7% of the female population, is it right that this cohort should command power over broader public behaviour and language? I accept that we should love, protect and respect all of our fellow travellers on planet earth, but in a democracy, surely the vox populi—the broad community sentiment—must decide what is correct about speech and behaviour, not a dissenting minority.

However, as I reflected further, I suddenly felt a flush of shame. What was I thinking? Political correctness was not something we could simply lie at the feet of the gay community. In my experience, gay men and women were more broadminded than the rest of us, and often more imbued with creativity and joie de vivre. No, the phenomenon of political correctness must extend way beyond issues around one's sexuality. And it does. It extends to a myriad of other areas of our lives.

Peta Credlin, former chief of staff of an Australian conservative Prime Minister and now a media commentator, has warned that the *"talons"* of political correctness have made it *"impossible to have an honest discussion"*—not just about sexual preference but also about other subjects which the 'correct few' have declared taboo—religion, climate change, race, gender identity and other descriptive areas of our language. In response to relentless political pressure from the correct few, recent government edicts have bordered on the ridiculous—including ones which have decreed that we should refer to *'chest feeding, not 'breast feeding'*, call *'breast milk'*, *'human milk'*, and fathers, the *'second genetic parent'*, apparently so we don't offend the LGBTIQ + rainbow community.

The term *'Judeo-Christian'* is now also taboo, because it has religious connotations. And *'nuclear family'*, meaning intimate family members—parents, siblings, children and grandchildren—is now offensive since families are more diverse and include gay couples and people estranged from their families. They should be called members of a *tribal culture*. It seems impossible to conceive that the word *family*, and the loving relationships it connotes, could be politically incorrect.

A TV presenter expressed similar alarm at the launch of academic Kevin Donnelly's book *A Politically Correct Dictionary and Guide* at the City Tattersall's club in Sydney, in front of a crowd that included former Prime Minister Tony Abbott. Credlin had been asked to speak and offered the view that, in Australian political discourse, "words matter, language matters, but who controls it matters most of all." She condemned the impact political correctness was having on public debate.

"Twenty-five years ago, when this fixation started to take hold of our discourse, we laughed. We even mocked it … We thought Australian common sense would see it off," she said. "Since that time, the initial tentacles of political correctness have become talons and have clawed their way into the various institutions and organs of Australian life," she added.

She praised Dr Donnelly for *tackling the way language is silencing us* and lamented that if one dared to point out *the obvious truth, that the Koran offers numerous justifications for infidels, you are immediately labelled an Islamophobe. If you question this new, leftist orthodoxy on any issue, you're not just wrong, you're a bad person*, she said.

It does seem, anecdotally, that *political correctness* has its roots in far left, left of centre or radical groups, which makes it unique for its assault upon people of conservative religious, social and political conviction, who deserve an equal place in any democratic discourse. But as political correctness continues its crusade to silence ordinary people, those who now push back against its insidious attack on our language and behaviour now include people from every walk of life and of every political hue, not just conservatives. It seems enough is enough!

Credlin, who I acknowledge is a well-known conservative, also noted that language had been *effectively deployed* by the same sex marriage campaign, using the term *"equality"* as a pejorative term. Equality is our birth right, but political correctness implies that opposition to social change is somehow bad, she said. This contradicts the very principle of equality. She argues that the same sex marriage issue has come and now gone, and there has been wide consensus validating it, but in a robust democracy, those whose religious beliefs prevent them embracing it have a right to religious freedom, not vilification.

I am a strong supporter of same sex marriage—I voted for it—and my view was supported by a majority of voters, confirming for me that our democracy is still alive and well. But like same sex marriage, there are many other controversial issues that need to be debated or are a social or political work in progress. A civilised public discourse will respect differences, particularly if supported by science or fact, around important public policies—not just same sex marriage, but other things, like climate change. Democracy provides a path to consensus not available to those living under authoritarian regimes. Civil discourse in a free and open society must surely be valued as something precious, and we should celebrate our freedom to differ.

Also present at the launch of Kevin Donnelly's book—*'How political correctness is destroying Australia'*—were former house speaker Bronwyn Bishop and cartoonist, Johannes Leak, whose illustrations appear in the book. Leak's father, an even more famous cartoonist, had been attacked for portraying an aboriginal holding a bottle of booze who could neither remember whether a boy standing before him was his son, or what the boy's name was. This satirical cartoon probed a deep social issue—the pervasive problem of alcoholism, domestic violence and dysfunction in aboriginal communities. As many cartoons do, like the Charlie Hebdo cartoon in France, Leak's cartoon had touched a raw nerve. It had reflected a harsh reality, a 'truth' no words could utter, supported by government statistics. But Leak's cartoon resulted in an outcry from the left and the public vilification of the cartoonist.

When speaking of his motivations in writing the book, Dr Donnelly cited the case of an American university academic teaching a class about *Huckleberry Finn*. He *was* attacked for using the word *'nigger'*. He said… *'it's in the book … a book written by a national literary hero, Mark Twain. How can I teach Huckleberry Finn without mentioning the 'N' word?"*

Dr Donnelly said that, as an academic, he was most concerned that political correctness *relied upon emotion rather than reason.* "As a teacher, this is the thing that I'm most upset about. If you talk about academic rhetoric, it is okay to use persuasive language, to appeal to experts … but to be reasonable, to be logical, that is what we argue for in our academic discourse. But political correctness is the opposite. It is more about emotion than logic. The expression … 'I think therefore I am'… has been a philosophical argument used to capture the era of enlightenment, but it has now become… 'I feel, therefore I must be right'. That, to me, is a serious problem," Dr Donnelly said.

Most of us will have experienced political correctness being weaponised to silence good humour, satirical commentary or words that are common in English usage. The following examples show how crazy political correctness has become:

- A UK recruiter was stunned when her job advert for *reliable* and *hard-working* applicants was rejected, as it could offend *unreliable* or *lazy* people.
- The BBC has dropped the terms *Before Christ* (BC) and *Anno Domini* (AD) and decided, instead, that *Before Common Era* and *Common Era* must be used.
- Throughout US local government and community organisations, terms using the word 'man' as a prefix or suffix have been ruled politically incorrect. A 'manhole' must now be referred to as a 'utility hole' or 'maintenance hole'.
- The European Parliament has introduced proposals to outlaw the use of *titles which indicate marital status*—such as *Miss* and *Mrs*—so as not to cause offence. The consequences of that are that *Madame* and *Mademoiselle, Frau* and *Fraulein*, and *Senora* and *Senorita* will also have to be banned when, as required by EU bureaucratic rules, the regulation is translated into those languages, as it must be enforced in the languages of member nations.
- Loveable cartoon kid *Dennis the Menace* has been given a politically correct makeover. The BBC has decided to take away his naughty water bombs, catapults, water pistols and pea shooters, because they incite people to violence and are thus politically incorrect.
- *Spotted Dick*—the classic English dessert—has been renamed. The traditional 'pudding' has been given the new title *Spotted Richard*, after UK Councillors feared the original, centuries-old name might cause offence.
- A school in Seattle has renamed its Easter eggs… S*pring spheres* to avoid causing offence to people who were not Christian or did not celebrate Easter.
- A UK council has banned the term 'brainstorming'—and replaced it with 'thought showers', as local lawmakers thought the term may offend epileptics.

- Gillingham soccer fans had offered celery to their goalkeeper, 'Big Fat Jim Stannard', who loved his nickname and was greatly amused by the joke. His nickname had brought him celebrity. The club, however, decided that taking celery into the ground should cease, not because of offence, but for health and safety reasons. As a result, fans were subjected to 'celery searches' with the sanction for possession of celery being a life ban from the Club.
- In 2007, in Sydney, Australia, Santa Clauses hired to appear in Department stores were banned from saying *Ho-ho-ho*. Their employer, the recruitment firm *We Staff* that supplies hundreds of Santas across Australia, allegedly told all trainees that 'Ho-ho-ho' could frighten children and be derogatory to women because 'Ho-ho-ho' was too close to the American slang word for prostitute.
- At some US schools, a Christmas tree must now be called a 'holiday tree'.

It is hard to believe that this nonsense comes from the minds of rational administrators. An article by David James, a PhD in English Literature and author of the musical comedy *The Bard Bites Back*, makes the following observations: "The push for politically correct language may be well intentioned, but its consequences are appalling. It can rob us of one of the most important of all human freedoms: the right to use words to mean what we want them to mean... to speak freely."

He goes on to say that, in prohibiting certain words, there is an assumption that the intention of the speaker is known by the listener. In literary criticism, this is called *the intention fallacy* ... the assumption that an author's intention can be readily derived from his words. He gives an example—a joke he wrote about Asian drivers, which was deemed to be politically incorrect, even racist. He tried to explain that the joke was meant to expose those who held such bigoted views. It was not directed at Asian drivers, but at those who had tarred all Asian drivers unfairly with the same brush—that was obvious from the context—but it was still deemed inadmissible. There could be only one possible intention—harm—no matter how much it was explained that this was not the case.

A similar thing happened in response to an article comparing burkas to nun's veils, following the banning of burkas on security grounds (i.e., when facial ID is required). '*Do we ban the nun's veil next?*' the article asked. While the question was offered rhetorically, in defence of Muslim woman subjected to these indignities, readers interpreted it as a *nun-bashing headline*, and thus politically incorrect.

Here is the problem. Political correctness relies upon making assumptions about another person's intent. That is, presuming to know another person's mind and political prejudice, simply by virtue of the casual use of a word, and sometimes even before they have spoken. When applied this way, pollical correctness becomes what is now popularly called *'cancel culture'*.

I experienced *cancel culture* first-hand at a dinner party in Sydney, when I explained that I was writing about the contribution made by Marcus Aurelius towards developing public policy. I mentioned my involvement with a series of public policy debates in Melbourne, which explored challenging issues of our time, like 'climate change'. The moment I mentioned the words *'climate change'* my host raised his hand and declared… *"Stop right there! I won't be lectured on climate change!'* I was shocked and embarrassed by the intensity of this retort and by the way it *'cancelled'* me. I thought I was addressing Marcus Aurelius his contribution to public policy, not climate change. I had no intention of arguing about that thorny issue.

My host was clearly passionate about that cause, but he had not only terminated my speech and misunderstood the context of my comments; he had done something far worse. He had presumed to know my views on climate change before I had even voiced them. He had assumed that I must be a denier. Perhaps he thought I was a fascist, and thus his political enemy. Had he read my chapter on climate change in this book, he would know that I express alarm about it. In presuming to know my mind before I had spoken, he was *cancelling* me.

Shakespeare's plays, the bawdiness of Chaucer's 'Canterbury Tales' and of Boccaccio's 'Decameron', Mark Twain's Huck Finn and many other works use language which would not pass today's politically correct standards. Their swearing, cussing and sexism would be totally unacceptable. Chaucer's villains enjoyed *a hot poker up the bum* and Huck Finn had to deal with *niggers*. Thankfully, the works of these great writers are not familiar to many of the younger generation, otherwise we might lose their works to political correctness and never be able to enjoy them or celebrate their greatness. Political correctness not only makes assumptions about the *intent* of words, but also about their *meaning*. Political correctness assumes that those who construct their own meaning from the spoken or written words of others—even if they are offered ironically, sarcastically or in jest—can assert that they have been offended and assume the sole right to define what those words can mean.

I will share another example of this. In 2015, I was called upon to speak at the Annual General Meeting of a bank, on whose board I sat. I wanted particularly to congratulate the women who ran three of its local community branches. Why? Because the branches were a bit unusual. They employed 35 female staff and only one male staff member and had traded brilliantly—in fact, in the top percentile, nationally. In politically correct terms I should perhaps have complained about gender inequity, but instead I wanted to congratulate the female staff on their wonderful performance. In my speech, I referred to them as our '*mighty Amazons from the local branch*es' (intending with this comment to reflect the heroic women in Greek mythology who could match or exceed a man's strength and courage).

It seems my well-intentioned remark, intended as a compliment, so offended some female staff members that they wrote to the 'chairman' (whoops…I have used another gender preferencing word … I should have said 'chairperson') demanding a written apology from me. We agreed that it would be easier for all if I apologised, rather than waste time educating the staff on the Greek classics or explaining that they had in fact been commended. Ignorance of Greek mythology had turned my congratulatory remark into an offence. The listeners had ascribed their own, different meaning to my remarks and asserted that I had offended them.

This perverse *right to feel offended* seems to transcend our right to *freedom of speech.* It represents an extraordinary attack on freedoms that are almost as fundamental as the freedom to think. "Language that is intended to be hurtful should, of course, be deplored," says David James, with a Ph.D. in English literature. He makes a point when he adds … "but there is a high cost associated with outlawing any language use because one cannot presage a speaker's intentions—that would require further evidence—or simply rule out a multitude of other meanings."

The very definition of English words is changing as common usage is redefined by political correctness. This was evident in the discourse surrounding Trump's Tweets and the vitriolic exchanges between Democrats and Republicans. We have seen how the act of presaging or presuming to know the mind of another person and aggressively opposing a view, rather than politely agreeing to differ, has created a new English phrase, explained in contemporary dictionaries as 'cancel culture'. This form of political correctness is defined thus, by *Wikipedia*:

Cancel culture (or call-out culture) is a modern form of ostracism in which someone is thrust out of social or professional circles—either online, on social media, or in the real world. Those subject to this ostracism are said to be "cancelled", while the person doing the 'cancelling' is said to "stop giving support to a person" or, as defined in Dictionary.com, to "withdrawing support for (or cancelling) someone after they have done or said something they consider objectionable or offensive".

The expression "cancel culture" has negative connotations and is commonly used in debates on free speech and censorship. The notion of cancel culture constitutes boycotting an individual (usually a celebrity and often a politician) who is deemed to have acted or spoken in a questionable or controversial way. For those at the receiving end of 'cancel culture', the consequences can be harsh, leading to loss of reputation and income that can be hard to recover from.

The emergence of another word—'Woke', which for centuries has been the past tense of the verb 'to wake'—is another example of how political correctness is redefining us—not just our free speech and our public discourse, but our very definition of words. The expression 'Woke' now has two meanings. The *Urban Dictionary* defines '*woke*' as "the act of being very pretentious about how much you care about social issues" and adds that "you will have found a fine specimen of a woke person if he or she triumphantly posts on social media that he or she has just signed an online petition which will really, really, really change the world!"

In seeking to understand the impact of *political correctness, cancel culture* and '*Wokism'* upon free speech, and with apologies to Dr James, I offer my own, personal conclusions about political correctness. I respectfully leave you to yours:

- Political correctness descends into authoritarian behaviour and aggression.
- If democracy, and a free and open society, depend upon protecting free speech, then political correctness is an unvarnished attack upon each of these ideals.

- Assertive intervention, to correct or censure another person's speech, is politically toxic and, at the very least, extremely rude, anti-social behaviour.
- A tolerant society will see language, spoken or written, in all of its beautiful cadence, complexity and polyvalence. Theatre and the arts depend upon that.
- We should cut people a bit of slack and look for the better angels in their nature rather than silencing them with a terse or cancelling rebuke.
- Civil discourse depends upon tolerance, not rebuke, and listening, not silencing.

And I make this final observation: What has happened to schoolyard banter? To the language we used to use when we were able to laugh and say ... *'Sticks and stones may break my bones, but words will never hurt me'*. Let's just man-up (whoops, I mean 'person-up') and respect the right of others to used rich language to express their views! Voltaire would applaud that, and I agree with him ... or her.

Chapter 15
Could Democracy Use a Makeover?

If you always do what you've always done, you'll always get what you've always got.
Henry Ford

Emerging flaws in democracy constitute a storm cloud on its horizon. Their menace now rolls towards us, threatening to undermine democracy as a system of government and challenging its promise of personal freedom. We should not shrink from the task of reforming it, though a reformist path will inevitably be a difficult one. Churchill will be remembered for his observation about reform. He put it thus: *...to improve is to change, so to be perfect is to have changed often.* The man who put it better, Henry Ford, dared to change the way things were done and created a revolution which changed our world forever. If Ford could lift people out of horses and buggies and place them in comfortable mechanical carriages, might we not also reform democracy, to take it from a horse and buggy science to a more efficient one?

Australia—A Case Study

There are two different sorts of reforms we could introduce in our quest to rescue democracy from its current dysfunction. The first ones are procedural, rather than cultural—that is, directed at reforming procedural anomalies which distort fair representation or impair democratic function. These reforms are probably easier to achieve because the other sort, cultural reforms, require fundamental changes in people's thinking and behaviour. Cultural reforms are no less critical than procedural reforms. Indeed, they may be more critical since they seem to be pulling democracy out of shape more brutally than its procedural dysfunction.

When I speak of 'cultural dysfunction', I mean things like the *Woke* movement, political correctness, the *Black Lives Matter* movement which, by its very name, is alienating. I speak of things like gender assignment and critical race theory, which is pervading our schools and seeking to groom and reshape innocent young minds in areas other than reading, writing and arithmetic. And I include the lunatic politics of the far-right as well—of movements like the *Proud Boys,* motivated by hate rather than logic. Together, these new cultural phenomena are condoning unspeakable behaviour and rewriting our language, without our consent. They are changes which are imposing new constraints upon freedom of thought and expression. I address the impact of these later in this book.

However, let us start by looking at the procedural aspects we could reform, to make democracy more functional and fit-for-purpose in a brave new, fast moving cyber world. We have considered the US system which, incredibly, has different electoral processes in each state and no uniform national electoral oversight by a national electoral commission. So, reforming mechanical aspects of the US electoral processes ought to be easy because its flaws are so transparent. However, attempts to garner bipartisan support for such reform are struggling to gain traction, as the red versus blue toxicity of the Trump era continues to poison the public discourse.

There are other democratic models, like Switzerland's, which is the most directly representative democracy, with each regional community, or Canton, electing a representative but no single politician, official or entity dominating, or having authority exceeding that of the electors, (not even a Prime Minister or President, since Switzerland has neither one nor the other. The heads of state are the people). However, most western democracies, including Australia's, follow a Westminster style, with two houses, making it a good model for exploring possible reforms.

In Australia the reform challenge is tough because the drafters of the constitution gave it durability. There have been several attempts to reform the Australian constitution, most notably in 1999, when Australia tried to change from a Constitutional Monarchy to a Republic, but and such change could only be approved by a successful, national referendum. Only eight of forty-four national referenda (18%) have succeeded. The referendum for a change to a republic failed for two reasons; (i) fear that a Presidential office might create a fifth column of power and (ii) constitutional protections, which made reforming it almost impossible. Before any change to the Australian constitution can occur, a proposal must first be approved (i) by a majority of voters across all states and territories and (ii) by a majority of voters in a majority of states (i.e., in at least four of the six). This provision was designed to ensure constitutional stability but has also operates to frustrate necessary reforms.

Of all the changes one could make to improve democratic function, reform of the Upper House, that is, the Federal Senate (and its state counterparts), is top of the agenda and that view is shared across the partisan divide. Former Labor Prime Minister, Paul Keating, was strident in his condemnation of Australia's Federal Senate, calling its members *'unrepresentative swill'*. Conservatives also share that view, as do political scientists and most voters, who lament that, when Bills proceed to the upper house from the principal organ of their democracy, the House of Representatives, they are subject to protracted delays, voted down by senators elected on hairline margins or opposed for no other reason than because an opposition party controls that house, though it is in minority in the lower house.

In 2013, Senator Ricky Muir called himself the 'Motoring Enthusiasts Party' and was elected, under an archaic, proportionate representation system, to the senate with just 0.51% of the vote. In May 2021, Wilson Tucker, of the *Daylight Savings Party*, in Perth, won election to his state's upper house with just 98 votes. Australia's 'accidental' politician flew back home to back to Australia from his job abroad to a firestorm of controversy, having been elected with so few votes. His upper house seat embraced a vast mining and pastoral region of Western Australia. He now represented it, even though he was employed abroad in an IT job and had little or no knowledge of, or interest in, mining or agriculture. His victory, with just a handful of votes, was attributed to his clever harvesting of preferences with the help of a so-called "preference whisperer", Glenn Druery.

The state's Attorney-General labelled Mr Tucker's election *an affront to democracy*. "The preference system, and preference whispering, needs urgent reform," he said, "and the federal senate may be just the place to start." There are no quick fixes or easy reforms of a nation's electoral machinery but, in Australia, several reforms were identified by the Melbourne-based, *Quaffers* public policy group as relatively easy ones which could achieve much. Many of the proposed reforms could, equally, be applied to other democracies to improve them:

Reforming the Upper House

First, for the reasons already outlined, one would logically start by reforming upper houses in two, important ways. To prevent upper houses *governing by negative proxy,* one could limit their role to *reviewing, not rewriting, legislation.* Well-constructed reforms might, for example, restrict senate authority to amending a bill on no more than three passages through the house. If at least one amendment were conceded on each passage of a bill, after three passages, and a minimum of three amendments, voting on the bill, so amended, would be considered carried.

One might also reform upper house voting rules and the flow of preferences to ensure that members have a genuine mandate. While preserving the desirable object of fair representation from each State, as intended by the existing system, one could require that upper house members meet *'a minimum constituency benchmark'*, expressed as a minimum percentage of the vote in their seat, before winning an upper house seat. This would prevent the election of politicians like Ricky Muirs who, with just 0.015% (1/10th of one percent) of the senate vote, was empowered to pass, or frustrate, nation-changing legislation. A *'minimum constituency benchmark'* expressed as a *hurdle rate* of say 5% of the vote—could be set for candidates aspiring to upper house seats. There is a precedent for this reform. After WWII, the allied Military Government gave Germany a new constitution. Fearing that the Nazi Party might rise again, they created a hurdle rate of entry, whereby no candidate could sit in the Bundesrat unless his or her party achieved 5% of the national vote. This ensured that MPs had a genuine mandate and, in the Australian context, would also address the absurdity of upper house ballot papers which are the length of a banquet table and a gold mine for *'preference whisperers',* who use algorithms, to *farm* preferences. I strongly advocate a 5% hurdle rate for entry into upper houses, so that those who influence our legislation have a genuine mandate and real moral authority.

Reforming Spending

In our quest to improve the functionality of democracy, we could also reform federal spending and the national budget process by establishing *'best practice'* benchmarks, or tramlines. An *Independent Budget Commission,* made up of distinguished people outside the Parliament with economic and public policy credentials, could recommend *'best practice tramlines'* for public spending, expressed as OECD averages, or perhaps international ratios of spending to GDP—to guide spending in key areas like welfare, defence, education, health, transport, communications and other portfolios. Spending benchmarks (with a + or—10% tolerance) would prevent spending motivated by political opportunism or corruption.

Reforming Public Policy (To Address Policy Myopia)

To correct what I call *policy myopia* (policies which cannot see beyond a single term of office and thus fail to address long term challenges), a universal flaw, one could establish a *National Horizons Commission* tasked with recommending fifteen to twenty-year and thirty to fifty-year national goals. Governments could then be measured against aspirational, nation-building goals and penalised, through the ballot box and by the media, for failing to address or meet them.

As China rises and the world order changes under our feet, we had better start thinking about the world we want to be part of in future, not just preoccupied with the one we selfishly covert now. Xi Jinping's recent speech talked about a three-phase process—raising China out of its feudal state, making it a modern, functioning society and returning it ultimately to a role of strong global leadership. Each of those steps was part of a patient, planned policy journey towards a future China's leader wants for his people. That vision was not constrained by a three- or four-year election cycle or by a consequent need to throw electoral sweetmeats at the feet of voters. If democracy hope to compete as a system of government, it has to develop the same prescient leadership and its leaders need to articulate a vision for the future that captures the hearts and minds of a nation. That, it seems to me, is a major failing in our current, materialistic, just-in-time version of democracy.

Reforming the Preselection Process

One could reform the preselection of candidates, to make politics a community calling, rather than a privileged career path, and recalibrate preselection criteria and political salaries to attract broader community talent. Think of pre-selections as an executive search process, designed to attract the best candidate by recognising and rewarding demonstrated capacity and career success outside of politics. Such a reform would attract high achievers, higher levels of parliamentary diversity and higher levels of professional competence. Why is it that lawyers and trade unionists still make up such a large cohort within our Parliaments? That is patently absurd and not representative of the general population.

Above all, despite popular sentiment not to do so, we could introduce pay scales which align politicians with their senior corporate counterparts, to motivate men and women of high standing to enter politics. Leaders of a nation have a heavy responsibility which needs to be acknowledged and properly rewarded. The cost of attracting good leaders should be loose change in the game of nation-building.

Reforming Campaign Spending

Finally, I would impose limits on campaign spending, eliminate anonymous donations and eliminate donations by vested interest groups. This would ensure a level playing field across the political divide, prohibiting hyper-funding by those who, necessarily, have their own, secular agendas. Such reforms would place all candidates on the same starting line, in the same footrace, and force candidates to win election on their own merits, not by dint of a well-oiled, well-funded marketing campaigns. Voters would choose candidates on the basis of the policies they present and their ability to articulate their case, rather than because of charismatic media campaigns. Candidates would have to articulate their case in their own tongue, and spell out what they stand for, without confected media language or slogans.

Chapter 16
Public Policy and Public Order

Do every act as if it were your last.
Marcus Aurelius

We take for granted the public laws, standards and regulations that direct our lives. The things they direct appear mundane—things like footpaths, to lift us out of muddy thoroughfares, clean drinking water, sewerage and the roads and highways that connect us and facilitate trade and commerce. These bring order to our lives, but we barely pause to acknowledge that delivering each one has been hugely complex. Developing, and then delivering public policy is like shooting rapids. One must first identify the policy challenge, then launch the policy discussion. One must then navigate complex political rapids before running the rocky shoals of cost-benefit analysis. Just when the way ahead looks clear, new obstacles appear, in the form of planning and engineering challenges and fiscal constraints on spending.

Over 2,000 years ago, the ancients, led by the Greeks and the Romans, are credited with bringing public order to the streets. They achieved order by developing public policies and enforcing them with laws, designed to control and regulate. Indeed, the prescient public policy thinking of the Romans still informs modern public administration. But the Romans had one major advantage over modern administrators. Their leaders were Emperors—benevolent dictators, not democrats—and were able to mobilise cheap human resources (slaves), impose military force to ensure compliance and obtain necessary finances, by simply commanding them.

They were unfettered by modern democratic considerations, like community consultation, environmental impact studies, human rights and other 'equity' issues. They could simply get on with the job. Enforcement laws in ancient times would not be tolerated today. They included harsh penalties, like the crucifixion of criminals, the banishment of tax defaulters and the stoning of adulterers (in Marcus Aurelius' Rome). Over the past 2,000 years, we have improved many aspects of public administration, but we cannot match Rome's brutal efficiency in enforcing compliance with public laws and regulations, which enabled Rome to simply get things done.

In its nascent form, the 'science of public administration' first appeared in Egypt in 2,600 BC when stone buildings appeared. Historians credit the development of science, particularly mathematics, for this sudden leap forward, as those sciences informed Egypt's extraordinary engineering and architectural feats. In Greece, public order was restored when Pericles overthrew the wealthy elite who ran Athens. They had progressively strayed from notions of 'public interest' and reshaped policy around maximising their own self-interest. His reforms allowed common people to have a voice and demonstrated that democracy depends upon enlightened public administration. Then, in 687 BC, the Greeks opened the first 'offices of government', so that public policy could be developed and administered. Their ideas about orderly government were then adopted by the Romans, in 509 BC. But public administration, on a serious scale, and a 'science of public policy', did not really find practical expression until the mature days of the Roman Empire, in around 27BC.

Before one can administer public policy in a practical way, one needs a metropolis—a centre of social and civic life—because that is where people come together, start carousing and behave badly. How did metropolises arise? It seems that public amenities were initially to blame—communal toilets, water fountains and livestock markets. These attracted people to hubs and brought them together in dense clusters, which became towns and cities. Denser populations, in turn, gave rise to demands for better access ways, better food and shelter and better water and sanitation. When people congregated, disagreements escalated, so laws were needed to enforce civil order. Decisions which delivered these things, made things safe and improved the human condition were codified and became 'public policy'.

Athens, one of the most important cities in the ancient world, offers useful insights into this process. The bustling main thoroughfare was the *Panathenaic Way*. For the annual celebration of Athena (the goddess of wisdom for whom the city is named), a procession of citizens from far and wide marched over a mile to the Altar of Athena on the *Acropolis*. In a macho society, men also gathered, on a regular basis, at three public gymnasia, training and preparing for the (naked) athletics competitions, held in the Panathenaic Stadium. The thousands of citizens who participated in Athens' fledgling democracy attended a popular assembly at the *Pnyx*, a hillock in the centre of the city. But the heart of daily life was the *Agora*, or marketplace, a sprawling complex of more than 200,000 square feet that traded daily essentials; oil lamps, fruits, meat, cloth etc. People began to enjoy interacting and congregating around these markets, so other attractions were soon added, most notably brothels, drinking taverns, and bathhouses.

The Romans vastly improved public policy when they merged it with engineering, building sturdy public roads, bridges, tunnels and aqueducts. Two thousand years later, these still stand as testaments, not just to Roman engineering, but to the evolution of public policy. Marcus Vitruvius, the Roman architect and military engineer who refined this science during the first century BC, is my hero. He took public policy to another level by establishing *standards*, as exemplified by his order that '*all public buildings must be executed in a way that takes account of durability, utility and beauty*'. Without knowing it, this organised man, with a prescient mind, was a pioneer, shaping public policy into a science with costs and benefits one could measure. He was also an author, and meticulously recorded his work.

Before him, the so called *Five Good Emperors*—Nerva (98 to 96 BC), Trajan (117 to 97 BC), Hadrian (138 to 117 BC), Antoninus Pius (161 to 138 BC), and Marcus Aurelius (180 to 161 BC)—were pathfinders in elevating public administration to the status of a science. They presided over Rome's most majestic days, progressively enhancing regulations to secure public order and amenity, gradually improving civic planning and administration, and continually expanding Rome's local, national and international infrastructure (including its roads, ports and fortresses).

Much of this book explores the rise of China. In my quest to understand more, I have studied more closely China's '*Belt and Road*' initiative and tried to understand whether its motives are genuine or sinister. In the process, I garnered information about the origins and complexities of this strategy. I learned, for example, that the correct translation from the Chinese text一带 一 路, is 'One Belt—One Road' and that those words were shorthand for a lengthier description, the 'Silk Road Economic Belt', first espoused by Xi Jinping in 2013. As I continued my research, I experienced a 'light-bulb moment', a moment of revelation like that experienced by Paul on the road to Damascus, which changed his life, and mine. From the deepest recesses of my brain, one question kept haunting me:

Could China's 'Belt and Road' be the same as Rome's network of viaducts and aqueducts? The same strategy as that implemented 2,000 years ago by the Romans, to extend their military and cultural influence across a vast empire? Were Rome's networks of roads, ports and aqueducts, and the cultural influences they left in conquered and compliant vassal states, the same thing as China's ambitious plans to expand its global mercantile and investment influence, including by building or investing in global infrastructure? Was China adopting a Roman strategy, to expand its culture into new territories, create new alliances and acquire vassal states?'

It seemed to me that the Romans had employed a very similar strategy—using their investments in roads, ports, and 'bridges—both real and figurative along which they could export to, or import from, each dominion a growing tide of commodities and technologies—an ancient equivalent of China's Silk Road. History teaches us that the Romans exported their road, bridge and highway construction techniques, their catapults and other military ideas, but were also great techno-maniacs, 'stealing' technology from other nations, like the Middle Eastern shadoof, for lifting water into irrigation canals, the waterwheel for grinding grain, the European crossbow and other weaponry, as they sought to expand their empire.

Like China's contemporary one, Rome's empire, was built upon marvellous engineering and cultural achievements, and marvellous infrastructure projects—its magnificent highways, aqueducts, bath houses and ramparts; Roman military disciplines, Roman laws and by-laws, and above all, Roman culture were the building blocks of empire, and Rome's equivalent of China's *Belt and Road* strategy created an empire which lasted for some 500 years.

If this strategy worked so well for Rome, why not for China? I offer the following additional information about the *'One Belt-One Road'* strategy which may help us to understand whether it is an enlightened or a sinister strategy.

- It was first espoused by Xi Jinping himself. It is therefore a plan in which he is deeply, personally invested. It was Xi himself who first described the strategy to the world, before it was really understood by his own CCP colleagues, as the *'Silk Road Economic Belt'* during an official visit to Kazakhstan in September 2013.

- It was immediately embraced by the CCP and is no longer just a personal ambition, having been formally adopted by the Chinese government and described as '*a national global infrastructure development strategy*'.
- Its stated goal is to invest in nearly 70 countries and international organisations, and to make it the centrepiece of Xi's foreign policy. The words 'belt' and 'road' were carefully chosen. 'Belt' is a contraction for Xi's original *Silk Road* proposal, drawing on the metaphor of the ancient Silk Road which, from 200 BC until 1700 AD, linked the east and west and, to be fair, greatly facilitated the flow of trade and culture in both directions.
- Xi's 'One Belt One Road' envisages overland routes for road and rail through landlocked Central Asia along historical trade routes of the Western Regions. But according to Xi Jinping, in a contemporary context, the word 'road'—as in 'One Road'—does not just refer to a land-based road network, but also captures his ambition for a '21st Century Maritime Silk Road', comprising 'sea lanes', including those connecting Indo-Pacific sea lanes, from Southeast Asia to South Asia, and from the Middle East to Africa—linking the existing network of land-based highways with existing and new sea routes.

China's Belt and Road Initiative includes investments in ports and stately buildings proclaiming China's might and architectural splendour—much like the Greek and Romanesque public buildings Hitler built to proclaim his 1,000year Reich. It includes railroads, highways, airports and dams—including the hydro-power dam China has built in Cambodia at the head of the Mekong, effectively controlling downstream flows. And it includes bold tunnels and bridges, like the 55-kilometre bridge linking Hong Kong to Zhuhai and Macau, and other, similar projects.

China is making impressive progress with this strategy while the west sits on its hands, unable to build competing, or equally grandiloquent infrastructure projects because China's autocracy is nimble, while modern democracy is massively bound up in red tape. Comparable western projects require a political decision, achieved against public opposition to it, community consultation, environmental impact studies, a tortuous wade through multiple layers of bureaucracy, and the attraction of private risk capital. China can bypass most of these tedious steps and just do it!

Most westerners would be alarmed to know that China's *One Belt—One Road* initiative was incorporated into its Constitution in 2017 and that a recent edict said that *'all such development projects, including ports, must have a dual civilian and military capacity'*. China's official media describe it as *'a bid to enhance regional connectivity and to embrace a brighter future'*. Like Goebbels edicts, the Chinese have become expert at putting a positive spin on any of their activities. The project has a completion date of 2049, which will coincide with the 100th anniversary of the founding of the People's Republic of China.

If those lofty words to describe it were genuine, China's Belt and Road strategy would have many laudable features. It is an idea which would be applauded, I dare say, if the west had thought of it first and it turned out to be genuine in its motives—namely, to bring nations together. Instead, China' aspirations for building a new empire—like Hitler's aspirations for a Third Empire, or Reich, are building a bow-wave of xenophobic angst in the west about China's real motives. Many worry that the nation we once called a *'sleeping tiger'* is wide awake, and its ambitions are creating an ideological gulf, rather than a uniting bridge, between the East and West.

Observers and sceptics alike, from non-participating countries, including the United States, interpret *'Belt and Road'* as a plan for a Sino-centric trade and geo-political sphere of influence. In response to this perceived threat, the United States, Japan and Australia have formed a little-known counter initiative, called the *Blue Dot Network* (formed in 2019). Moreover, on 21 April 2021, Australia's Foreign Minister, Marise Payne, said that Australia would be *'pulling out of the Belt and Road initiative completely'*, a strange retort, since we were not ever formally included in it.

But I digress. We have asked the questions *'Where did public policy come from? And how did it evolve?'* China's *Belt and Road* strategy may provide an answer. If it is the same as the strategy which first came to prominence under the Roman's, combining autocratic rule, military might and territorial ambition, we had better beware, for with it, the Romans were able to build the greatest continuum of government in history.

The combination of assertive rule, military capacity and a desire to spread cultural influence worked brilliantly for Rome, and these elements appear succinctly in the rise of China and its One Belt—One Road' ambitions. And it is now openly acknowledged as a 'public policy'—one which has been formally adopted into law by the Central Committee of the Chinese Communist Party.

One is forced to the conclusion that the Chinese model is shaping a new world order in which democracy seems bound to become, if it has not already done so, less dominant and less competitive as a system of government. That troubles me greatly. Not just because democracy is now demonstrably less efficient than autocracy at delivering services and outcomes, but because of the threat China's autocratic model implies to hallowed western values—like freedom of thought, speech and expression and the right to aspire to happiness and personal fulfilment. I am forced to the conclusion that western democracies, if they are to survive and compete, must answer some confronting, philosophical questions:

- Is China's system of government, despite its autocratic harshness, a more efficient system of government and public administration?
- If the answer is to that question is *yes*, is democracy still 'fit for purpose'?
- Could China's *One Belt—One Road* initiative, like the ancient Silk Road, unite nations rather than divide them, and distribute trade and economic benefit?
- Will that initiative, as it unfolds, be positive or negative for world peace?
- Or is China's *One Belt—One Road* initiative a wolf in sheep's clothing? Whether we can answer those questions positively or negatively, the answer will have consequences, not just for the survival of democracy but for the way democracy delivers public policy. Public policy is the critical element which builds and sustains public cohesion. That is demonstrably true for China as it is for America, Britain or Australia. What then does that mean for democracy, if it doesn't measure up as a system of government? It means that we must treasure public policies which preserve liberty and elevate the human condition and eschew those in other regimes which subjugate or oppress. For those qualities make democracy, with all of its other shortcomings, fairer, more humane, more just and therefore a superior system.

There is, however, a sting in democracy's tail. Precisely because it is so open, transparent and accountable, it is more easily penetrated and corrupted by internal malignancies, including Plato's 'sense of entitlement'. Good public policy should regulate these things, in an exquisite arm-wrestle with public sentiment. My next chapter thus examines public policy in more detail, beginning with the rhetorical question: *Is public policy the same as politics?*

Chapter 17
Without Policy Clothes, Democracy Walks Naked

The biggest challenge in public policy is to know when and how the world has changed.
Richard Lamm

This book was originally to be about public policy. Writing it should have been easy. I had organised, chaired and recorded policy forums for some 15 years. These papers would be collated and used to demonstrate how public policy shaped society. That was my intention, but as I began, the world around me began tugging at my sleeve. It became apparent that public policy was not a rational or linear thing but, rather, something that was hammered into or out of shape on a political anvil. By 2020, it was changing at warp speed, and with it, the world we lived in. China had emerged from nowhere to assume a commanding presence on the world stage. Donald Trump was rattling democracy's cage and shaking the foundations of its governance. His *'Twitter-texts'* were more like explosions from a blunderbuss—firing a volley of *'policy stones in the rough'*, unpolished by public debate, unedited by cautious minds and unfettered by due process.

Trump was twittering like a canary, while Britain stumbled like a blind man through Brexit, juggling that event with the coronavirus. These new phenomena were distorting my policy world faster than I could write about them. Democracy, too, was being sorely tested, as public policy, which typically evolves methodically, over time, like a tortoise rather than a hare, was unable to find a timely response to such rapid-fire changes. Weighed down by political toxicity and bureaucratic intransigence, public policy seemed to waddle behind a fast-moving reality, like a duck with a limp, always pausing to absorb a new crisis or react to the political buffoonery which cluttered its pathway, and finally arriving too late to do much about it.

The public theatre surrounding the US election was unfolding on one side of the Atlantic while, on the other, Brexit and the coronavirus were bedevilling British democracy. To the south-east, a Chinese dragon had awoken from a deep sleep and was rising, becoming assertive, and building new momentum in its march towards empire. Russia, too, was busy in a more clandestine way, deftly administering toxins to political dissidents and cyber-intruding into western politics. Finally, the institutions which underpinned our rules-based world order seemed to have lost both their voice and their authority. Did those things, together, signal that democracy was crumbling, or was democratic dysfunction the product of increasingly bad public policy?

In a moment of clarity, it occurred to me that governments would walk naked if they were not clothed in tidy public policy. That the one, good governance, was dependent upon the other, public policy. When these two were functioning at their best, they walked hand in hand. So, it seemed to me that, if we were to rescue democracy from its present dysfunction, we should ask men and women of good conscience to rise above their political prejudice in search of good, a-political public policy. That would require that we reach across the aisle in a common cause—to rediscover civil discourse and rescue democracy from the malign forces which threaten it. Above all, good governance requires that we sift public policy from the moving sands of political prejudice and media spin.

In writing this book, I have tried to set aside my own prejudice, to give all sides of an argument equal air, and resisted favouring one political view over another. But when the subject is contentious and it might have been safer to remain ambivalent, I have chosen not to be so, as that leaves you, my readers, in a state of flux. Instead, I dare to express a view in favour of one argument or another. Many of you will disagree with particular views I share, but that is, after all, the nature of democracy. Without a miscellany of views, democracy's compass can never find true north. To function properly, it *demands* open debate. That is its lifeblood. And each of us is privileged if, by an accident of birth, we live in a democracy, for the forces which oppose democracy don't allow citizens that privilege. They simply silence dissent and coerce adherence to a faith of their own making.

Writing this book has been like journeying through a foreign land, where sunsets are streaked with new colours, sunrises stream blinding light and dark clouds gather over distant horizons. I am troubled by an emerging world order which I don't yet understand and by changes which proposes a new social contract between people and their rulers—influences which are threatening my Westminster model of democracy. Is public policy the one constant we can rely on to guide us forward?

If men and women of good conscience are to rebuild a civil discourse, the best way to do this, I think, is to find comfort in public policy—to assess and discuss social issues on their merits and allow good policy, informed by fact or science, from whatever side of politics it comes, to triumph over political prejudice and spin. To rise above what I will call the *pernicious 'Ps'*—political toxicity, partisan prejudice, political spin and populism. For most of us, particularly those driven by strong tribal loyalties, that may a bridge too far, but it is a journey worth taking.

Is Good Public Policy Good Governance?

Having decided that public policy is what holds societies together, I began researching where it came from and how it evolved. I wanted to bang that information into my keyboard, to better inform and reassure myself that democracy was safe, because it farmed input from many minds, letting free speech enrich the thought process and stimulate public debate. However, my research raised more questions than it answered.

'What does 'public policy' really mean?' Is it made in a top-down fashion, by rulers, or in a bottom-up fashion, by citizens? 'Is 'public policy' just 'another word for 'politics?' Is it a science, and if so, 'how did it evolve?' Does government—be it a democracy, a dictatorship, a communist state, a monarchy or some other form—determine the shape of public policy, or does public policy *shape government*? I decided that public policy must always have been central to the rise and fall of nations, *irrespective* of their system of government, and likely followed, rather than spurred, the conflicts and conquests that created nations.

One thing is certain. Nations which rise to greatness rely upon public policy to *sustain* their greatness. Military capacity alone does not do it. Winning wars and invading others might be a great way to extend one's boundaries and acquire territory, but a belligerent warrior state cannot achieve lasting greatness or social order without sound public policy. Public policy builds lasting social cohesion, creates order and regulates behaviour. It straddles a nation's administrative, civil, legal cultural, religious and even its military landscape, to achieve national cohesion. Public policy also makes things work …codifying everything from engineering standards to public health, and from rail connectivity to defence spending. It is the glue that binds us and maintains social order. It is not surprising, therefore, that the civilisations which first developed a science of public policy were the first to rise out of their crude, agrarian-subsistence and become civilised.

There is evidence that public policy, around things like irrigation channels, land ownership, chariot construction and military training, made the Egyptians, Assyrians and Greeks great (the Greek word *demos* or *common people eventually* gave rise to the term '*democracy*'). The Romans, whose Plutocracy endured for 500 years, was buttressed by a strong fundament of public policies. Rome's Marcus Aurelius was important because he not only refined the science and practice of public policy but also wrote down his thoughts about it, for the benefit of future generations.

Public policy is not always a force for good, and not all nations which rose to greatness were benevolent. There were many malign regimes, like Genghis Khan's blood-thirsty raiders, Hitler's third Reich and Hirohito's Japan, where public policy was a major ingredient in forging social complicity and retaining public cohesion, even in an evil cause. Those regimes took people with them on a perverse policy ride, despite policy immorality—including an entire German folk, who loved culture and classical music but hated Jews. The atrocities committed by those regimes remind us that public policy is, in the end, a raft of legal, cultural, social and moral planks constructed by rulers, both good and bad, and can have both *benevolent* and *malevolent* consequences, depending on the policy direction a government takes.

We may all agree that maintaining greatness—for example, a Roman or a British Empire's greatness—requires the ability to sustain social order and cohesion. But greatness cannot rely solely upon good public policy. If it is to endure, a great nation must also defend itself against the forces aligned against it. Military capacity must therefore be an intimate precursor to national ascendancy, and military might, commensurate to the greatness of a nation, essential to sustaining its power and dominion. The 'rise and fall' of Rome makes that clear and it remains as valid today as it was back then. Superpower status is not just about public policy's role in securing social cohesion. It must be anchored in military power.

Arms races, in their various ancient and modern guises, have always been about achieving domination or building a defensive capacity against such domination. Public policy must therefore always have a room in its house for defensive, or offensive military postures, including military alliances. This should remind us that, in the present age of rapid technological advancement, military technology is evolving in parallel with Wi Fi, Bluetooth and other ubiquitous technologies which pervade our modern lives. Along with those which deliver civil amenity, many insidious threats have emerged—invisible cyber intrusions which drift silently through time and space to capture our thoughts and spy on our actions, more lethal missiles, microwave and magnetic pulse weapons, which cause moral outrage, etc. But I ask this question: if remaining great means combining public policy with a potent military capacity, what happens if one of those two pillars fails?

Just as Nations Rise, They Can Also Fall

The process by which nations rise to greatness must surely have a counterpart process, by which they fall from it. But if good public policy and administration are critical to a nation's rise, is the reverse—bad policy and administration—responsible for a nation's decline? History is again informative. It teaches that administrative dysfunction and moral decadence are common precursors to the decline of empires. Why should this not apply, equally, to our modern superpower equivalents? If a fall from greatness is foretold by moral decline, decadence or corruption, are these in evidence? In which nations do we find them? And do they signal an imminent decline? Phases of ascendancy and decline have occurred many times before and will occur for as long as man occupies his planet. Many observers perceive that we are in a transitional phase right now; one which is dividing global power into two opposing camps—democracy versus autocracy.

What will our world look like in 50 years-time? Is American leadership of the free world in decline? Is Britain a spent force? Is China's ascendancy assured, or is it fragile, as the world rebalances its response to it? Will 600 million middle class Chinese add a thirst for democracy to their penchant for French wines and Ferraris?

I would pay a king's ransom for answers to those questions. As I contemplate the future, my image of it is clouded by a swirling fog of uncertainty, for the rise and fall of nations is as assured as the continuum of history. Nations are always in a state of flux, tending to rise or to fall according to the fortunes that shape them. Their transition to greater or lesser nationhood is a work in progress. Time will tell whether the US can regain its charismatic leadership of the free world and whether China can sustain its rise to global superpower status ... or indeed, to continue its march towards empire. There may even be a third outcome, a balance of power like that which existed last century and was shattered when Archduke Ferdinand was assassinated. What if, once again, the powers of the east and the west align in an arm wrestle for supremacy, the precursor to similar, cataclysmic global conflicts?

We must hope that our modern institutions, calculated to preserve a rules-based world order, prevent a repeat of that sort of madness. Indeed, as I reflect on the matter, it seems to me that the thing which keep us all in line is not politics, which is plagued by passion and volatility, but public policy, which operates as a soothing balm, to maintain equilibrium. It did so way back in Egyptian times and has done so in all the great civilisations which have followed. Sane public policy always operates to curb insane politics. Public policy preserves social order and keeps the wheels of government turning, when hot heads try to distract us. It is a moderating force.

If I am right that public policy is critical to good governance and to maintaining social cohesion, and if one can call it a science, where did it come from? How did it evolve? I attempt to answer those questions in my next chapter, and hope to reveal some secrets about ourselves, where we have come from and where we are headed.

Chapter 18
Can Policy Rise Above Politics?

*The secret of freedom lies in educating… the secret of tyranny,
in keeping people ignorant.*
Robespierre

Roman rulers, and the engineers who oversaw their public works, might have 'rested on their laurels', to coin a Roman phrase. But they could not, because they were subject to the irresistible force of public sentiment—*politics*. It was political pressure which drove them to continually improve methods and invent new ones, and to experiment with new materials and techniques. This process was greatly assisted by the global reach of the Roman empire, which allowed emperors like Hadrian to observe, appropriate and apply distant technologies for the benefit of Rome. Today we might call that a 'theft of foreign intellectual property', for that is precisely what it was, and technology was not legally protected back then, the way it is now.

Roman rulers and their agents observed the world around them and borrowed (or stole) from it without apology, to modernise bridge and aqueduct construction, improve weapon systems, build machines that better harnessed the power of water, and improve the administration of their empire. The introduction of the Roman wheeled plough, for example, dramatically increased agricultural production, making food grain and wine the new currencies of empire. As public policy merged with technical innovation, Rome's military, engineering and organisational skills generated so much wealth and prosperity that an elite class emerged. Standing above the masses, *Patricians* were a highly influential lot and, in their turn, exerted even greater political pressure upon rulers to improve their lifestyle, secure Rome's borders and cement Roman domination of Europe and the Mediterranean.

While these observations support the idea that public policy and politics are the same thing, on closer inspection, it is clear that they are *not*. Indeed, they are strange bedfellows, coexisting in a state of exquisite tension. A powerful autocrat, for example, running his nation centrally, might define public policy as that which he and his elite, power-sharing cronies deem it to be, whatever that may be—not what the people themselves might want. Some hold that present day China is an example of this, demonstrating how public policy plays out in a closed rather than an open society.

Like Rome's Emperors, China's leaders can '*command*' physical, human, and financial resources, without being very troubled about the governance and accountability issues that bedevil democracy. And they can create and impose draconian laws to enforce compliance without incurring the wrath of civil libertarians or human rights activists. Because China limits or controls these and other aspects of life (free speech, international trade and investment, intellectual property rights etc.) it is a 'Command Economy'. We have seen that, with other centrally planned economies, including India, Brazil and Cuba, China and the command economies now control some 58% of world trade. If democracy has unwittingly ceded mercantile dominance to the command economies, it had better wake up and respond!

Is Political Dysfunction Distorting Public Policy?

We have seen that China's autocratic regime, unfettered by western notions of public interest or by human rights, equity, environmental or other sensitivities, are able to progress economic development projects efficiently, while democracies, which are required to serve the will of the people, must first wrestle through a myriad of public consultative, legal, planning and other bureaucratic processes before gaining approval to proceed. In democracies, these things, intended to ensure equity and justice, conspire to constrain progress. By way of example, in the Victorian town of Kilmore, a town bypass has been debated for 18 years but is yet to be built.

The culture of '*not in my backyard*' pitted two lobby groups against each other—the '*west is best*' and the '*eastern route*' lobbies. Bumper stickers supporting one route option or the other appear on local vehicles. Much fist clenching and writing of angry letters to the editor ensued. After 18 years of so-called community consultation—democracy's *Achille's heel,* and a constraint which drags like a sea anchor on progress in democracies—a bypass route was finally agreed. In seeking to please all sides of the debate, a compromise had been found, resulting in a route which looked more like a crankshaft than a straight line. One stretch of bypass first directed traffic away from, then later back towards the township, largely defeating the purpose of the whole project. After eighteen years of tiresome public conflict, work on the bypass was yet to commence. By way of comparison, during those same eighteen years, China had completed 7 high-speed rail systems (bullet trains), three new cities, doubled its port capacity and become a great military power. God help democracy!

While this book largely cites Australian policy aberrations, like the Kilmore bypass, the dilemma remains the same in other western democracies. It matters not whether you are sitting in a democratic boardroom in Sydney, in New York or in London, or in an autocratic boardroom in Beijing, Pyongyang or Moscow. The task of distilling good policy out of the swirling mist of competing interests is a similar one, but the ability to act decisively and with dispatch to deliver outcomes is decidedly different in each. Examples of bad public policy can be found in either system, but they are most apparent internationally, when there is a clash of interests and cultures, in the institutions which shape or regulate our international community.

Most of us would agree, for example, that the decision by the World Health Organisation to accept China's early assurances about containment of the coronavirus, which delayed the WHO's release of public health warnings to an unsuspecting global audience, was a catastrophic failure of public policy, with massive, global consequences. In assessing the coronavirus threat as a small outbreak in one Chinese town, the WHO made a critical error of judgement and failed in its duty of care. Bad policy allowed an insidious pandemic to invade a global landscape. So, bad policy can have very serious, very malign consequences, whether in a small, local government context or in a transnational context.

Some would hold that Australia's call for an investigation into how the virus escaped was bad policy. It certainly was from Australia's point of view, as it had an extraordinary sting in its tail—the heavy price paid by Australia's in cancelled or lost trade with China. Few nations questioned the morality of Australia's quite reasonable request, but many questioned China's terse response. One immutable fact is clear. Even policy decisions which seem to radiate common sense, seem axiomatic in their logic and should rise above politics, can fail to find traction in an autocracy.

Good public policy does not happen easily. It must be extracted as one might extract a stubborn molar tooth, because it must first rise above political differences. That requires political courage, informed leadership and decisions based upon incontestable fact and science, not political self-interest or spin.

Chapter 19
Toxic Language—Hate Speech, Virtue Signalling and Other Toxicity

Rudeness is the weak person's imitation of strength.
Eric Hoffer

On 6 January 2021, I awoke at 5 am to a chorus of birdsong. A pink dawn greeted me as I paddled through the peaceful halls of my Australian farmhouse towards the kitchen. I passed the TV in the library and decided to check how a more troubled society in the US was facing its day. Had Trump yet come to grips with his election loss? Had things settled down now that the Democrats had finally won both Senate seats in Georgia, gaining control of both the upper and lower houses? It was time, surely, for the US to heal its wounds and make its new year a better one.

In Washington, it was 1.00 pm. I clicked on the world news and was greeted by a tirade of inflammatory rhetoric from lame duck President Donald Trump, indifferent to the manner in which his language was inciting to violence a crowd of thousands of angry demonstrators, waving banners proclaiming—'Stop the Steal', "Make America Great Again" and 'I am with Jesus and Jesus is with Trump'.

T-Shirts carried rightist slogans. The crowd included 'Proud Boys', far-rightists waving Confederate flags, wearing military fatigues and carrying improvised weapons. Bandanas and clubs made the thugs obvious, but they were accompanied by civilised looking people who ought to have known better. Archetypal Republicans, the quiet, middle-class establishment Americans we had come to associate with that party, were nowhere in evidence. They may have been looking on gravely, disturbed or outraged by Trump's trashing of their Republican brand as he appeared on TV touting fanciful statistics to support his delusional claims of election fraud. His words were delivered angrily, in a tirade of what could only be described as hate-speak.

The beacon-light of democracy that had always emanated from the US Capitol was all but extinguished that day, as world leaders, too, looked aghast at the damage Trump was inflicting upon his country's brand, its prestige and its leadership role in world affairs. Speaking ahead of Trump, his faithful allies, Rudy Giuliani and his two sons, had fanned the same, false bonfire of delusion, repeating allegations of election fraud. Giuliani urged his supporters to *"wage trial by combat,"* while Donald Trump Jr. railed against the Republican Congressmen and women who had declined to support Trump's embarrassing charade.

"We're gonna walk down to the Capitol," said Trump, "and we're gonna cheer our brave senators and congressmen and women… but we're probably NOT gonna be cheering so much for some of 'em, because you'll never take back our country with weakness. You have to show strength and you have to be strong." Those words rose to a treasonous level.

As a result of Trump's propaganda, the Capitol was then stormed, requiring the evacuation of the Senators working inside. There, a brave and more dignified Republican—Vice President, Mike Pence—had been chairing certification of the *real*, not *fake*, election outcome. The result had withstood hurdles in the courts and in the legislative chambers. Both institutions had affirmed the integrity of the process prescribed by America's founders, albeit one in need of some revision. Pence had ignored his deranged boss's instructions, salvaging whatever dignity he could.

History has shown that lies, repeated often enough, become fact in the minds of an accepting audience. We have seen this phenomenon many times before. Lies and distortions are the hallmark of controlling regimes, not democracies. They are the metaphorical bullets fired by manipulators—for example, when they are fired as war-time propaganda by men like Goebbels who, in March 1945, aroused global condemnation over the bombing of Dresden when his SS controlled German Red Cross reported 202,040 deaths in the attack. The real figure was just 20,204 but the Nazi propaganda machine had simply added a zero to achieve its goal. When lies are accepted as fact, democracy is shattered.

The phenomenon of public dis-information was once unique to war—indeed referred to as a propaganda war—but it has become ubiquitous to society with the advent of new communications technology. Man has found new ways to whisper or shout his false messages electronically, using cyber-speak to reach a new, 'virtual' public. Included in his new cyber-rhetoric is a careless mix of information and misinformation, delivered over a myriad of cyber channels and emerging on shiny screens that project images and texts from hand-held, robotic and other devices. Man has produced a new threat to democracy that operates like a silently virus to infiltrate and weaken it. Some might argue that the vastly increased number of communications channels has broadened, rather than diminished free speech. That it has made democracy stronger, not weaker. That is fine for speech which informs the public debate, but what if it is toxic, or simply confected truth and lies?

The environment in which a dignified Westminster system once operated, not just in the UK and the US but in other hallowed cathedrals of Democracy, has arguably changed so fundamentally, that democracy has yet to figure out how to adapt to it. When did the insidious cancer of hate-speech first seep into our politics, replacing the intellectual jousting, clever wit and repartee which once rang though the halls of our Parliaments? I decided to investigate whether the ancients, too, had hurled toxic abuse at each other as they spoke publicly in defence of their points of view. I was surprised by what I found. The ancients, too, beginning with the Greeks, had used direct, toxic language when seeking to tear down a political opponent. But clever wit and genteel wisdom were more common and elevated the debate.

In that ancient melting pot of democracy, which was still finding its way, no two-party system had evolved, so political attacks, when they occurred, were directed randomly at people who misspoke or events which were opposed, rather than along tribal, or what we now call party lines. Back then there were some astonishing philosophers who could calm the masses and bring sense and reason to civil discourse. Would that we had such statesmanlike examples in our modern discourse.

Consider these gems of ancient wisdom, which informed civil discourse without resorting to personal attacks:

"The real destroyer of the liberties of people is he who spreads among them bounties, donations and benefits."—Plutarch

"When you are offended by another man's fault, study your own failings. Then you will forget your opponent's offence."—Epictetus

"Wealth is something to be properly used, rather than boasted about. As for poverty, no one need be ashamed to admit it: the real shame is in not taking measures to escape from it."—Pericles

"Those who have virtue in their mouths, and neglect it in practice, are like a harp; they emit a pleasing sound but are insensible to their own music."—Diogenes

"Toil is no source of shame; idleness is shame."—Hesiod

"We hang petty thieves and appoint great ones to public office."—Aesop

"Society is well governed when its people obey magistrates, and when magistrates obey the law."—Solon

And the following from Aristotle:

"The worst form of inequality is to make unequal things which are equal."

"We praise a man who feels angry on the right grounds, against the right persons, in the right manner, and at the right moment."

"Republics decline into democracies. Democracies degenerate into despotisms."

And from the wisest of them all, Plato, whose wisdom informs this book: "The most virtuous are those who are innately virtuous without seeking to be so."

"Good people don't need laws to tell them to act responsibly, while bad people find ways around the law."

"Justice means minding one's own business, not meddling in other men's affairs."

"When there is an income tax, the just man will pay more and the unjust one less, on the same amount of income."

"Our object in the construction of the state is the greatest happiness of the whole—not that of any one class."

"Only the dead have seen the end of war."

"The curse of me and my nation is that we always think things can be bettered by immediate action of some sort, of any sort, rather than of no sort at all."

"Knowledge becomes evil if the aim be not virtuous."

"This is the root from which a tyrant springs; when he first appears, he is a protector."

These gems indicate that civilised discourse was prevalent in ancient times as it was in contemporary times when wit, mirth and repartee resonated across the halls of Westminster. But civil discourse has always had a counterpart—

pugnacious abuse and cheap point scoring. Xi Jinping, Putin and others must be delighted by democracy's present toxicity. They could be forgiven for thinking that they are witnessing democracy in its death throws. In a more genteel age, men and women in public office delighted their audiences, as the ancient Greek philosophers had done, with a discourse which was civilised, poetic, simple and beautiful, and which made its political points masterfully without attacking another's personality. Consider these:

"Politicians and diapers should be changed often, for the same reason"—Mark Twain.

"Better to remain silent and be thought a fool than to speak and remove all doubt."—Abraham Lincoln.

And from Mark Twain: "Suppose you were an idiot. And suppose you were a member of Congress. But I repeat myself."

"A politician is a guy who will lay down your life for his country"—Texas Guinan.

And from Churchill: "Winston, you are drunk!" And his reply: "Yes madame, and you are ugly ... but tomorrow I will be sober!"

Ronald Reagan, in response to criticism that he was too old: "I want you to know that I will not make age an issue in this campaign. I am not going to exploit, for political purposes, my opponent's youth and inexperience."

Where this clever repartee once rang, recent US politics has preferred verbal abuse and pugilism; words which attack rather than delight. But the ancients were also capable of this, proving that political pugilism is as old as time itself. Perhaps mankind simply comprises good people and nasty people and we must discern them.

Historians have found evidence that political debates in ancient Rome were also redolent with harsh words and personal attacks, at least as hateful as the hate speech we find on today's internet. "Attacks, which the Romans termed 'invectives', contributed that word to the English lexicon and were an integral part of the public life of Roman senators," explains history professor Dr. Martin Jehne of the Dresden Technical University. Jehne found that, although Roman politics sounded rough, in Rome's hierarchical society there were agreed rules. Politicians were permitted to ruthlessly insult each other, but in the popular assembly, by agreed convention, politicians refrained from abusing the common people. The people, however, were allowed to insult politicians (oligarchs and plutocrats). In a profound division of rich and poor, this served to limit the power aspirations of the elite.

So, in ancient Rome, politicians and the public rarely took abuse very seriously. It was all part of the game, and therefore not a reasonable comparison with contemporary political toxicity. "To compare ancient invective with its modern counterpart is misleading," says Jehne. "There was a certain Roman robustness in dealing with abusive communities which dampened excessive toxicity and required that invective also give way to real facts."

Slander in the Roman Republic (509-27 BC) was a commonly used political foil and went quite far. According to Jehne, "The famous speaker and politician Marcus Tullius Cicero (106-43 BC), for instance, defended his supporter, Sestius, by publicly accusing his enemy, Clodius, of incest with his brothers and sisters." There were hardly any limits to crude language assaults in political disputes. According to the historian's findings on ancient discourse, "withstanding and overcoming insults ultimately has a politically stabilising effect."

In today's world, the Trump era undoubtedly saw political toxicity rise to new levels, and the language used by some is now enough to make educated observers cringe in disgust. So, where does that leave us?

I hope we can agree that, whether in ancient or in today's public discourse, the language people use when addressing each other *does* matter. Civilised people prefer gentle language over crude invective and this difference is a benchmark in polite society which separates civilised people from ruffians and those of low intellect or bad manners. Most contemporary politicians agree with that sentiment, even those who serially abuse their own sanctimonious standards of civility.

Recent examples suggest that something in our civil discourse has changed to alter the temperature of our public language. Here is my theory: I think it is the ability we now have to broadcast our views anonymously, or in a cowardly fashion, without having to stand in an opponent's presence and look him in the eyes. The coward excuses his toxic rhetoric by broadcasting it from a hiding place—using new technology to distance himself from the hurt or angry look he invokes in the eyes of the people he offends. The new tools we use might be nest described as *'cyber-megaphones'* or *'cyber bully pulpits'* and there are many examples of them. They are cheap to access and immediately at hand. They are Facebook, Twitter, Instagram, Tik Tok and a host of other techno-robotic devices, designed to remove personal interface or emotion as one lashes out.

These enable cowards to broadcast unedited swill and bald-faced lies, with no public adjudicator to correct them ... and this 'cyber distortion' is tearing at the fabric, and the decency, of our political discourse. Politicians who try to tap into the sentiments of their own political base, too, are now bewildered as they struggle to separate political ideology from the sentiment they encounter on the hustings, which is informed, or more often, misinformed by a hailstorm of distorted truth emanating from social media. How can we protect democracy's hallowed place as a system of government, when its ground rules are changing so radically beneath our feet?

And it is not just uncensored cyber-voices outside our Parliaments that threaten democracy.

Separating Fact from Fake News

Even the business of newspaper and television broadcasting has been tainted. In a capitalist free market context, these mainstream media have chosen sides, seeking to capture a 'leftist' or a 'rightist' market share. In doing so, they bias their reporting and edit stories to better fit the narrative disposition of their target audience. Research has shown that left-leaning and right-leaning people watch TV channels and read newspapers that reinforce their already cemented political prejudice or may do so to feed their anger and allow them to rail against their ideological opponents. But the same research also indicates that the impact of television and newspapers bias upon voting intentions is almost neutral.

However, the ubiquitous use of social media to communicate 'fake' news, and the emergence of 'cancel culture', 'political correctness', and what I term 'cyber-megaphoning' are not neutral in their impacts. They incite people. If the fake news, or bald-faced lies they represent as fact, are believed by naïve audiences, they do indeed shift public sentiment and influence voter propensity to lean one way or the other. We saw this in the way Trump's often absurd tweets built an army of some 50 million loyal supporters. This cyber distortion is now a real threat to democracy.

In today's cyber world, the once dominant, or mainstream platforms—the floors of our Parliaments, and the better-informed print and TV media—have become junior partners in the communications business and must now compete with and cut through a media blizzard created by a host of competing, amateur broadcasters—*Twitter, Facebook, YouTube, Instagram, Parler* and similar platforms—which operate subtly to shape, and often distort, public sentiment.

The ability of one person, with sufficient following, to assert questionable facts and move the public discourse in a particular direction is best illustrated by President Trump's use of *Twitter* to make his own, sometimes insightful, often dubious case, while declaring all opposing views 'fake news'. The term '*cancel culture*' is often loosely attributed to the left, but Trump elevated it to an art form and made it a tool of the right wing, too, which he enlisted in his Republican cause at a fraction of the cost of paid advertising, and which amplified his unwillingness to entertain any dissenting view. I offer some examples of Trump's sometimes deranged public Tweets:

'Sorry, losers and haters, but my IQ is one of the highest—and you all know it! Please don't feel so stupid or insecure. It's not your fault.'

'Healthy young child goes to doctor, gets pumped with massive shot of many vaccines. Doesn't feel good and changes—AUTISM! Many such cases.'

'Every time I speak of the haters and losers, I do so with great affection. They cannot help the fact that they were born fucked-up!'

Wokism And Virtue Signalling

'Wokism' is defined by Wikipedia as a 'Marxist inspired movement that started with well-intentioned people who wanted to stop racism and injustice. It morphed into a cult that silenced those who disagreed, using social humiliation to silence opponents and graduating to violence through movements like Black Lives Matter.'

In a 2020 article, Sean Masters, a respected creative advertising director, offered an interesting insight into the way *Wokism* (an evolving word with no clear definition in the English language) and *virtue signalling* were operating to shape our discourse. He said ...

I've been building brands for 20 years and I've never seen anything like 'Woke'. It's a mistake to think this dangerous ideology comes from a bunch of disorganised radical students who are 'virtue signalling' wherever the wind takes them. It's better to think of it as a highly sophisticated, lifestyle brand. Let's look at the elements needed to create a brand.

First, you need to know your market. A strong, loyal and plentiful customer base is essential. Tick! With no faith in capitalism, nor hope of owning a home. Along with the death of religion, which makes people rail violently against the system and look for something new to believe in. Tick! You need a brand promise. Woke offers a sense of moral superiority, a group identity, freedom from personal responsibility and a victim mentality. Tick! You need a brand personality that people can identify with. Tick! You need a mission statement that sets out core brand objectives. Tick!

The tenets developed by "anti-racist" educators, among them the Woke high priestess Robin Di Angelo, include... that "Racism must be identified, analysed and challenged. That means, to not act against racism is to support racism." You need a brand book that explains how the brand behaves and relates to the world. Tick! Apart from Di Angelo's 'White Fragility', there are 'How to Be an Antiracist' and 'Between the World and Me'—handbooks for embracing Woke.

You need a brand strategy to dominate the competition. 'Cancel culture' is chillingly effective, constantly creating widespread moral outrage. In advertising, we talk of the "customer journey" that maps the experience with the brand, and "full funnel" marketing that builds awareness. Tick! The media strategy—and the budget for buying media exposure, is solved for you. Woke is already in all media, free of charge—in The Guardian, on SBS and the ABC and even on commercial programs like The Project. They have all bought the product. Woke is so powerful that tech giants like Facebook, Google and Twitter have colluded to ensure that if you're not on brand, you're out. People have been "permanently suspended" from Twitter for so-called "hateful conduct". Think of Woke as a Masterbrand, like Unilever, with sub-brands under it.

Tick! The four brand pillars of Woke are gay, trans, gender, and race. Sub-brands need a visual identity—a logo. The gay logo is the iconic rainbow. Trans has the tripled Venus and Mars design. Tick! Each brand needs a high-impact tagline. Tick! For gender, it's "Believe Women". For race, "Black Lives Matter" and going to a kneeling position at major events. A brand needs a social media strategy. Woke is without peer. It goes viral. Tick! The zenith for any brand is word of mouth, where your customers do the selling for you. Woke has countless brand ambassadors, spruiking and hash-tagging. Brands need point of sale. Here's where the highly organised anti-racism industry, valued in the US at over $10bn, swings into action. Tick! They offer DIY manuals with instructions on *how to buy in. Not buying in carries the threat of termination for workers, with the epithet—you are a racist, bigot or white supremacist.*

'In reality,' says this respected marketing executive, 'Woke threatens to undermine the values of Western civilisation', but he thinks the 'Woke' brand a masterpiece of ingenuity. 'Not bad for a bunch of blue-haired Uni students,' he says, and warns us not to underestimate its danger to democracy. If Masters is right in his analysis, the 'Woke' and 'virtue-signalling' movements have evolved enormous power to penetrate the marketplace of democratic ideas and values, and they do so outside the conventional institutions, like our Parliaments, normally used for public policy discussion and debate.

Cyber Distortion and International Risks

If *Wokism* doesn't trouble you enough in a national context, imagine how much more troubling it is when it operates, hand in glove with its cyber disciples, across a global landscape, as an avowed enemy of democracy. Cyber platforms are an increasingly worrying new frontier. Not only do they work to attack or distort our civil discourse, but they have also made us increasingly vulnerable to hacking by foreign agencies and to the seeding of concocted fact by malign forces wanting to further incite an audience or skew another nation's public and national discourse. If the extent of cyber meddling Russia and China stand accused of is true, the new cyber-frontier is 'warlike'. Cyber-babble constitutes a real and present danger to informed, public debate, undermines public trust in western media sources, and subjects' voters, who are the life blood of democracy, to an unfiltered flow of tainted information, making it increasingly difficult to separate fact from fiction. As the Australian PM recently noted, the most insidious face of the cyber bully is, in fact hidden from view, since cyber platforms enable anonymous cowards to target their hate language at susceptible people from behind dark shadows. Evidence now confirms that juvenile and teen cyber-bullying is actually increasing youth suicide.

In its domination of the communications market, and its ability to push a miscellany of subjective, private agendas, social media has become a dominant voice in shaping public sentiment, drowning out the voices of elected representatives. The chambers which, for centuries, were the cathedrals of western democracy—the houses of Parliament and their counterparts around the free world—are now pipsqueaks compared to the loud voices generated by cyber platforms. These are imposing a sort of techno-autism over public debate, which was once practiced face to face, by candidates prepared to stand up and be counted—on soap boxes in parks and on street corners. Where are those honest front-line democrats?

Are Science and Fact Now Casualties of Political Spin?

Cyberspeak is now so effective in crowding out the face-to-face contest of ideas that even the reliable 'pub test' must be threatened by the forces which now influence it. Is it still a reliable barometer of public sentiment, or is it, too, influenced by fake science and news? The contest between fact and fake news, between science and social prejudice, is evident in the debate around 'climate change'. Readers will recall that this controversy began decades ago when scientists warned mankind about 'global warming'. This, in turn, fuelled a global sense of urgency and a thirst for deeper research, in an area of science which all qualified observers agreed was fraught with uncertainties, since weather science is driven by 'chaos theory'. The public policy response by governments around the world was swift.

With few exceptions, national governments were moved to increase their funding of deeper research into this existential threat. With much increased funding of it, a flurry of new scientific and academic research ensued. Those undertaking this work were not of one mind, of one discipline, or even of one branch of science. They included data collectors and analysts, those skilled in modelling and calculating mathematical probabilities, chemists, physicists, and geologists, who saw the world through different lenses. Some geologists thought in geological timeframes, millennia, not in decades or centuries, and defended carbon as the most important, life-supporting element on our planet. There seemed to be no single, authoritative branch of science. Hence, a collective effort, across a number of scientific disciplines, would be needed to refine and more accurately quantify the climate problem.

Two things happened. First, the institutions which depended heavily upon funding of their research, raised their hands and competed strenuously for a share of this new bonanza. Secondly, as competition for funding exploded, creative new areas of research emerged. With the efflux of time, outcomes differed from initial findings. This was the case when the dire predictions of the University of

East Anglia were not met, and had to be corrected, with an apology for having manipulated data. 'Global warming' became 'climate change', to better fit the narrative.

Fuelled on one side by a doomsday culture, which may be right in its premise, or by denial, on the other side, new social heroes emerged, bringing passion and politics to the debate. Both sides selectively cherry-picked the bits of science which reinforced their prejudice or supported their narrative. The term 'climate sceptic' became a derogatory term, though scepticism is the starting point for all good science (as with Galileo's assertion that the world was round, not flat, which nearly cost him his life). Passion can be dangerous! It was the global threat of climate change, and the controversy which surrounded it in 2006, which prompted a Melbourne public policy forum—*Quaffers*—to choose this subject for its inaugural debate. Its first public policy paper, summarising the debate, and other public policy papers offered in this book illustrate how men and women of good conscience can, if they try, rise above political prejudice in their search for truth and balance.

Truth is sometimes buried beneath the debris of loose rhetoric. It generally lies somewhere near the median of views, but science and fact, rather than conjecture, must be the mediators of sound debate, and only fools now deny the balance of science which affirms that our climate is changing. And following the charismatic speech of a young, autistic Swedish schoolgirl to the United Nations—infused with passion—two generations of young people are now persuaded, while scientists continue to argue, that climate change is the challenge of our age. Climate change has morphed from a science into a religion, whose disciples have been sent out to preach its gospel of doom and have built a global church of converts. Any political party which fails to embrace this religion will be doomed to political ignominy.

While the silent majority must be trusted to separate truth from falsehood and to allow informed science to rise above uninformed passion, history is littered with examples which demonstrate the reverse—that passion is a more powerful force than science and can have both good and malign impacts upon democracy. Throughout history, passion has been the most powerful driver of social change, as it was, for example, when the English barons rose up against King John's iniquitous taxes, when French peasants overthrew the Louis kings, when Russian peasants revolted, when women marched in legions, demanding voting rights and when slaves were freed following a passionate speech in the British

Parliament by William Wilberforce. Simply put, passion is the locomotive which drives, and steers, democracy most often fuelled by the hot coals of public issues affecting the human condition.

The politician's role is to translate public passion into good public policy and to guide the legislative response. That can be a delicate balancing act—balancing a need to calm public passion with a need to inform legislation with good science and fact, not emotion. Democratic governments always seek to appease voters on important issues, like climate change. That is axiomatic to their political survival. But beware the passion that is misinformed, misdirected or has unintended consequences. It can corrupt democracy, particularly when it is laced with lethal intent. Legislators would do well to put public passion to one side as they reflect on their legislative response—to remove the debris of falsehood and consider unintended consequences before they, too, embrace excessive public passion.

History is littered with examples of the locomotive of public passion gathering steam and rushing forth into the legislative night, oblivious to the consequences. Hitler and Goebbels, for example, were masterful manipulators of public passion. Goebbels even went so far as to acknowledge this fact on several occasions, as he crafted a passionate, National Socialist following by whipping up public hatred of Jews. Consider these disturbing but logical quotes from Goebbels:

"It is the absolute right of the State to supervise the formation of public opinion."

"If we are attacked, we must defend ourselves with guns, not butter."

"Think of the press as a great keyboard upon which a government can play."

Against this background, consider the following nationalist sentiment which, on 1 July 2021, as China celebrated the 100th anniversary of the founding of its Communist Party, dripped from the lips of China's leader, Xi Jinping. *"The people of China are not only good at burying the old world, but they have also created a new world,"* he said. Xi went on to say that the people of China would never allow foreign forces to bully, oppress, or subjugate them. *"Anyone who dares to do that will have their heads bashed bloody against the Great Wall of steel forged by over 1.4 billion Chinese people,"* he said, sparking applause from an invited audience of 70,000 gathered in the massive Tiananmen square in central Beijing.

Xi's extraordinary display of nationalism and use of inflammatory rhetoric signals a new age of Chinese assertiveness. His words are hauntingly familiar. They channel and echo those of Hitler, as Germany rose. They channel Goebbels' manipulation of thought and re-engineering of society. But wait, this phenomenon is not unique to China and other despotic or autocratic regimes. That same social engineering is alive and well right now, in our schools, here in the west.

Are Schoolteachers Selling Knowledge, Or Propaganda?

Goebbels, a master of propaganda, would be proud of the way educationalist are following the example of the *Hitler Youth* program. Recent reports indicate that teachers have taken it upon themselves to become social engineers, to cancel the role of parents and instead, assume their role. Where our classrooms were designed to be forums for teaching literacy, science and mathematics, precious gifts of knowledge that equip our youth to succeed in life, they have become bully pulpits, urging our kids to question their sexuality, demanding that they become passionate climate warriors, and teaching them to feel ashamed of their whiteness (which connotes white privilege) or blackness (which connotes social inferiority or victimhood). Critical race theory and virtue signalling may have their genesis in the United States, but they have become mobile and are spreading like a virus to classrooms in other countries, like Australia, where they invade school curriculums. This cancer challenges the very fundament of an egalitarian society and the Judeo-Christian values which have guided the development of western democracy.

How did this insidious cancer find such fertile soil in our learning institutes and why have teachers, who are supposed to champion the quest for knowledge and prepare young minds in maths, science, English and other essential disciplines, decided to become social architects? They are not paid to do that work! I am outraged by *critical race theory*, which is invading educational institutions. If you Google the term, you will find it defined as *'a branch of the European Marxist school of critical theory'*, with the qualification that *'critical race theory is an academic movement which links race and racism to the exercise of power in society'*. How dare teachers assume a Marxist mantle and lecture our kids in that tainted ideology!

Unlike the Civil Rights movement, which at least attempts to work within the structures of American democracy and within the laws governing civil discourse, critical race theory attacks those very structures, ignoring constitutional law, and legal reasoning. Critical race theorists are adamant that American social life, political structure, and its economic systems are founded upon race and bigotry. In the eyes of critical race theorists, racism stems from the dominant role race plays in American life. They hold that there have been significantly different legal and economic outcomes for racial groups, depending upon the individuals race and colour and based upon a subconscious hierarchy of racial supremacy, in which privileged whites sit at the top. Apparently, if you are born white you should be ashamed of yourself and if you are born black you should understand that you were born a victim.

Critical race theory plays identity politics with the same panache as a concert pianist might play a grand piano—and with unbridled zeal. It relies upon anti-racist protests at universities and movements like *'Black Lives Matter'* to demonstrate how racism is at work in each of us, a contradictory logic which suggests that racism is turned on its head and now plagues white people. Its full-frontal attack upon traditional family values has captured national attention and inspired defiant white parents to flock to school Parent-Teacher Nights, demanding answers from their School Boards as to why teachers are feeding Marxist bile to their children.

It is not enough that you are NOT a racist. As Boston University professor *Ibram Kendi* writes in his book *'How to be an anti-racist'*, the only way to satisfy a critical race theorist is to undo racism by *"consistently identifying it, describing it and dismantling it."* Self-avowed anti-racists are not only expected to push for equity (including equality of outcome) but are also asked to look for it and expose racism in everyday life. Robin Di Angelo, author of 'White Fragility', writes "The question is not—'did racism take place?' but rather—'how did racism manifest in this situation?'" Anti-racists are thus challenged to find racial bias in every aspect of life, ranging from discussions in the classroom to interactions between work colleagues. But the most invasive form of this new social manipulation is in the classroom, where the student is a passive receptor into whose mind this bilge is pumped by those in control.

Are University Campuses for Social Engineering?

In the wake of the death of George Floyd and the subsequent *Black Lives Matter* protests, many universities have bent to the will of campus activists and groups demanding anti-racist action be taken by them. Colleges and universities have responded in different ways. Several universities now proudly proclaim that their admissions process is more "equitable", since they have scrapped standard admissions tests and, in one case, added a 'diversity plus equity' scorecard to application forms. The US media has reported other changes to address *implicit bias*—in response to critical race theory, including the following initiatives:

So that students, faculty leaders and staff may better understand what they now term *implicit bias*, institutions of higher education have required them to undergo training, group orientations and *anti-racism, diversity and inclusion* classes.

To educate the broader public about alleged racial bias in long-standing institutions, critical race theorists are pushing for changes in curriculums, ranging from mandatory classes on anti-racism to forced instruction and initiatives to *'embed anti-racist ideology in classroom teaching materials'*. US university administrators have also clamped down on academic freedoms, revising their codes of conduct and commitments to academic freedom by inserting prohibitions on *hate speech* and *racist language*, however subjectively that may have been defined.

US institutions have donated money to student chapters of the *Black Lives Matter* movement, or directed students to attend political meetings, to placate activists who now routinely cajole them into taking such action. Academic institutions have poured millions into research on critical race theory and racism, ranging from grants and fellowships to fund the establishment of new, anti-racist institutes. Some have even compiled lists of ideological teaching resources, like *'How to be an anti-racist'* and *'White fragility'* and provided them free of charge to students.

Some institutions have not taken action to mandate curricular changes or to fund critical race theory research, but those that haven't are under pressure to do so. They have had to agree to anti-racist *action committees* and been asked to rename supposedly offensive buildings—that is, those named after *white supremacists*—to placate students. Buildings named after George Washington are targets, since he owned slaves, and so too are those associated with Abe

Lincoln, who they say didn't emancipate slaves until halfway through the Civil War. This is destroying true history.

In late June 2021, I watched a televised report from the US which broadcast a video clip of a brave American mother standing at a microphone in a school hall. She began in a calm voice, politely seeking answers from the school board about why her kids were being told they should be ashamed of being white, why they were being told they should question whether they were really male or female, if they felt uncomfortable in their bodies and why, instead, the teachers, in whose trust parents placed their children, were not teaching Maths, Science and English literature. This caring parent, asking these entirely reasonable questions, was repeatedly asked by the school headmistress to resume her seat and hold her tongue. Each time, she defiantly asserted her right to speak out, and needed to progressively raise her own voice to command attention and override attempts to silence her. She was finally joined at the microphone by another mother, who explained that it was not the role of the school board to discipline parents. It was the parents who had elected the school board and who paid teachers' salaries. As crazy as it sounds, the response to this rational comment was mixed. Half of those in the school hall rose and applauded, while another half of the parents—mostly black parents—refused to do so.

If we cannot agree that teaches are appointed to teach, rather than to be self-appointed social psychologists and social engineers, our democracy is doomed! Surely the hallowed halls of our schools are not the place to explore LGBTIQ options with our children, or to be proxy parents, instructing kids who were accidentally born white that they are privileged and should be ashamed. It is not the province of teachers to tell black or Hispanic kids that they are inferior, predisposing them to a mentality of victimisation and defeat before they have even reached adulthood.

If democracy stands for any value, it is that we are equal, whatever our colour, race, religion or ethnicity. As the US constitution asserts, '*we hold it as self-evident*' that each of us—white' black, brindle or otherwise—is deserving of equal respect and love from those with whom we share our planet. Prescriptive movements like critical race theory, black lives matter, the woke and the cancel culture fraternities are surely calculated to divide rather than unite, and they are achieving that brilliantly!

Chapter 20
Money and Democracy

No man's life, liberty or property is safe while ever the legislature is in session.
Mark Twain

Studies consistently confirm that policies which favour free trade and open markets—that is, free-market economies—tend to maximise innovation, grow local and international markets, and generate national wealth. That is only true, however, when there are also strong anti-trust regulations and 'fairness' laws to prevent monopolies, oligopolies, transfer pricing, tax avoidance and other distortions. Democracies with free and open markets generate national prosperity, raise all boats on the same economic tide, and thus maximise per capita GDP. That is why it in the most common form of liberal democracy within the OECD and the economic philosophy embraced by governments of both conservative and liberal-socialist ilk.

It is a less-known fact that, in 1901, when Australia was protected by '*Most Favoured Nation (MFN)*' tariffs and had, as the world's leading supplier of wool, wheat, beef, sheep-meat and a host of other agricultural commodities, become a warehouse of supply to the British Commonwealth, Australia enjoyed the highest standard of living in the world. The saying evolved that *millionaires rode on the sheep's back*, and that was true. In 1949 a single bale of Australian fleece sold for a record £197, enough at that time to buy a brand-new Mercedes Benz.

That utopian world changed as the British Commonwealth devolved and new global competitors emerged, forcing Australia to lose it most favoured nation (MFN) status, shed its protectionist mantle, so that it could become more competitive, and diversify away from its comfortable colonial markets into broader markets for new commodities, like minerals and metals and elaborately transformed manufactures.

In recent times, global markets have evolved further, this time into much different creatures than ever before, as new institutions, like the so-called *Tech Giants*, radically reshape global wealth and lubricate the transfer-pricing industry, to avoid national and supra-national tax and legislative imposts. These new hybrids are distorting the benefits of western free market capitalism and demonstrating that, when too much wealth resides in the hands of too few, rather than being equitably distributed, the free-market system is corrupted. Even capitalists agree on this.

In 2007, the richest 1% of the American population owned 35% of the country's total wealth, and the next 19% owned 51%. The top 20% of Americans owned 86% of the country's wealth and the bottom 80% owned just 14%. It appears that a number of agencies—the *Tech Giants*, major media groups, pharmaceutical oligopolies, industrial cartels, so-called command economies and protected trading blocs—had jointly and severally contributed to this disturbing trend, bending markets out of shape and distorting the fair and equitable distribution of global wealth. Wealth creation is essential to growth and prosperity and a good thing, but when it benefits few, disenfranchises many and weakens democracy, it becomes a monster. When it tilts the playing field, it creates and feeds public unrest and undermines social equity.

Even the most conservative voices in our democracies now concede that too much wealth in too few hands is a dangerous thing and that personal wealth can negatively influence our public discourse. In Australia, one billionaire, Clive Palmer, has funded $50 million dollar advertising campaigns to promote his own political interest through his own United Australia Party, acting as a puppeteer for those candidates he funds to do his bidding. This is what I call proxy-democracy—democracy that is purchased by one vested interest with significant financial means. There have been similar examples in the US, most notably Michael Bloomberg who spent just over $US 1 billion on his race through the Primaries, albeit unsuccessfully.

Outside of the political arena, personal wealth generated in the business sector can be a positive contributor to national wealth and prosperity, provided the footloose capital and employment it generates is applied in the national interest, rather than in distorting or controlling markets. At a national level, prosperity is a good thing and contributes to a better lifestyle for citizens, but it also amplifies the gulf between rich and poor nations—the North-South disparity—as underdeveloped and developing nations lag further behind, muting the voices of the poor in global affairs and making them and their leaders more susceptible to corruption.

Paradoxically, the share of global economic power held by the so-called *highly industrialised* nations (all of them democracies) is dwindling as China, India, and other newly industrialised nations rise. Between 1990 and 2017, China's GDP per capita increased 16-fold—that's right; by 1,600 %, driven by a new phase of market penetration and globalisation that has unlocked enormous wealth.

However, research shows that the distribution of benefits has been uneven, with most accruing to global entrepreneurs, transnationals or workers in the rising countries and economies. Low to medium-skilled workers in long-industrialised democracies, like the US and Britain, have gained relatively little from the expansion of wealth. In fact, their jobs have been lost to increased foreign competition and rapid technological change. On the positive side, the rise of prosperity in China has lifted over 400 million of its citizens out of poverty and created a 600 million-strong middle class, creating many new market opportunities for western exporters.

Can Economic Self-Interest Be Defended?

Many informed observers are concerned that democracies are now drifting apart, rather than coming together in the shared cause of expanding economic cooperation. Some are now working at cross purposes. This is because, in the face of China's rapid rise, many of them have, almost unwittingly, developed an unhealthy dependence upon China and are now at pains not to offend China for fear of trade consequences. That, in turn, has enabled China to use trade coercion as a tool in its global diplomacy and tended to further undermine the rules-based world order.

This demonstrates that there is, indeed, a causal link between free trade, free markets and the preservation of democracy. Democracy needs defending when traditional champions, like the United States, are stumbling and economic alliances can serve that purpose. But defence of democracy can also have an economic sting in the tail, particularly for nations with a case of what I will call *acquired economic dependence* on China. They must choose their words carefully so as not to offend. So, the values which serve peace, prosperity, and freedom are under serious threat, and that threat extends well beyond trade and commerce into many other areas.

A new offensive against freedom of expression, amplified by what I will call *'digital authoritarianism'*—is worrying. A recent *'Freedom on the Net'* report found that ... *'China is now exporting its model of comprehensive internet censorship and surveillance around the world, offering training, seminars, and study trips as well as equipment that takes advantage of artificial intelligence and facial recognition technologies. The internet is taking on the role of a 'virtual public', and as the cost of sophisticated surveillance declines, Beijing is able to spread its totalitarian models of digitally enabled social control. This poses a major risk to democracy'*.

Moreover, some twenty-four countries around the world, including heavyweights like Russia, China, Turkey, Iran, and Saudi Arabia, have recently targeted dissidents abroad with harassments, like extradition requests, kidnapping, and even assassination. The attempted assassination of Russian dissident, Sergei Skripal and Saudi Arabia's murder of journalist Jamal Khashoggi in Turkey, have put a spotlight on the pursuit of critics by authoritarian regimes. Beijing's policing of opinions and enforcing of its views via motherland-faithful Chinese citizens and communities embedded abroad, has led to brutal inhumanity, including the repatriation of Uighurs from countries where they have sought refuge and the surveillance of Chinese students at foreign universities, using facial recognition.

Together, these worrying developments suggest that democracy, as an open social system, is under serious threat. I am forced to the conclusion that Democracy is losing ground and may even be broken. Let us explore that frightening possibility.

Is A Lust for Democracy Organic in Man?

Historically, democracy has always seemed to spring from the loins of oppression or injustice. Oppression or injustice, in turn, has inspired demands for freedom. These two forcess—injustice and a thirst for freedom—have worked to build new democracies, just as molten lava boils to the surface of the earth, erupts as a volcano and claims new ground. Does that mean that democracy is more than just a codified system of government or an abstract, intellectual concept? Could it be organic—an immutable force of nature that boils up within us? There is rich evidence of this, not just in historical events, but in recent events, which indicate that the universal promise of democracy is still a powerful aphrodisiac for mankind.

In 2018, *Freedom House* researched the innate need inside us for personal freedom, which is an emotional locomotive for democracy. It found that Angola's new president, João Lourenço, had acted swiftly against corruption, reduced the malign influence of his predecessor's family and granted the courts greater independence.

In Armenia, demonstrators had forced the resignation of Serzh Sargsyan, who had evaded limits on his term as president simply by moving from the presidency to the prime minister's office. The people were not impressed. After an election in 2020, a reformist majority in parliament removed him, pledged to promote transparency and made politicians accountability for corruption and abuse of office.

In Ecuador, President Lenín Moreno ended the antidemocratic practices of former president, Rafael Correa, by granting the media and press new freedoms and passing a referendum to restore presidential term limits.

In Ethiopia, the monopolistic ruling party, in response to three years of protests, was forced to instal a reformist prime minister, who lifted a state of emergency, released political prisoners, and created space for more public discussion of political issues.

In Malaysia, voters threw out corrupt prime minister Najib Razak and his tame political coalition that had governed since independence, clearing the way for a new government and for steps to hold Najib and his family accountable.

In each of these nations, politicians were forced to respond to organic demands—organic uprisings, for want of a better word—by people passionate about achieving democratic change and standing up to forces of coercion or

---

The Best and Worst Democracies
(Freedom House 2017 survey: Weighting: 10 = full democracy; 0 = authoritarian state)
Top Ten: Norway (1), Iceland (2), Sweden (3), New Zealand (4), Denmark (5), Ireland (6), Canada (7), Australia (8), Finland (9), Switzerland (10)
Lower Rankings: US (21), India (53), China (151), Saudi Arabia (159), Congo (163), Syria (166), North Korea (176)

---

oppression. People have continued to strive for freedom, dignity and accountability, including in countries where the odds of achieving those things seemed insurmountable, and that is good news for democracy.

Partisan Bias

Later in this narrative, I explore the role of *public policy* in building strong nationhood. If democracy is to function justly, to strengthen social cohesion and to inform effective government, good public policy must rise above partisan prejudice. When it does not, as we have seen in recent American politics, it breeds dysfunction. I hold this conviction quite strongly, and it is borne out in the examples of the Roman and British empires. That is why, in addressing public policy issues, politicians must strive to let facts and science inform the discourse and present both sides of an argument, so that the voter can distil, from disparate arguments, the merits of a proposal. Rising above partisan bias is a difficult contract for each of us because it asks us to rise above our political egos. However, partisan bias is not only natural in a democracy, but essential to it, for without it there can be no contest of ideas.

Equally, the quest for civil discourse means that political differences should be tolerated civilly—for example, the discourse over controversial issues like the size of immigration. Differences are essential. They are the very bedrock of democracy. Some assert that the left tends to embrace social justice issues more passionately, or more emotionally than the right. Some hold the reverse, but the needle on democracy's compass solves that for us but settling on an electoral true north. But leftist rage seems to have distorted that compass, for example, in the *Black Lives Matter* movement, attacking police brutality so effectively that police numbers have been significantly reduced—arguably a very bad public policy outcome. In doing so, they have also given the right side of politics a charismatic new, law and order platform for the next poll, which will appeal to many voters and be counterproductive to the Black Lives Matter movement. The right has, similarly let its rage distort democracy's compass, for example when the Proud Boys movement marched on the Capitol, trashing and respect for that cathedral of democracy. Fortunately, democracy operates like a shock absorber—or perhaps an invisible hand of justice—to settle such affairs and return public sentiment to a rational, mean position.

Democracy needs champions of social justice to voice their concerns, even when their passion rises to a level of prejudice. In a democracy, passionate views will always find a political counterpoise and tend to evolve in the public discourse into a more rational, dispassionate debate. Both sides are entitled to put their case and to air it publicly. Both sides of an argument can have greater or lesser merit and, in a democracy, the majority view, contested and won at the polls, must ultimately prevail.

The current turmoil on America's southern border provides a poignant example of how liberal immigration policies, espoused by those with misguided humanitarianism and concern for desperate people fleeing poverty, can increase, not reduce human suffering. As a consequence of misguided politics, detention centres packed with women and children have popped up all along the length of America's southern border. This makes robust public debate across the political divide essential to finding the most humane and pragmatic solution. Democrats or Republicans alone cannot decide immigration policy. The vox populi will ultimately do it for them. If either gets it wrong, a mix of public outrage and practical expediency will decide the correct immigration settings. And if that fails, the next general election will decide the issue.

The cancer of corruption in public life is subject to the same scrutiny and brutal public diagnosis. During the last US election, for example, assertions were traded on both sides. Democrats railed about Trump's conflicts of interest (he was rightly targeted for being in violation of the *Emolument Clause* in the US Constitution, because of a federal government lease over his *Old Post Office Hotel*, and for his breaches of anti-nepotism laws). There were countervailing claims of conflicts on the part of Democrats, including Biden's conflict over his son's dealings in the Ukraine and the actions of the *Clinton Foundation*, which had raised unexplained millions.

The allegations about Trump's and Biden's conflicts resonated equally, across the political divide, but professional journalists and political commentators are held to a higher standard and must rise above political bias. As independent arbiters of democracy, with an unedited power to sway public opinion, they must choose their words carefully. For corruption has no partisan owner. If a political leader is corrupt, or is a dud, democracy has some effective levers for removing him from office. The same escape is not offered to those ruled by a Stalin, a Putin or an Xi Jinping. Indeed, one might argue that it was an invisible hand of democracy which so deftly removed Donald Trump from office when the polls initially had him romping home. Elections are corrections! That is how democracy finds strength as a system of government and why credible elections are essential to the health of a democracy.

It troubles me greatly therefore, that America's ballot system is so disjointed. That it has no uniform, national, independent oversight or arbitration. The 2020 US election demonstrated how dysfunctional that system can be (compared with the systems operating in comparable western democracies, like Britain, Canada and Australia, with uniform rules and independent, national oversight). It is puzzling that the US has no national Electoral Commission, but rather, voting protocols which varied from state to state, and even more puzzling that electors tolerate that situation.

This dysfunction is difficult to understand in a nation capable of so much sophistication—in manufacturing, space exploration and in so many other fields of endeavour. Why is it unable to design and implement standard election safeguards?

Media Reporting and Election Bias

The 2020 US election was also remarkable for the way it pitted 'team red' (Republicans) against 'team blue' (Democrats) in a contest which looked more like a Superbowl than an election. Media hype, and media bias was rampant, on both sides. But while Trump allowed his feverish 'Twittering' to lead the charge, the right insisted that the mainstream print media was overtly leftist in its bias. The left asserted the same media bias, against the Democrats and their candidates. Both were right, but the thing which made the 2020 election different was the toxicity of its language, which reached new heights and breached all standards of civil discourse.

Trump's claims of election fraud remain fanciful and unproven, but a feature article in Time Magazine, on 4 February 2021, was equally fanciful in its braggartly claim that 'a secret conspiracy had saved democracy'. In self-congratulatory language, it reported triumphantly what it called a 'shadow conspiracy to wrest back democracy from the brink'. If what Time magazine described was true—a conspiracy involving normally conservative corporations and leftist trade unions, acting in concert to ensure a Biden victory or, in the event of a loss, to trigger mass demonstrations—it admits to a corruption of the US electoral process. In sponsoring the TIME article, the Democrats may have kicked an 'own goal'. In any true democracy, elections are a contest of ideas. Both sides must have an equal say, and the information machinery must function equally for all voters and contestants.

The conspiracy pact so proudly reported was formalised in a terse, little-noticed statement from strange bedfellows—the U.S. Chamber of Commerce and the US Trade Union movement, published on Election Day. Both sides had come to see their conspiracy as a clever bargain—inspired by the summer's massive, sometimes destructive racial justice protests in which the forces of labour came together with the forces of capital to keep the peace and oppose Trump's so-called assault on democracy. The TIME article said ...

"For more than a year, a ... coalition of operatives scrambled to shore up America's institutions as they came under attack from a remorseless pandemic and an autocratically inclined President. Much of this took place on the left, but it included contributions by so called nonpartisan and conservative actors, desperate to stop a Trump victory. It was an election so calamitous that no result could be discerned at all, a failure of the central act of democratic self-governance that has been a hallmark of America since its founding."

It went on to say ... "The conspirators work touched every aspect of the election. They got states to change voting systems and laws and helped secure hundreds of millions in funding. They fended off voter-suppression lawsuits, recruited armies of poll workers and got millions of people to vote by mail. They successfully pressured social media companies to take a harder line against disinformation and used data-driven strategies to fight viral smears."

One might ask by what authority an organisation operating in dark shadows outside of the political process and running no candidates, came to judge which party it thought was deserving and which was not? That decision is meant to be made by the people, via the ballot box, not by special interest groups operating behind closed doors. If what the Time article asserted was true, it amounted to a confession that the election was tainted. TIME continues:

"That is why the participants want the secret history of the 2020 election to be told, even though it sounds like a paranoid fever dream—a well-funded cabal of powerful people, ranging across industries and ideologies, working together behind the scenes to influence perceptions, change rules and laws, steer media coverage and control the flow of information. They were not rigging the election; they were fortifying it."

Not rigging an election, but fortifying it? Please explain to me how that works! That statement was breath-taking in its hypocrisy. It supported a view that US democracy was at best broken, at worst, in tatters. Secret cabals. *Black Lives Matter* and *Proud Boy* movements. Virtue signalling using social media. These things were central players and altered the face of the US election process. They signalled alarming democratic dysfunction.

Can One Buy an Election?

Even more alarming was the amount spent on campaigning. Total spending on the 2020 US election was an eye-watering $14 billion, twice the sum spent on the 2016 election. Moreover, while Trumps Twitter campaign exploited a highly effective medium, it was also highly cost-effective. Indeed, the Democrats spent twice the Republican sum ($9.3 bill versus $4.8 bill). Was it the emotive intervention of the so-called *secret cabal* that enabled the left to *steal* an illegal victory, as Trump asserted? Is that a fanciful interpretation which insults the intelligence of US electors? Did toxic language from both sides fire up the public so much that people flocked to polls in larger numbers than ever before? Or was it the staggering dollar spend that drove them there? We will never know, but the shameful process could not have occurred in any other, self-respecting democracy without invoking public outrage of offending a long-established legacy of electoral fairness and regulation.

The huge sum invested in the 2020 US campaign, and its distorting influence, are difficult to imagine in other democracies, where campaign budgets are more modest. A conspiracy to 'save' democracy, by a coalition of the elite, the Labor movement and the capitalist establishment, is the sort of thing one might expect in a banana republic, not a highly developed nation with a strong system of law and justice. The smug claims by *Time* magazine should trouble us greatly and warn us that democracy is in terrible trouble.

Together, these events reinforce the case for limiting election funding, not just in the US, but in all democracies. They make a case for funding each candidate equally, on a seat-by-seat basis, to ensure that representatives are elected on the merits of the ideas and policies they expound, and that their case for election is delivered in front of audiences, in town halls and on street corners... not via munificent media campaigns. Let men and women aspiring to public office tell us in their own words what they stand for and articulate what they propose to do in our Parliaments, so that we may know their intellect, the sincerity of their words and their motives for serving their nation.

When one considers the gravity of a political appointment, it ought to require a probing search for talent, such as is faced by any senior executive. Not be based upon one-liners, or redolent with political catch phrases fired at us via text messaging, Twitter campaigns, on television screens and over other communications media, to overwhelm us rather than allow us quiet moments of reflection on what each candidate stands for. So, here's what I concluded: Democracy IS broken ... at least the functional version its founding fathers intended, to harmonise our lives.

I believe our leaders must find new political courage to address the forces which assail democracy—the cyber babble, virtue signalling, political correctness and other phenomenon which have invaded our modern, political landscape. At the risk of sounding a bit biblical, democracy needs a saviour, but I see no sign of one ... no hands at work to reform our outdated electoral processes or adjust our electoral machinery to meet the dictates of our new, cyber world. Where are the prescient minds, searching for new ways to safeguarding our democratic institutions as they struggle to adjust to the new influences upon them? How can democracy address its new community of cyber-citizens, who seem to have replaced conventional voters, and how can we regulate the new communications media, which seem to reach through our eyeballs into the deepest recesses of our brains to shape our thoughts. How can we defend ourselves against the cyber invective which now distorts our reality? Is there an *unsubscribe* button? Where is it?

We are bedevilled by these dysfunctions at a time when forces opposing democracy—in places like China, Russia, the Middle East and other parts—continue their relentless missions to impose their different values upon us. Are we sleepwalking into disaster?

Chapter 21
'Policy Flat-Earthers'

Nothing in all the world is more dangerous than sincere ignorance and conscientious stupidity.
Martin Luther King, Jr

Sometimes, political passion assumes such momentum that it takes over, like a tsunami wave, sweeping all before it and taking others with it, even when the facts informing the emotional response are false. The kind of passion which comes with sound knowledge and conviction is to be admired, but those who come armed with ill-informed passion, faux indignation, and faux righteousness, indifferent to, or ignorant of flaws in their logic, are dangerous people. I call them *'Policy Flat-earthers'* because they mimic their C16th counterparts, the religious zealots, who were passionate in their conviction that the earth was flat, and that the sun revolved around it, despite Galileo's evidence that the reverse was true. Galileo was a social leper. A scientific voice in the wilderness. Nobody wanted to hear his truth.

Flat-earthers are found everywhere, passionately expounding their views ... most often at dinner parties, after a few drinks, at public meetings seeking celebrity and on *Twitter*. Shaping, or misshaping the public discourse. Their misinformed zeal is usually innocent, not malign, but it threatens democracy. It also raises an interesting philosophical question. Do they have the right to express their strongly held views, even when those views are misinformed, or simply wrong?

If we subscribe to a free and open society, in which freedom of thought and expression are immutable tenets, we must reluctantly grant them that right. But equally, we have a right to politely disagree and to correct any factual error. In formulating public policy, those with a legislative duty of care should let 'experts' check and inform their views, to ensure that the science or facts that guide them are not tainted by religious zeal or political prejudice. Plato expressed the view that educated people should manage affairs of state, not plebeians, or as some call them in the modern vernacular, 'punters', a politically incorrect view these days and one which holds little sway since nowadays everyone has at least a basic education. In Plato's era, that was not the case. Slaves and plebs were truly uneducated.

At the level of individual discourse across a dinner table, however, demanding evidence to back a passionate claim is provocative, intellectually precocious, and considered rude by most of us. Law students understand that *'ignorance is no excuse'* but, clearly, voters do not. Exquisite tension thus exists between fact and uninformed political passion. As civilised beings, most of us choose to avoid contradicting *flat-earthers* in public, because telling them that they are wrong may humiliate them, cause them offence or risk an angry escalation. Uninformed passion is thus one democratic dysfunction we must live with.

A policy debate in 2015, about *'carbon sequestration'*, demonstrated how misinformed some political passion can become. Let me share details of that debate with you. Back then, the Quaffers policy forum was still striving to improve its understanding of climate change. To get to the bottom of the CO_2 problem, it decided to invite an expert to explain the best way to sequester carbon. I contacted Adjunct Professor Tony Richardson, of Monash University, who was expert in the field and passionate about carbon sequestration (capturing and holding carbon). I thought he would be a great speaker, and he did not disappoint, suggesting that we rename the debate: "Reducing CO_2: We Wood if we Could".

Professor Richardson opened his keynote address with the extraordinary claim that "Trees are not really trees. They are Carbon Factories." He explained that billionaire Richard Branson had offered prize money of $1 million to anyone able to demonstrate the best solution to sequestering carbon, to tackle climate change. The professor joked that *Branson could save his money. Trees would win hands down. Nothing else came close!*

According to Professor Richardson, there are many good ideas for sequestering or reducing carbon, but most of these have long lead times, confirming that *'trees are still the smartest short-term fix'*. The professor's research into *Forrest Offsets* showed that, between year 3 and year 20, new plantation trees sequester over 400 tonnes of CO_2 per hectare, almost exactly equal to the '*Kyoto Assumption*' on necessary action to stall global warming. Debunking some popular myths, he said that, while old growth forests are valuable, and there are good reasons for protecting them, they are not much good at sequestering carbon.

"Trees sequester carbon very efficiently—but only for about 17 to 20 years between the ages of 3 and 20. After that, they flat-line," he said. "So, the 'Green' lobby,' who will not let us clear land for plantation forests or cut down any trees at all, are actually cutting off their noses to spite their faces.

"In their passionate opposition to cutting down trees," he added, "they are seriously misinformed. If they embrace the threat of climate change, like all good environmentalists, they should understand that their opposition to plantation forests is stalling efforts to reduce atmospheric CO2 (i.e., their flawed logic fails to answer the threat of global warming, which they passionately embrace). We are smarter to start new plantations, harvest them after twenty years and then sequester their carbon once again, in tree-based products. Trees do not last 100 years. Most rot or burn down well before then, emitting carbon when they burn."

He went on to explain that most plantation trees are harvested for use in the construction, furniture and related industries, providing additional sequestration.

"On top of the 400 tonnes of carbon sequestered by the average forest tree as it grows, we can extend that period of sequestration immensely when the tree is transformed into a product. House frames and furniture items are particularly effective 'carbon-sinks'. They hold their carbon for a very long time—often for 100 years after the felling of the tree. Even at the end of a tree's productive life—when its timber is no longer sequestered in a piece of furniture, a house frame or floorboards, it is returned to landfill, which sequesters it for several more decades.

"While much may be achieved with better energy science (for example, electric trams, electric cars, cleaner fuels etc.), long lead times are required to achieve critical mass with these. Professor Ross Garneau's 'call to action' across all options was a good idea, but 'time' is the critical factor, so we need to put 'tree smart' policies up front and make a start right now," he said.

Professor Richardson conceded that there were other public policy challenges—around available land, land use and costs—in promoting new plantation forests, but carbon trading could balance these out. For example, coalfired power generators could be given carbon credits for sponsoring new growth forests.

"While soil and the oceans (e.g., plankton) remain the two biggest natural carbon sinks, neither of these are areas where we humans can make much difference," he said. "In stark contrast, trees are very efficient carbon sinks and man can act now to expand their capacity, with immediate returns in the fight against CO2 and climate change," he added.

"So," he concluded, "to passionate environmentalists, I say this: Study and understand the science around plantation forests. Rethink your position and become informed climate warriors." I was moved by this logic and became a disciple, but several years later, it barely rates a place in the climate debate, and I despair that any discussion of carbon sequestration is immediately stifled by the anti-carbon lobby.

Google-Literacy

Beyond the scourge of scientific ignorance on the part of those who passionately oppose things on the basis of their acquired expertise, there is another, insidious force at work in democracies, amplifying the spread of misinformation, with worrying impacts upon public policy and civil discourse. The internet now allows anyone with a modicum of computer skill, research and become an expert. We have seen this play out in two prominent areas of public policy—the COVID-19 pandemic and the climate change debate. In each of these critical areas, those with a particular political agenda, or with a prejudice they wish to reinforce, have been able to cherry-pick bits of data that reinforce their beliefs. They then use this data selectively, to appear learned, erudite and to speak with authority.

"We've been living in a world of misinformation for a few decades, but the reach is out of this world with new platforms," said Sarah Evanega, director of Cornell University's Alliance for Science, dedicated to correcting misconceptions. *"And this, at a time when people look to political leaders to help them think about issues, including science. Political leanings and prejudices are making people susceptible to specious scientific arguments."*

Under the burdens of political urgency and public anxiety about issues like climate change and Covid19, scientific journals are pressured to rush their work and cut corners on data which would normally be more carefully vetted before being published, according to Jennifer Zeis, director of communications at the

New England Journal of Medicine. "This is unusual—we're not a 'news-breaking' organisation. This really stretches our resources."

Research by John Cook, communications expert at George Mason University, showed that one of the biggest predictors of whether someone is likely to deny climate change or COVID-19 was the person's political affiliation. His research showed that political leaders significantly influence attitudes about climate change. The same is true for COVID-19. An overwhelming majority of Democrats wear face masks, and social distance, while only a minority of Republicans do the same. This political polarisation is "*a tragedy,*" said Cook, pointing to Donald Trump's early, persistent dismissal of wearing masks and social distancing.

Indeed, in the lead up to the US election, if you wore a mask you were a Democrat and if not, a Republican. Mask wearing became a badge of political affiliation, replacing health science and making it less important than political loyalty—a national tragedy. In an early analysis of COVID-19 misinformation, researchers at Oxford University found that while most fake news about the pandemic was spread by average users of social media, politicians or celebrities received much more attention and engagement on their posts and could sway the masses.

"*A single, non-expert with a large platform, whether a celebrity or a political figure, can have a disproportionate impact upon popular sentiment,*" says Cornell's Evanega. That was especially true for COVID-19, she said. In a study published by her, she and her team analysed 38 million pieces of English-language content published between January 1 and May 26 2020. They exposed over a million news articles that had spread or reported misinformation about the pandemic, including false articles on miracle cures, drugs etc.

To illustrate how another malaise, *information deficit*, can distort public policy, consider this: The coronavirus has prompted governments around the world to print money and invest trillions in ameliorating its effects, while a much larger public health issue remains hidden in plain sight—one which has persisted for years. This massive health issue could be immediately eradicated with the simple application of a small part of the trillions in funding directed at Covid 19 (relief for the unemployed, assistance for small businesses etc.)

According to UN agencies—the WHO and FAO—in 2021, six hundred and ninety million people (690 million) were malnourished and 440 million of them died from hunger. There is a vaccine for hunger. It is called food! It works straight away and has no side effects! Instead of investing trillions in the fight against Covid19, with its 99% survival rate, how much more could humanity achieve if it invested just a tiny part of those trillions in solving starvation, for that is all it would cost?

When politicians get their priorities wrong and ignore other public problems, life starvation, which have no votes for them, this information deficit, or worse still, misinformation, plague democracy and cripple its functionality. People struggle to discern what is important from what is trite and what is real from what is false.

In a study published in *Psychological Science,* two groups were presented with headlines giving false information about the coronavirus. The first was asked how likely they were to share the news, while the second was asked to determine the headline's accuracy. 32% were more likely to share misinformation than they were to rate it as accurate. In a second experiment, participants were asked to judge whether a headline was accurate before sharing it. This small change, to make participants think more critically, made them 3 times more likely to spot misinformation.

"On social media, people focus on how much their friends and followers 'liked' their post, rather than its accuracy," says David Rand, a researcher at the Massachusetts Institute of Technology, who studies the spread of misinformation. Texas Tech Uni's Hayhoe thinks "productive conversations are possible. First and foremost," she says, "there has to be mutual respect. Both sides must strive to find common ground; something to agree on," she says, "to move towards a solution." In a practical context most would say "Good luck with that!". It is the principle upon which the Melbourne-based *Quaffers'* public policy debates rely, and I am very proud of that legacy, as are those who joined me in forming *Quaffers*.

Flat-Earthers And Unintended Consequences

If we look carefully, we can find many examples of misinformed passion corrupting public policy. In a typical scenario, the focus on one issue becomes so intense that it blinds the policy advocate to other, often more serious, unintended consequences. Seeing public policy in black and white terms is fraught with danger. When policy makers adopt a blinkered approach, other complexities tug at the honesty of their policy. Uninformed zealotry, when it finds expression in public policy, almost always creates havoc in its unintended consequences, and not only distorts the original purpose of the public policy but also its impact upon good governance.

One of the best examples of this was the decision, in 1935, by the Australian Bureau of Sugar Experimentation, to introduce Cane Toads into Australia from Hawaii. Native to Central and South America, the toads were introduced to control the native *grey-backed cane beetle* (*Dermolepida albohirtum*) and *French's beetle* (*Lepidiota frenchi*). The cane toad is one of Australia's best-known, introduced pests. It has since spread all the way to remote north-western Australia, has no known predators in its new, Australian habitat, and has had a serious impact on the ecosystems of northern Australia.

Another example of unintended consequences was clumsy politics in New South Wales, Australia, around protecting koalas. In this case, several competing policy positions were running in parallel, mixing the policy metaphors and confusing the intent of the draft legislation. In turns out koalas were just one part of the policy contest, which included an important public infrastructure project, a wider state planning issue, an environmental issue, a climate change issue and, finally, an issue affecting farmers and their production of food and fibre. Attempts to find agreement on a public policy position satisfying everyone were futile from the very start.

Scientists explained that habitat was one of the smallest risks to the koala. The biggest risk was *Chlamydia*, a sexual disease rampant in the species which was killing them much faster. Bushfires were bigger koala killers, making policies around forest fuel loads critical. Moreover, while the legislation applied across an entire state, koalas did not inhabit much of that space, preferring mountain tops where they were less exposed. Not only do koalas indulge their appetite for over-breeding but they also destroy their own habitat by eating it bare. These policy complexities were barely raised although they were hidden in plain sight.

But in cases like these, even if democracy sometimes gets it wrong, when policy debate makes transparent an important moral or ethical issue, it is courageous. Policy complexities epitomise the contest of ideas and make democracy special. Even if a preferred policy position does not run the political gauntlet and win through, the fact that it is able to be put is hugely important. Public policies which offend social justice, send bulldozers through villages or are insensitive to koala habitats do not burden autocratic regimes, like China or Russia. Democracy can be imprecise in its public policy deliberations, but those with a strong social, moral or ethical case must be heard. That is surely, a higher cause, and a small price to pay, even if we sometimes get practical aspects wrong.

Chapter 22
Who Governs—Politicians or Bureaucrats?

Bureaucracy gives birth to itself and then expects maternity benefits.
Dale Dauten

Throughout history, there has been exquisite tension between the competing arms of government—the voters, the parliamentarians, the judiciary and the bureaucracy. Bureaucrats are supposed to deliver the policy decisions of elected governments, as their servants. In the constellation of power and authority within democracy, the bureaucracy is supposed to sit on the bottom rung, having no executive power and no elected mandate. But bureaucrats often wield power disproportionate to their role as agents of government and can, by proxy, direct affairs over which they have no public mandate or authority. Granted, there are instances when they must operate without government direction, during election campaigns and periods of transition to new policy settings and new governments. Bureaucrats must keep the wheels of government turning and thus govern by default.

Few would argue that the public sector—the bureaucracy—is crucial to the task of delivering outcomes and administering the affairs of state, but how should it be resourced for that function compared, for example, to the resourcing of political office, of law and order and of other democratic functions? Bureaucracies are routinely criticised for their size, cost, waste and inefficiency and for their tendency to inertia. Reforming a bureaucracy, and its often-entrenched policy ideas, can be like reversing an ocean liner. That is because bureaucracies have a tendency to develop their own, internal political culture, particularly in the social justice portfolios where political passion collides with ideology. Bureaucrats can even resist, or stall, a new government's policy agenda. To that extent, the bureaucracy is not just another cog in the public policy wheel, but the driveshaft of the machinery of government. At its best, the bureaucracy initiates good public policy and recommends policy settings to its Ministers. At its worst, it offers stubborn resistance to policy dictates it is required by its political masters to embrace but is reluctant to support. These tendencies have earned the bureaucracy the nickname *'The Swamp'*, invoked by politicians and the general public alike to describe its ineptness or disloyalty. That gives us pause to contemplate where the term 'drain the swamp' first arose.

One's first impulse is to associate the term with Trump and the last US election. However, it first emerged when malaria was abundant in the US and Europe, alluding to attempts to kill mosquitos, to combat malaria and to prevent the spread of disease. Given that background, it is not surprising that it soon became part of the political vernacular. The first person to use the phrase politically was a Democrat, Winfield Gaylord, not Trump, as some may think. In 1903 Gaylord said: *'Socialists are not satisfied with killing a few mosquitoes ... from the capitalist swamp. They want to drain the swamp'.*

Trump may have been inspired to use the phrase by Ronald Reagan who, in 1980, called for action to *'drain the swamp'* of its bureaucracy in Washington. He was partnered in that sentiment by Margaret Thatcher whose attempts at reversing nationalisation of UK enterprises and at introducing fiscal austerity were strongly opposed by left-leaning bureaucrats and public sector employees, who felt they might be held to a higher standard of performance if government enterprises were privatised. Trump's use of the term became a chant following toxic political exchanges about alleged collusion with Russia, corruption associated with both Obama's, and Clinton's previous administrations, and both Trump's and Biden's alleged conflicts of interests. These were to be investigated (or buried) by senior bureaucrats during the ensuing couple of years, becoming a serious distraction from the business of government. The most notable example was the controversy surrounding FBI Director Comey, who seemed to be doing the previous government's bidding, and did so in the heat of an election. That raises the philosophical question whether the bureaucracy has an executive role in government or is just a benign agent of it.

Stereotypes about public servants, as they are characterised in sitcoms like *'Yes Minister'*, or proclaimed by those who wait in line for services which are denied them by bureaucratic red tape, fail to recognise the magnificent contributions of the many fine public minds and intellects which grapple with complex policies, resolve problems in complex areas like public health, science, education, the law, monetary and fiscal policy, trade negotiations and the like. The services of these public heroes are critical to the proper functioning of democracy.

There are as many reasons to trust as there are to distrust the bureaucracy, but in the final analysis, it is an essential and powerful tool of government. Its reach into society is so pervasive that it must always be accountable for its actions and its contribution to democracy will be heightened by an enlightened partnership with, rather than cynical contempt for, government. In a democracy untainted by politicisation of the bureaucracy or by public corruption, the bureaucracy draws much of its authority from Acts of Parliament and is thus a calming, steady-as-she-goes force in a democracy. Political agitation to change policy settings usually takes place outside of the bureaucracy, which is conflicted by its own involvement, and ultimately judged by independent arbiters—voters—before changes find expression in new Acts of Parliament.

In the final analysis, a bureaucracy's effectiveness in delivering good democratic government is only as good as the direction it receives from its political masters, and the capacity of successive governments to influence its policy role and direction. An enlightened Minister of state will *negotiate* the policy direction with an enlightened Department head, whereas an autocratic government will *command compliance*. Therein lies the difference between a democracy and an autocracy ... not in the individual merits of the bureaucrats ... since, in either system of government, their only function is to serve their political masters.

While recent events have raised questions about US *democratic dysfunction*, the 'Westminster system' is not without its own dysfunction. For example, when political appointments are made over the heads of professional bureaucrats or when undue influence from outside the Parliament corrupts bureaucratic processes. We see that when property developers or media Moghuls contribute large sums to political parties or officials to sway public decision making—in a tender for major works, for example. Thankfully, a fair and equitable system of law and justice will safeguard democracy against that dysfunction. Law and order must underpin a true democracy and be the final arbiter of its moral authority.

That quality is patently lacking in non-democratic or pseudo-democratic regimes, where the justice system fails to identify and punish corrupt or aberrant public sector behaviour. There is nothing new in the dynamic contest between fair and just government and the forces of corruption. Law and order have always had to triumph over corruption, as they did in Marcus Aurelius' Rome and in King John's England—while in autocratic regimes like Russia and China, that quality is missing, or at least obscured by other motives (e.g., Xi Jinping's anti-corruption campaigns were used as a pretext to remove political opponents).

There are different ways to measure a public sector's contribution to democracy, but some of those measures are inept. If one looks, for example, at things like the percentage of people employment in the public rather than the private sector, we cannot do so in a vacuum, without allowing for things like the public sector's contribution to labour market stability, its impact upon national productivity or its role in delivering necessary but uncommercial services to meet social justice dictates. This applies in areas like public health, public transport, public education and national defence. A morally responsible democracy must invest in these things, even when they require heavy subsidy.

When we compare the size and cost of national public sectors against international benchmarks, the results may surprise critics of communist and centrally planned economies. At first blush, communist states and centrally planned economies seem to have much fatter public sectors. One would expect that to be the case in a communist state. If we measure China and India, for example, the crude employment figure is around 70% of the workforce, compared with Australia and the United States, at 18% and 15% respectively. But those high percentages are deceptive because, in Russia, China and India, they include employment in state trading enterprises, which are businesses and in other countries, would likely be privately owned. When these are stripped out, the relativities are closer. In 2019, a ranking of public sector size by country was produced by the OECD and the ILO. Their findings are given below. Note the close similarity between Russia and the Scandinavian states:

Percentage of workforce employed in the Public Sector—2019:

Country	OECD (%)	ILO (%)	Mean (%)
China	70	70	70
India	69		69 ('organised workforce')
Norway	35.6	32.4	35.2
Denmark	32.9	29.6	32.3
Singapore	32		32
Russia	32		32
Sweden	29.9	29.2	29.4
France	28	20.5	24.3
UK	21.5	21.5	21.5
Belgium	21.5	21.1	21.3
Canada	22.4	20.2	21.1
Australia	20.4	18	19.2
Italy	18.3	16	17.2
South Africa	17.4	16.9	17.15
Argentina	16.9		16.9
USA	17.6	13.2	15.4
Austria	15.2		15.2
Malaysia	15.1		15.1
Germany	15.3	12.9	13.1
Brazil	12.1	12.3	12.2
NZ	13.4	11.5	12.4
Japan	12.9	7.7	9.1
Philippines	9.1		9.1

Note: Disparities, and similarities in values across democratic and autocratic regimes may be explained by the differences in government architecture which exist between free market and command economies and by differences in welfare programs.

- In China, India, Russia, Cuba and other command economies, most enterprises are '*state owned*' and therefore regarded statistically as public sector employers, skewing the statistics. Many of their western counterparts—in manufacturing, for example—are private enterprises.

In India and China, if we strip back their percentages by removing government trading enterprises, the figure falls to an astounding figure of around 10%.

- In democratic states with significant social welfare architecture—in Scandinavian countries, for example—the size of the public sector is an unreliable measure and needs to be seen against the disparate tax, welfare, retirement, health and other social benefits provided by NGOs whose employees operate as proxy agencies of government.
- Within the OECD, France (28%), Britain (22%) and Canada (21%) have larger public sector employment than Australia (at about 20%). The USA is lower, at about 17%. New Zealand—admittedly a much smaller economy—puts all OECD nations to shame, with only 13%. But comparisons are meaningless unless they include things like national public sector economic dividends, productivity etc.,—measures which are impossible to quantify in portfolios with a human services or social justice, rather than an economic, mandate.
- The size of a bureaucracy alone is thus an unreliable measure of either economic efficiency or democratic function. One might hold that the ultimate test of a true democracy is its humanity—the way a nation's citizens care for each other, the happiness of its people and the presence of a fair and equitable system of law and justice. These far better measures of democratic function and of the moral authority a government draws from its people, than the size of its bureaucracy.

Chapter 23
Fiscal Governance

Government...can be summed up in 3 short phrases: If it moves, tax it. If it keeps moving, regulate it. If it stops, subsidise it.
Ronald Reagan

A fundamental aspect of public policy—particularly *new* policy decisions—is that, no matter how well-founded a policy may be, it comes at a cost to the public purse. Rarely does an existing policy make way for a new one, so that its impact is cost neutral, though some policies *can* deliver budget efficiencies. The way that public funds are collected, managed and spent is thus a key indicator of the moral strength of a government, and for that matter, of democracy. Conversely, poor fiscal governance quickly erodes a democracy and broadens the scope for corruption.

We will all agree that democracy, if it is to be a fair and equitable system of government, must defend its sacred values—like freedom of speech and assembly, the right to vote and a range of other human rights. But those noble things cost money and money corrupts people. A fair and equitable democracy relies on eliminating financial corruption. If you want evidence of just how corrosive fiscal corruption can be, look no further than an excellent book published by *Karen Dawisha* entitled *'Putin's Kleptocracy'*, which evidences the way Putin and his oligarch cronies have syphoned billions from public coffers for their own benefit. We also saw that in Marcos' Philippines and we see it in a number of other states.

For that reason, the purest and most successful democracies, in my view, are those whose systems of law and justice are untainted, robust and come down heavily on corruption, for laws are the final arbiters of public accountability and good, governance and over the way public money is collected, administered, and spent. Good public policy, too, must include fiscal discipline. When fiscal discipline is lacking, funding can be misdirected, or eaten up by administrative or other project costs, which dilute the policy's effectiveness so much that little of the intended public benefit is lost. Policy is not measured solely by its intrinsic merit, but also by the fiscal discipline which accompanies it, to ensure that public funding is invested efficiently.

In the present age, we see clear differences in the way that democracies approach fiscal discipline, compared to autocracies, like Russia and China. From the outset, in a democracy, public policy settings and funding need the imprimatur of the people and the legislature—sometimes via the ballot box—and are frequently based upon esoteric or subjective benefits, which are difficult to measure. These include things like environmental benefits and social amenity. Autocratic regimes do not always care about those things, face the same public sensitivities or rebukes or necessarily factor in the additional time and cost penalties, faced by democracies, which meeting the will of the people entails.

Our democratic processes are more complex because they deliver justice and equity, which come at a cost. Most autocracies, by comparison, are command economies whose governments intervene in markets. They may save time and money by skirting around our democratic processes, but they lack the fiscal discipline of Adam Smith's 'Invisible Hand' which tends to deliver efficiencies not always seen in autocracies, like open, competitive public tenders which make bidding process keen and deliver design, management and cost efficiencies. Most autocratic regimes do not encourage these checks and balances. Their fiscal disciplines tend to be imposed, not tested by the market for their economic viability, because autocracies demand public conformity, whatever their moral, fiscal or social consequences.

British Prime Minister Winston Churchill's legacy of statesmanship was largely shaped by his inspirational wartime leadership and speeches that lifted a nation's spirits and enabled Britain to triumph in its darkest hour. He is not remembered for his fiscal indifference, or disdain, for those who would limit his wartime spending, in particular, the Exchequer, which was seriously concerned about his profligate spending, the horrific cost of the war and its impact on Britain's empire.

The fiscal impact of WW II on Britain was so crippling that it is thought to have reduced its global power status and ended the era of British empire. Its' lend-lease arrangements—loans from the US which financed a massive ramping up of navy, military and other war related procurement and the cost of incurring long-term debts, are still being repaid. According to public records, Britain's wartime debt repayments do not cease until 2031, 80 years after the end of hostilities. How do we measure profligate spending in public policy terms? Well, one might hold that it turns on the morality of the policy driving the debt. War is indifferent to smart economics and fiscal conservatism. Britain had to be saved at any cost. There was no point in costing the alternative—surrender to a Nazi oppressor and loss of national sovereignty.

In many ways, the coronavirus pandemic has the same fiscal characteristics, as a war, except that it is not confined to a few wartime protagonists but is a global phenomenon. Governments around the world have chosen to ramp up their health services, to keep the wheels of their economies turning, to sandbag their decimated airlines and their tourism sectors, to save people's jobs and to stimulate economic activity by throwing money at them all. That cost is already in the trillions and climbing and does not include opportunity costs, like the cost of 'foregone output' which, in October 2020, was estimated by the International Monetary Fund (IMF) at US$28 trillion by 2025. That estimate relied upon a vaccine cure being found to end the pandemic by 2022, which is by no means certain as new strains of the virus emerge and vaccine distribution is compromised by political interference.

Is Fiscal Diligence A Political Legacy?

Churchill's legacy as a wartime hero and saviour of democracy will never be eclipsed, despite his profligate spending. Whitlam, on the other hand, was judged to be so profligate that the opposition blocked a money supply bill and forced him out of office. But a Whitlam policy legacy remains … in important areas like university funding, gender equality, no fault divorce legislation and recognition of China, which changed the face of his nation, most would argue, very positively. Unlike Churchill, US President Donald Trump will be remembered for a deficit in statesmanship, or at best, a patchwork policy quilt stitched together from a rag-tag of positive and negative achievements. History will likely remember Trump's use of social media to spin his own message, his exaggerated rhetoric which often stretched the truth, his spurious claims to suit his own political self-interests and the abusive language he aimed at his opponents—legacies which demeaned the office of President. However, a balanced account, ignoring his personality, should also record important things that he may have gotten right.

His impact on the US economy, on coal-miners' and farm jobs for example, are still playing out.

There were some memorable things which Trump got right. For example, his creative approach to normalising relations between Israel and several Arab States. His unconventional policy approach achieved a breakthrough in a stalled process, which no other politician had been able to achieve. In any other mere mortal, such a triumph would have earned a Nobel Peace Prize. Many would also hold that Trump's questioning of what he called 'The Washington Swamp'—the bureaucratic swamp which he wanted to drain, including 'the Washington establishment'—was a positive initiative, because it reminded voters that the will of the people always transcends the power of the bureaucracy and of the lumbering, all-powerful public muscle it flexes.

In public policy terms, Trump's questioning of the Washington establishment applied a metaphorical 'spirit level' to it, to ensure that the bubble in the 'public spirit level' was in the median position and that the tail (the bureaucracy) was not wagging the dog (the American people). Putting the 'Washington Swamp' on notice also reminded bureaucrats that their salaries were a charge to the public purse and that they therefore served at the will of the people, not at the whim of their own, internal policy agendas. If democracy derives its moral authority from the will of the people, it is axiomatic that the public sector must always be subject to close public scrutiny and be able to demonstrate that it can and does serve governments of any persuasion with equal, non-partisan loyalty and efficiency.

So much for bureaucrats. But what about politicians? They, too, sometimes forget who they serve. They horse-trade with opponents on the hill in Washington, and in similar forums around the world, looking for compromises and, in the process, delivering less than ideal public policy outcomes for the people who elected them. Are they not also corrupting good public policy? America's fiercely contested *Covid Relief Package* offers some useful insights into this phenomenon.

In late December 2020, Republican Congressmen and women capitulated on important matters of principal, to avoid a money bill crisis which would potentially cause a shut-down of government over the Christmas period. Neither Democrats nor Republicans wanted to face the ire of the American public by denying them a family Christmas. They had already been denied freedoms by being locked down during the pandemic. That would be political suicide, for either party. As Christmas approached, the $900 billion *Coronavirus Relief Bill* needed to be passed ... and urgently. When the threat of angry retribution from the voting public became palpable, both the US House of Representatives and the Senate eventually agreed to pass the bill, setting aside months of pugilistic rhetoric and partisan differences. It seems that *Santa,* not the upper house, eventually passed this bill, and the gratuitous gifts it included.

The relief package was wrapped in a $2.3 trillion, 5,600-page "*Coronabus Bill*" which included a $1.4 trillion *omnibus* bill, to fund the federal government for the forthcoming year. The bill was approved in the House of Reps by 359 to 53 and in the Senate, by 92 to 6. Those margins were sufficient to dissuade any normal President from exercising a veto, or challenging convention. But Trump was a man with little regard for convention and was determined, even in the last days of his office, to stand his ground and bring his nation to its fiscal knees. He ultimately relented. However, on closer inspection of the Bill's consequences, Trump's opposition to some terrible aspects of the Bill was well founded.

The Bill's main policy thrust was to deliver three things—a $600 a week additional jobless benefit, a subsidy for hard-hit businesses, like restaurants and movie theatres, and extra money for schools and health care providers. However, in the ensuing battle over the Bill's content, the legislators lost sight of its main purpose. They overshot the mark. The political horse-trading demanded by the Democrats distorted its main policy intent.

Included in its 5,500-plus pages were multiple, non-pandemic related measures, such as the establishment of two Smithsonian museums: a Smithsonian *American Women's History Museum* and a *National Museum of the American Latino*. The package also contained $2 billion for the *Space Force*; $35 million in *sexual abstinence programs for kids*; and *tax breaks for those who own racehorses*. It included provisions to end *surprise medical billing*, authorised *flood control and water-related projects* and assisted *fish breeding*. It also provided that Federal Reserve emergency lending programs would expire on December 31, for businesses and for state and local governments, as Republicans believed these amounted to government interference in the private sector.

While these non-Covid related measures were domestic outlays, the Bill also contained some weird international payments—$ 85.5 million for Cambodia, $ 134 million for Burma and a staggering $1.3. billion for Egypt and its military, most of which commentators conceded would be used to buy Russian military equipment! A further $505 million would go to Belize, Costa Rica, El Salvador,

Guatemala, Honduras, Nicaragua and Panama and a further $25 million would go for *democracy* and *gender equality* programs in Pakistan. These were perversions of the Bill's purpose and perversions of public policy. Unvarnished political point scoring.

The outgoing President was angry. In policy terms, he had good reason to be. Those of us who subscribe to the idea that fiscal measures must be targeted, morally sound and responsible would agree. Trump refused to sign the rescue package, demanding instead that the bill increase payments to US$2,000 per citizen, rather than the proposed $600. This seemed crazy, since the $2,000 he proposed was identical to the figure earlier proposed by the Democrats, which Trump's own party said was too much and opposed. However, on closer inspection of Trump's counter proposal something interesting was revealed. It was fiscally more responsible!

Although Trump's proposal required a much higher per capita payment, the net difference in public in agreeing to $2,000 per head instead of $600 per head, was almost negligible, because demands from the Democrats for funding of many unrelated causes had distorted the cost of *administering* the Bill. If the more diverse Bill were approved, each aspect would require action by a different government agency, adding significant costs to the Bill's implementation. If, instead, a single '*Covid Relief*' payment had been agreed, only one agency, the Federal Reserve, could administer the task of giving each American $2,000, making the cost of the Bill's implementation much smaller, and the $2000 Vs $600 amount, budget neutral.

This demonstrates how bad fiscal discipline can corrupt good public policy, resulting in large portions of government outlays being absorbed in bureaucratic and administrative costs, rather than flowing directly to the intended beneficiaries. It also demonstrates that we must assess public policy dispassionately and see it on its own merits, rather than judging it through the lens of personal animus or political prejudice. That requires a neutrality few of us possess.

Returning to the question of fiscal responsibility and whether public money is ours, or magically becomes someone else's after we surrender it as a tax or other contribution—this fiscal ambiguity is not just a government problem. It affects other public entities. An investigation into the operations of the American Red Cross demonstrates this. The American Red Cross falsely claimed that 91% of the donations it received were spent on delivering services. The Red Cross

CEO went so far as to say that he was very proud of such a low overhead. However, when the public interest organisation, *ProPublica*, began digging into his claim, the Red Cross removed the spurious figure from its website and refused to *"clarify"* the apparently fraudulent assertion. The very reverse had been true.

ProPublica found that the Red Cross' own financial statements proved that its overheads were significantly higher. Fundraising ate up 26% of every dollar and *management and general expenses*—a major part of most organisations operating costs—were either not made transparent or not included in the calculations. Some $2.2 billion of the organisation's expenses—80% of its spending—went into its *blood business*, not into *disaster relief.* Only 14 % went to *disaster relief,* despite public statements that this was *the principal focus of the organisation's work.*

To be fair to Trump—or more likely his advisers—he recognised the same fiscal lunacy in the Covid Relief Bill. He understood that its' political concessions would dilute benefits to ordinary Americans because so many sections of the bill were not related in any way to the relief the Bill was intended to deliver. On the cusp of leaving office, Trump defiantly argued that the rescue package was a disgrace. Alas, his lack tactless manner, lack of statesmanship and desperate timing made his otherwise well-reasoned case futile. Wide public antipathy towards the man had blinded people to his entirely reasonable criticism of the bill's wasteful elements, which he had correctly assessed. Those literate in the fiscal game saw the same demons in the proposed legislation. They did not mince words, agreeing with Trump about the disgraceful waste elements. However, by then Trump's credibility was so damaged that, despite corruption of the Bill's intent, he caved in and signed it.

"This so-called Covid Rescue Package has nothing to do with Covid," said Trump. "Lots of money abroad, and to lobbyists and special interests," he railed. "I ask Congress to change the bill and throw out the bribes and other unnecessary things."

Republican Senator Rand Paul addressed the Senate prior to his colleagues' vote on the $900 billion coronavirus bill and told fellow Republicans who backed the stimulus that they were "no better than the Democrats they criticised, who align themselves with socialism. If free money was the answer…if money really did grow on trees, why not give more free money?" he said. "Why not give it out all the time? Why stop at $600 a person? Why not $1,000? Or $2,000? Maybe these Free-Money Republicans should join the Everybody-Gets-A-Guaranteed-

Income Caucus? Why not $20,000 a year for everybody, why not $30,000? If we can print money with impunity, why not do it?" he added. "When you vote to pass out free money, you lose your soul, and ... abandon any semblance of... fiscal integrity."

I like Senator Paul. His point was well made and morally sound. Public money is just that, and public debt is *the people's* debt. It is galling when politicians seem to say '*What is a billion dollars here or there? It's not my money?*'

... or perhaps ... '*It's just part of a stimulus package*'. We taxpayers *must* care if we wish to hold the public sector to account and instil fiscal discipline. The *Covid Relief Bill* approved spending worth US$ 1.4. trillion—yes *trillion, not billion.* For the uninitiated, one trillion dollars is $1,000,000,000,000,000,000 (i.e., ten to the eighteenth power). I shudder to think how that sum would be viewed through an Australian, Canadian or even a British lens, rather than an American fiscal lens. To put the word '*billion*' into context, and to help you judge whether you want your politicians to spend your billions, consider this: A billion seconds ago, it was 1959.

A billion minutes ago, Jesus was still alive.

A billion hours ago, our ancestors were living in the Stone Age. A billion days ago, no-one walked on the earth on two feet.

And shockingly, a billion dollars ago was only 13 hours and 12 minutes, at the rate that the Australian government is presently spending its consolidated revenue.

Government Debt and Welfare Dependence

If a middle-ranking nation like Australia spends $1 billion dollars every 13 hours 12 minutes, how does it replenish those funds to maintain budget equilibrium, how does it compare with similar nations and are those funds spent wisely? It will surprise many to learn that Australia raises consolidated revenue from one of the highest tax bases in the OECD. It collects the following, eyewatering array of taxes:

Stamp Duty, Tobacco Tax, Corporate Income Tax, Personal Income Tax, council rates and taxes, unemployment tax, fishing licence tax, petrol and diesel taxes, inheritance tax (a tax on a tax), alcohol taxes and excises, the G.S.T., property taxes, service charges, social security tax, vehicle licence and registration taxes, vehicle sales tax, workers compensation tax and a new miscellany of CO2 Taxes.

If you find that a staggering tax base, consider this: *not one of those taxes existed 60 years ago,* when Australia was one of the most prosperous nations on earth. Back then, Australian families were much more self-reliant and supportive of each other. Thank God we have moved on from the old, misogynistic idea that *'the little lady should stay at home and mind the kids'*, but it remains important to try to understand how our culture has shifted so radically away from self-reliance towards a welfare state. Consider for a moment the following, shocking truths:

Sixty years ago, Australia had no debt—not one dollar—and the largest middle-class in the world. Mothers stayed at home to raise kids and played tennis and bridge, or simply cooked and house-cleaned while they waited for hubby to come home and pay the bills. Back then, dads and schoolteachers used a belt across a kid's arse, with impunity. Kids did what they were told to do. It really was so!

Back then, 'Boat People' were kids sailing dinghies on our harbours, not illegal immigrants. Back then, if you did the crime, you did the time. A criminal's life was uncomfortably spartan. Prisoners had no special rights, TVs, radios, comfortable beds, three hot meals a day or workout gymnasiums. These more Spartan times are abhorrent to modern thinking, particularly on social justice, gender equality and other grounds, but that society really existed, and it remains a legitimate case study.

If we focus on fiscal policy and leave social justice out of the equation, we must grudgingly concede that this was a self-reliant society in which families accepted responsibility for their own welfare, without relying upon welfare payments or government subvention.

As global populations explode and an ageing demographic threatens to exhaust national superannuation and savings reserves, it may be useful to consider which policy elements of that previous, more self-reliant social order reduced welfare dependence. That might suggest some fiscally responsible pathways—ones without a misogynistic fault line—to prevent us realising Plato's assertion that democracy leads to a sense of entitlement. Policies which lubricate self-interest and place it above the public good or the national interest ought, logically, to be resisted else we venture down Plato's forbidden path and augment an attitude of entitlement.

Do Conservatives or Socialists Show More Fiscal Restraint?

There has been a popular misconception in Australia that Labor racks up debt to finance its social justice agendas, leaving successive deficits for Conservatives to pay down. This has been exploited in campaign rhetoric. Upon closer examination, however this analysis is too simplistic. It does not take account of inherited, exogenous, rather than real-time endogenous impacts, like inherited structural debt, investment streams that continue from another party's political initiatives like '*The Future Fund*', which governments inherit from previous administrations, fluctuations in the rate of inflation and shifts in global financial and currency markets, which impact a nation's debt ratio. Former Labor Senator, Stephen Loosely puts it thus:

"All my life, like most social democrats, I have been lectured by conservatives about the profligacy of Labor governments with the public purse. There have been exceptions, of course, but the overwhelming reality of Australian politics is that, compared to other nations, both sides of the aisle have been subdued and sober with public finances."

Like its US and European counterparts, Australia's Reserve Bank argues that, provided growth exceeds inflation, we shouldn't be troubled by the size of the national debt. But what if something like a coronavirus comes along? The world has been turned upside down by the coronavirus and it has caused Australia's Liberal Conservative party to trip up on its own, political catch cry, one which it regularly invokes in its attacks upon the left: *"Where's the money coming from?"*

At the moment, as Loosely puts it, the conservatives are *"spending with Argentinian abandon."* One could be mistaken for believing that conservative Treasurer Josh Frydenberg's budget had been prepared by a socialist government. Other OECD nations are also becoming profligate spenders, in their frantic attempts to keep employment robust and businesses buoyant during an unparalleled pandemic. That has required a spending frenzy which more closely resembles Churchill's which almost bankrupted Great Britain in its fight against Nazism.

Labor's shadow minister for finance, Jim Chalmers, correctly noted that *"under the current (Liberal) government net debt has doubled."* By July 2018,

Australia's net debt was A$341 billion, up from A$175 billion in September 2013, when the Coalition took office. That's an increase of A$166.5 billion, or 95%, over five years. To put that in context, in Labor's last term (2007-13), a six-year period that included the Global Financial Crisis, net debt rose by about A$197 billion—only A$30 billion more than has been the case under the current 5-year Coalition government.

To be fair, we must remember that, over time, a government's debt reflects the deficits (or surpluses) it inherits from past governments. One thing is clear. The Covid 19 pandemic has weakened the sturdy grips nation's traditionally have on their fiscal levers. It has done so across a global landscape and across the political divide, indifferent to the politics of any Treasurer, President or Prime Minister. Spending is conducted with the same abandon as a turkey shoot or a paint-ball skirmish…and we don't yet have the invoice for this profligate fun, or any idea how we will pay for it.

Corona-debt is a creeping cancer, that will require a painful convalescence.

Chapter 24
Can Democracy Prevail?

Divide and Conquer!
Gaius Julius Caesar

Where to from here? We have looked at the architecture of democracy, at the forces which seem to be attacking it, at the relationship between democracy and public policy in righting the ship of state and at the way in which new cyber and other highways of communication have created a 'virtual public', giving it voting rights which it was never intended to have. We have considered the rapid rise of China, the challenges from autocracies and the emergence of other economies, like India, which now play a more dominant role in political and economic affairs. We have seen an apparent loss of authority by the institutions which, after WWII, were put in place to secure a 'rules-based world order'. There is no doubt that our world is wobbling on its axis and looking for a new equilibrium. On the balance of evidence before us, I am persuaded that democracy *is* losing ground. Its seductive promise to defend human dignity and freedom is struggling in the face of new attacks upon it, to diminish that promise. Unless we defend that promise, and those hallowed values, we may find ourselves subject to the will of nations which do not share those values.

It is worth looking back through history to the last time there was a seismic shift in the world order. That might help us understand how that seismic change occurred, how the free world rallied to counter it, and what we can learn from that experience, as we attempt to bring order back to our troubled world.

The last seismic shift in global power commenced in August 1934, when Hindenburg died and Hitler became both Chancellor and President of Germany, an absolute ruler, and commenced a dramatic rearmament of Germany. Just eleven years later, in July 1945, the leaders of the U.S., Great Britain and the

Soviet Union gathered at a palace in Potsdam to hammer out yet another plan for a new world order. Ironically, to avoid inhaling the smoke and fumes still rising from a landscape of rubble and wartime destruction, some of the Potsdam delegates wore face masks like those which now protect us from the coronavirus. Churchill glowered at Stalin, understanding that the man sitting beside him represented an insidious threat. Stalin would divide, not unify, and impose borders which Churchill later described as an *'Iron Curtain'*. These three men would calmly carve-up Europe, seismically changing the landscape and creating a new age, dubbed the *'Cold War'* era, which prevailed for three-quarters of a century (until 1991, with the dissolution of the Soviet Union).

Bloomberg recently provided a report on a newly opened exhibition to mark the 75th anniversary of the Potsdam conference. At the exhibition, 21st century contemporaries wearing similar face masks—this time protecting them against a virus, not the ashes and smoke from the war ruins—pondered the consequences of those decisions 75 years ago. Even as those 21st century protagonists wandered through the Potsdam memorial exhibition, the geopolitical map of the world was being redrawn yet again—not only as a consequence of the emergence of new military and economic powers, but also because of the coronavirus, which German Chancellor Angela Merkel described as the biggest challenge of our era.

As Bloomberg put it, *"Governments are confronting a health crisis, an economic crisis and a crisis of institutional legitimacy, all at a time of heightened geopolitical rivalry. How those tectonic shifts crystallise over the next period will go a long way to determining the post-virus era. Trends that were already apparent pre-Covid-19 have intensified and accelerated. A fast-rising power, China, is growing more assertive and jostling with countries from Canada to Australia. The U.S., the one superpower that has remained at the top table since Potsdam, is increasingly self-absorbed as the virus rips through its population and economy ..."*

Rory Medcalf, head of the *'National Security College, Australian National University'* says: *"A lot of structural problems in the international order are becoming much more apparent."* With a convergence of multiple pressure points, from failures of leadership to a lack of trust in the truth and veracity of information ... *"it does add up to a kind of perfect storm,"* he said. *"The big test is really whether we can get through let's say the next decade without these crises coming to a head."*

Seventy-five years ago, Potsdam was the focus of a new, ideological struggle between Communism and Capitalism. Its human face was the subsequent 'face-off' between Moscow and Washington, culminating in the Bay of Pigs and a close brush with a nuclear war. The Soviet Union had emerged from WWII a new superpower, while the U.S. had announced widened the gap by demonstrating an even more awful military advantage, when it dropped atomic bombs on Hiroshima and Nagasaki. Today, we see a hauntingly familiar standoff between the U.S., other western democracies and Xi Jinping's China, which former Secretary of State Henry Kissinger has described as *"the foothills of a new cold war."* Australian Senator, General Jim Molan, agrees and historian, Niall Ferguson, thinks we are already there.

Medcalf has written a book titled *"Indo-Pacific Empire"* which looks at strategic rivalry in our region. He says that the defining issue is not just how the U.S. responds to the rise of China, but whether *"middle players"* including India, Australia, Japan and Europe, are prepared to take risks to defend the international world order and work together to do so.

In August 2014, I attended a policy forum in Melbourne on emerging defence threats. Participants supported Medcalf's view about the need for a coalition of middle-ranking democracies. For my part, at the forum I proposed a new defence pact, which I called a JAPINDA Pact, to buttress Australia's ANZUS Treaty with the US by adding India and Japan into the mix (and possibly also Indonesia) to localise the alliance, build confidence in regional security and increased deterrence.

A number of speakers held that new alliances were essential because the United Nations, formed in 1945 to prevent wars, had become largely dysfunctional. Russia and China, two of the five veto-wielding powers, routinely blocked resolutions. Meanwhile conflicts with Beijing were, as one commentator put it, suddenly and bewilderingly to be found everywhere. China was locked in a tussle with the West, over freedom of navigation, with Australia over the origins of the coronavirus, with Canada over the detention of the Huawei executive Meng Wanzhou, and with India, over a long-standing territorial dispute over their common border.

More recently, Japan, Australia and the EU have moved to reduce their supply chain dependence on China, not just because of China's territorial ambitions, propensity for disputes and bold investment behaviour, but also because of the controversy surrounding the coronavirus. Germany, Britain and

Australia have all enacted legislation to protect against predatory investments from China and an EU policy paper on competition has supported the view that… *'Chinese investment with a geopolitical, instead of a purely mercantile purpose, is becoming "a huge threat'.*

Meanwhile, a new national security law which China has imposed on Hong Kong has spurred global concerns about Beijing's interference in the former British territory's independence. U.K. Prime Minister, Boris Johnson, has called for an earlier decision—permitting China's Huwei to participate in Britain's 5G network—to be reversed, to exclude it, prompting a warning from China that the decision would have *'consequences'*. Johnson's government also offered three million Hong Kong Chinese a fast track to British citizenship. Ulrich Speck, a senior visiting fellow at the German Marshall Fund, described China's stance on Hong Kong as a metaphorical *'Berlin Wall'*—recalling the blockade of Berlin by the Red Army in 1948-1949.

According to William Choong, senior fellow at the Yusof Ishak Institute in Singapore, *"tensions with Taiwan, in the disputed South China Sea and in the East China Sea have been heightened by a hyper-power display by China. In the Chinese mind, the U.S. has lost its mantle of leadership in the Asia-Pacific, if not in the world,"* he said. *"So, China does see it as an opportunity to press home its advantage in our part of the world."* Choong has also voiced concern that a confrontation between the U.S. and China, or between Japan and China, could turn to open conflict if some *"trigger-happy commander on the ground decides to push a button."*

History is littered with unintended consequences, and the Potsdam Conference had its share. In Potsdam, over 2 weeks, Truman, Stalin and Churchill basically decided Germany's future. That was a pretty short time span for such momentous decision-making. They also debated Poland's borders and took positions that would have far-reaching consequences for the Middle East and for China, Japan and Korea, that are still playing out in those theatres.

Here are some examples: Shifting Poland's border west to compensate for territory carved out of the east, which led to the displacement of some 20 million people. Creating a precondition for war on the Korean peninsula. By 1950, war had broken out between the Communist north and the US-backed south. Many of the other fault lines established in Potsdam are still there today, and the cultural and economic fault lines created have been further accentuated by the coronavirus. Constanze Stelzenmueller, a senior fellow at the *Centre for the*

United States and Europe at the Brookings Institution in Washington, says *"where there have been flaws and weaknesses, the pandemic has ripped through with particular brutality."*

The Sudden Rise of Corona-Vira-Tocracy

If the rise of China, the attendant shift in global power and a resultant weakening of the post-war, rules-based world order are not enough to make you wonder about the future, the coronavirus, a seismic event with unintended consequences for democracy, has added another dimension. Some democratic leaders have become so autocratic in their exercise of a newly acquired power over people's lives, supported by health officials looking more like storm troopers, that they have become autocrats. Indeed, Putin and Xi Jinping would be proud to call many of them comrades.

Political populism, apparent from the polls which show that politicians who fiercely protect local constituents by applying tough lockdowns, raise their popularity with local voters to stellar new levels. The West Australian Premier's popularity hit 90% after he refused to open his borders to interstate and overseas guests. The Queensland Premier saw how popular that made her counterpart and did the same.

The CV19 crisis is destined to be with us for some time, but frustrated citizens unaccustomed to the way government by health-proxy is now ruling their lives, are beginning to push back. The trouble with government-imposed lockdowns, apart from the fact that they deepen economic hardship and create new mental health risks, is that they turn democracy on its head, robbing people of their democratic right to freedom of movement and association.

Plato described this circumstance perfectly when he said: *"This and no other is the root from which a tyrant springs—he first appears as a protector."* If and when we get on top of this virus, we must pray that our political leaders will be able to break their addiction to a newfound authoritarianism. A health-driven power over every aspect of our lives, closely approximating the powers of repressive, autocratic regimes, is unhealthy for democracy and a serious attack upon personal freedoms.

When we add to the impacts of the coronavirus the many other, fastmoving parts that are forging a new social contract and a new world order, we have genuine reason to be concerned. Rory Medcalf, of La Trobe University thinks that there is an analogy for what comes next. For him, the closest analogy is the pre-war period of the 1930s. *"Whatever is happening,"* he says, *"we are on the edge of a gathering storm. We have a pretty good idea where it will come from. It's just that we don't yet know what the storm looks like or how it will break.*

Chapter 25
Accountability—A Window into Democracy

The government's view of the economy can be summed up in a few short phrases: If it moves, tax it. If it keeps moving, regulate it. And if it stops moving, subsidise it.
Ronald Reagan

One of the distinguishing features of a genuine democracy is the requirement that politicians answer to the people for the policies they introduce, the priorities they set and the way they spend their money. Democracy provides transparency into those things and ensures that corruption is held in check, in stark contrast to the autocracy we see in China and the Kleptocracy we see in Russia, where Putin and his oligarchs are cut into every deal. (For an excellent book on this, I recommend *'Putin's Kleptrocracy'*). There are shades of grey in pseudo-democracies—in places like Indonesia and the Philippines—where long-standing cultural practices accept, almost fatalistically, the need to bribe officials, or grease the palms of government officials to get things done, and privileges are granted to a small coterie of plutocrats and their families. Philosophically, the people's money (their taxes) should be reinvested in their happiness and welfare, not find its way into the pockets of officials.

If the genuineness of a democracy is measured by the moral authority it derives from its people, that should be regulated by the polls, which operate like a weather barometer to measure the public response to government policies—to a government's law-and-order record, its transparency and its efforts to ensure fairness and equity. It seems logical that we judge governments not only against the values they defend but also by the direction and priority they accord to public spending, which, in turn, helps us to measure and rank democratic function or dysfunction.

An analysis of the funding of government departments and agencies will tell us lots about the way a government orders its priorities and serves (a) the public good and (b) the national interest. One could start by looking at things like public health, education and welfare. But in the context of the rise of China and the potential impact that might have upon democracy, I prefer to begin by measuring defence spending. It is the biggest ticket item in most national budgets, and it indicates a democratic nation's capacity to defend its sovereignty and protect its values.

Other metrics are available around the amount a government spends on delivering services and infrastructure and the ratio of its spending on wages and salaries compared to delivering public works and services. This latter measure is commonly used to indicate whether a bureaucracy is bloated, and whether it supports private sector involvement in project and service delivery to achieve cost and structural efficiencies. By benchmarking these things against other governments, we can see relativities that tell us a story about good or bad governance.

In 2020 a report by *Statista*, a statistics agency headquartered in Germany, reviewed global defence spending. With spending totalling $US 732 billion, the United States ranked first. China ranked second, as it has done since 2008. The US spent about 38% of the global military spend that year ($US 1.92 trillion). In 2019, United States military expenditure amounted to 3.4 % of US gross domestic product (GDP), placing the US lower in national spend on a per capita basis than Russia, which spent 3.9 % of its GDP, and Saudi Arabia, which spent 8 % of its GDP.

According to Congressional Budget papers, US defence outlays will rise from $US 625 billion in 2014, to $US 781 billion by 2024. Between 2013 and 2022, the US is projected to spend $US 392 billion of this total on nuclear weapons and $US 97 billion on missile defences compared with 100 billion on the environment and health.

The military advantage America holds over China and Russia is reassuring, but why the bias in US spending towards so many nuclear weapons? If we believe that the US will maintain its role as a defender of democracy, a conventional rather than a nuclear capacity would seem more logical if most of its adversaries are non-nuclear or arming themselves with an array of new conventional weapons—new navies, interdiction missile systems and land-based military capacity, instead of nuclear warheads, which are outlawed by the UN.

Moreover, the US and other nuclear nations each have enough nuclear warheads to destroy the world several times over. America's nuclear might is reassuring, but it will mean little should any protagonist simply ignore the size of its nuclear deterrent by choosing a nuclear first strike. If that should happen, all of us, and this book, will be pointless. We can destroy humanity with a fraction of the current US nuclear arsenal.

So much for defence spending. What about other areas of government spending and the way in which spending aligns with or clashes with wealth creation versus welfare spending initiatives? Is a capitalist, free-market approach to fiscal policy better than socialism, albeit the kind which spends lots on flattening income disparities and ensuring social justice for all? That seems a question worth exploring.

Chapter 26
The Right to Vote

Power tends to corrupt, and absolute power corrupts absolutely.
Lord Acton

In a democracy, it seems axiomatic that power should be exercised from the bottom-up, (i.e., by the people) rather than from the top down (i.e., by a politician, or perhaps a dictator). In the lead-up to an election, politicians are all ears, but in between elections, they seem to grow deaf and have trouble hearing the plaintive cries of their constituents. After all, they are only held accountable periodically—at the end of each electoral cycle. One can measure the proximity of an election by the width of a politician's smile, by a heightened willingness to eyeball locals and engage, as if the distance between the electorate and the Parliament has been miraculously shortened. In the final analysis, if a politician's performance on the hustings or during a term of office is substandard, there is a price to pay at the ballot box. So, in a democracy, politicians are all, ultimately subject to the will of the people.

Universal Suffrage

The term 'universal suffrage' is always conflated with a woman's right to vote, but in fact it means precisely what it says—that all *adults* have a right to vote; not just women, but all women and men, and from all walks of life, not just a privileged group in society (as was the case for most of our planet's pre-history). When we talk about the idea that all politicians should be subject to the will of the people, do we mean subject to the will of all of the people, all of the time, or only to some of the people some of the time? Are some voters more influential than others and so command much more attention because politicians see them as 'make or break' supporters?

Have you ever considered that there are *special* voters who politicians feel they need to impress to stay in office? For example, coal miners in a town where jobs depend upon support for the coal mining industry, or perhaps workers in a vehicle plant whose continued operation depends upon government subsidies. Sometimes political energy is focussed selectively, not applied universally. The right of *all* people to choose their leaders, regardless of their wealth, income, gender, social status, race or ethnicity (with exceptions around issues like mental capacity), must surely be fundamental to democracy, but that breadth of voter entitlement is a recent event.

Universal suffrage—the right to vote—first appeared as an idea and a democratic construct in 1793 under the *Jacobins*, who believed in equality and personal liberty and led the revolution which toppled King Louis XVl of France. It was a difficult concept at that time, since only people well connected to the royal court had any ability to express a view about government and if they did, they had to do so carefully. If they got the politics wrong, they could lose their heads. It was not until recently that the vox populi (the common folk) were given a vote, although that cohort initially excluded women, and it is only recently that women were given a vote. We had to wait a little longer for other cohorts, like ethnic minorities and Australian aboriginals, to be given a vote. So, the term *universal suffrage* has only recently been given finally had real expression.

Since women have always been 50% of the population, it is staggering that it took not just centuries, but millennia for them to have a say in public affairs. Mao Zedong was an avowed supporter of women. He acknowledged that they must have a say in a nation's affairs because, as he put it, "*women hold up half the sky.*" But this fundamental right was not present in the ancient world, or even in our more contemporary political evolution. It was not until 1893, in New Zealand, that women were granted the right to vote.

The concept was later extended, but only to *adult male voters* in some new democracies and eventually to every *adult* voter, in most democracies. However, when we apply the test of 'universal suffrage' to the 195 nations and 60 dependent territories which populate our planet, only 80 nations, or 31%, meet that test; that is, allow universal voting, (NB: albeit the age at which a person becomes eligible to vote varies, from nation to nation, between 18 and 25). In some countries (mostly Islamic states) it remains so that only men can vote. But when we use 'universal suffrage' as a measure of democratic legitimacy, we mean *everyone's* right to vote—not some esoteric, socialist, conservative, gender preferencing or other variation on that theme.

Compulsory and Non-Compulsory Voting

If democracy is the voice of the people, what if only a third of the people vote and the rest remain indifferent? Is the result of that vote representative? Is it democratic? The Australian experience offers us some insights. It owes its relative stability and success, I think, to three special qualities—its compulsory voting system; its fiercely independent administration of law and justice and the existence of an independent, national authority to regulate elections—fairly, uniformly and nationally.

Australia's compulsory voting system sets it apart from most other western democracies. It maximises legitimacy of the result by maximising voter turnout. Moreover, while in many nations members of the judiciary are elected (for example, in the US), making them political, in Australia and more generally across the Westminster system, laws are enforced by an *unelected*, and therefore fiercely independent judiciary. It is this independent and clinically efficiency system—largely removed from the taint of political process—which enables Australian law enforcement agencies to hold all governments, Federal and State, to account, even when a government tries to abuse its constitutional power.

Finally, sitting calmly above the hailstorm of political controversy as election day approaches, a national regulator—the AEC (*Australian Electoral Commission*) clinically and dispassionately administers the national, or state poll, ensuring that its rules are applied uniformly at every voting booth across the state or nation conducting the poll.

The AEC ensures that each elector can vote only once, in the same way, and that his or her name is ticked off an electoral roll—where every voter must be registered. The electoral roll ensures that no duplication, or false or misleading conduct, can occur. Then, as voting closes and counting starts, AEC officials allow scrutineers from all parties to watch them count every vote—at every booth, uniformly, across the state or nation. While vote counting from booths located all over the landscape is manual, totals from each parochial booth are quickly transferred electronically to a tally centre, so that election outcomes are often known within 2 hours of the polls closing.

Only 13% of the 200 nations which grant all of their citizens the right to vote have compulsory voting, while 85% do not enforce voting. So, what are the merits of compulsory voting versus non-compulsory voting, and does it matter that the way democratic elections are held, scrutinised, counted and declared differs so much?

In an earlier chapter, I express astonishment that the USA, a nation which, for most of the last century has stood as a democratic exemplar—a *'light on the hill'* for the free world—and whose technical genius has landed men on the moon, has such an inept electoral system. With no independent Electoral Commission to ensure one, national, uniform system of voting, how can fair elections ensue? And how is it possible that such a clever nation still tolerates electoral machinery that is archaic, contestable and differs from state to state? We have seen first-hand how this plays out on the hustings in Trump's allegations of vote rigging and fraudulent counting.

History instructs us that most uprisings against ruling governments, including revolutions, have been ignited by a belief that elections were rigged—a banana republic phenomenon which has now infected over 50 million Americans, persuaded by Trump that his election was stolen. This unprecedented mindset, across a staggering proportion of the US electorate, is a frightening precursor to future toxicity and instability in the US. Indeed, a poll conducted immediately after the last US election indicated that 40 % of Republicans would follow Trump should he establish a break-away party. Trump has since said he will not do so, but he has clearly highjacked the mighty, establishment Republican party, fracturing it, infecting it with a separate stream of political zeal and possibly condemning it to years in opposition—all of that damage off the back of an assertion that the election was rigged.

David Kilcullen agrees with me. A counter-insurgency expert, former military officer and advisor, professor of political studies at the University of New South Wales and at the University of Arizona, Kilcullen has authored books on this subject. He says that the rise of a new right in the US poses a serious threat to mainstream democracy. Even more worrying is his contention that this phenomenon is not confined to the US, but is global, and is matched by the rise of a new and equally militant left. What happened to the silent majority who used to coalesce around a moderate and sane political centre?

Campaign Budgets and Undue Influence

If we agree that democracy derives its moral authority from the voice of the people, how does the US voting system achieve representative fairness when campaign budgets are not regulated, households are selectively door-knocked to mobilise voters, and voters are bussed in to vote. How can that system vouchsafe a representative voter sample—that is, citizens casting their votes spontaneously, privately, and without undue influence or suasion? That argues elegantly, I think, for compulsory voting, to ensure a representative outcome.

According to William C.R. Horncastle, Department of Political Science and International Studies at the University of Birmingham, spending on US elections eclipses the annual total economic output of some small countries. The total spending by candidates, political parties and independent campaign groups in the 2016 race was US$6.5 billion—comparable to the GDP that year of Monaco, Kosovo or Liechtenstein, and more than double that of Liberia.

The 2020 election cycle smashed previous totals, with the Centre for Responsive Politics estimating that it would reach a total spend of about US$11 billion. That sum is approximately equal to the 2019 GDP of Equatorial Guinea or Chad.

Cost of US elections (adjusted for inflation) $US billion—Source: Centre for Responsive Politics:		
Year	Congressional Races	Presidential Race
2020	5.674 bill	5.163 bill
2016	4.451	2.576
2012	4.134	2.958
2008	2.949	3.322
2004	3.068	2.620
2000	2.511	2.126

US campaigns have traditionally been funded by donations to candidates, prompting attempts to impose funding ceilings to ensure a level contest. But in 2010, the US Supreme Court ruled that *'restrictions on campaign spending by corporations and labour unions were unconstitutional and limited their free speech!'* However, the party with the biggest campaign budget is able to buy more advertising time and thus sway public opinion. The same phenomenon exists in other western democracies, most often when trade unions or big business decide to enter a campaign to defend their own, sectional interests. This argues forcefully, I think, for a legislated cap on campaign spending, or a '*same funding for all*' policy, under which the state grants each candidate an equal allowance and makes external contributions illegal. Funding constraints of this sort would force candidates to rely solely on their powers of intellect and articulation, give them no place to hide and require that they are elected on their own merits.

Is Compulsory Voting Less Democratic Than Laissez-Faire?

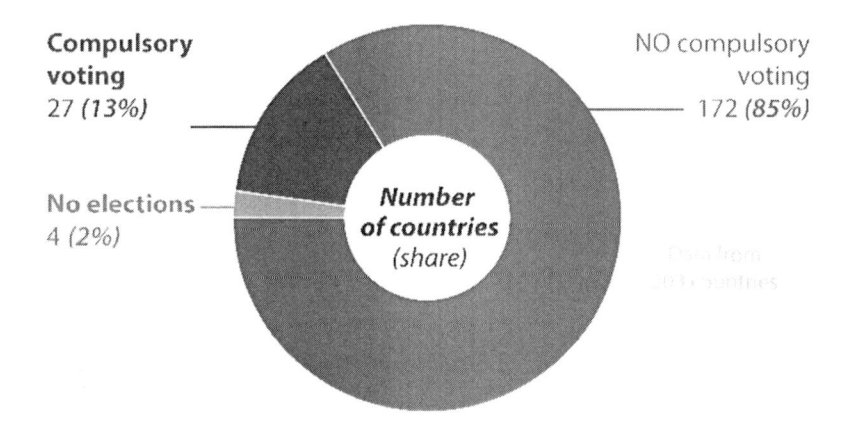

Compulsory voting
27 (13%)

No elections
4 (2%)

Number of countries (share)

NO compulsory voting
172 (85%)

In most democratic governments, participation in national elections is a right of citizenship, rather than a legal obligation. However, compulsory voting is not a new concept. It was first introduced in Belgium, in 1892, then in Argentina in 1914 and Australia in 1924. Advocates of compulsory voting argue that governments are more legitimate when higher proportions of the population vote for them. They make the point that compulsory voting also has an educational impact and improves political literacy. Political parties derive financial benefit from compulsory voting, since they do not have to spend resources convincing the electorate to turn out and vote for them. If democracy is government by the people—by all of the people—then each citizen should have an equal say in electing the nation's leaders.

The main argument against compulsory voting is that it is not consistent with the freedom usual associated with democracy. Forcing people to vote could infringe their free will. Is a government more legitimate if the higher voter turnout is against the will of the voters? It has been shown that forcing people to vote results in a slightly higher number of invalid, blank or donkey votes, compared to countries with no compulsory voting. But the difference in donkey and invalid votes includes 'accidental' errors and is statistically so small as to be negligible. This does not impact in any statistically measurable way the legitimacy of the overall vote, of the democratically elected MPs, or of the ruling government's outcome.

In Australia, the penalty for not voting is nominal and a small price to pay if you are travelling abroad or fail to lodge an absentee vote. Since compulsory voting requires that every eligible adult must head to a local booth (usually a high school or college campus) on election day (commonly Saturdays), election days assume a holiday atmosphere and bring communities together. Rotarians, fire fighters, Red Cross and other volunteer groups run *sausage sizzles* and other fund-raisers outside voting booths. Volunteers hand out voting materials outside booths and assist each another to set up and take down election-day paraphernalia. A conservative volunteer might ask a Labor volunteer to hand out his 'how to vote' cards while he or she visits the loo. This gregarious behaviour is common, helps to develop respect for political opponents and promotes civil discourse.

Studies have shown that non-voters are statistically irrelevant to the outcome, so compulsory voting delivers a more representative vote and a more accurate polling of national sentiment. In 2016 the effective participation rate was measured by the Australian Electoral Commission at 82%. In the US that figure is about 40% lower (although it rose to an all-time high in the 2020 campaign).

What Makes an Elected Government Legitimate?

Trump's plaintive cry that the US election was rigged may have been fanciful, but if it achieved anything, it focussed attention on the issue of legitimacy. I am drawn to the conclusion that, if a democratic government hopes to govern with moral authority, to enjoy a genuine mandate from electors and be answerable to them, and if its power is to be appropriately constrained, it must tick the following boxes:

- It must limit campaign funding, to prevent lopsided funding by vested or sectional interests, seeking to 'buy' an election or unreasonably shift public sentiment.
- It must strive to achieve a truly representative result, by maximising voter participation. This could be achieved by making voting compulsory.
- It must establish a uniform, national voting system and appoint an independent arbiter (e.g., a Federal Electoral Commission) to manage all elections.
- Any parallel, executive office (e.g., the US Presidency) with powers which compete with those of members of the legislature, elected by a national plebiscite, (a general election), must be held in check by making that office ultimately answerable to a national assembly (e.g., a house of representatives).
- Political and administrative institutions must be subject to a fiercely independent system of law and justice, which provides remedies if those institutions stray.

Chapter 27
Does Democracy Look the Same Everywhere ... And Does It Speak with the Same Voice?

The further a society drifts from the truth, the more it will hate those who speak it.
George Orwell

Most modern democracies are constitutional monarchies, with a king or a queen, or republics, with a President (though there are variations on that simplistic description and many regimes which call themselves a democracy do nothing, in the way they behave, to earn that exalted title). Some democracies have Governors, a hang-over from colonial times, but in modern practice, the governing power in nearly every democracy resides with the legislature—that is, with the joint and several powers of the upper and lower houses of an elected federal or state Parliament, not in monarchs or presidents who operate as *legal instruments with limited, reserve powers*. In constitutional monarchies, the most powerful statesperson is thus the Prime Minister, not the monarch, and the Crown's role tends to be ceremonial.

Most models also elect representatives to an upper and a lower house, the lower house leader being head of state. In some democracies, a head of state with the title '*President*', may be popularly elected, with an accompanying political power base, but many Presidents are appointed, not elected. Presidential (or Gubernatorial) power may be potent (as in the USA) or impotent (ceremonial), as in India and Australia. In India, for example, the Prime Minister is the national leader and most powerful statesman—traditionally a Hindu—while the President holds a ceremonial office and is, by convention a Muslim, to balance religious sensitivities.

In a third variant, which includes several pseudo democracies, the power is shared, or may be vested in a President, subject to moderate or perhaps firmer limitations upon his or her power. But when great power is vested in an individual, it is often accompanied by cronyism and corruption. We saw this in Stalin's Russia, in Idi Amin's Uganda and in Marcos's Philippines and we see it today in Putin's Kleptocracy. History demonstrates that power which is unconstrained by the voice of an elected national assembly, or not earned by an honest, transparent election process, is invariably corrupt and usually malign.

Switzerland has a unique system of government, considered the closest system in the world to a *direct* democracy—that is, one in which citizens, not politicians, rule and may challenge laws voted by the federal assembly. Switzerland's Executive, Judicial and Legislative organs are organised on federal, cantonal and communal levels. Remarkably, unlike other democracies, Switzerland does not have a President or a Prime Minister. The country's citizens sit at the pinnacle of power.

In another variant, the Constitution of the Government of Singapore provides for an *Executive* branch of government, made up of the combined offices of the President and the Cabinet of Singapore. Although the President can use personal discretion in the exercise of certain functions, usually as a check on the Cabinet, the President's role is largely ceremonial. The Cabinet, comprising the Prime Minister and other Ministers appointed by the President on the advice of a majority of the Ministers, is the vehicle which effectively runs the Government. The Cabinet is, in turn, formed by the political party that wins a simple majority at a general election.

In some hybrid models, a potent, power may be discreetly shared or reside quietly, rather than visibly, with a 5th column of power—for example, a power-sharing arrangement with a military General and his army, with a religious leader (an Ayatollah, as in Islamic states), or with a monarch (as with the King of Thailand).

Military Juntas are a rare exception. However, this unsavoury system still exists in Myanmar and some West African states. Indeed, something very unpleasant happened on September 5, 2021, which was the day Colonel Mamadi Doumbouya, formerly an officer in the French Foreign Legion, led a group of soldiers to overthrow President Alpha Conde, of Guinea. A country of about 13 million inhabitants with French as its language, Guinea is reputed to have the world's largest bauxite reserves, a major requirement for producing aluminium.

In addition, Guinea also has a sizable amount of gold and diamond deposits, as well as reserves of crude oil.

The coup plotters showed scant regard for international opinion when they executed their sinister moves on a day when there were special foreign visitors—especially football players and FIFA officials, visiting for the 2022 World Cup match between Guinea and Morocco. Despite the presence of those and other officials, the coup plotters went ahead and overthrew an elected president. They had risked a backlash from the Economic Community of West African States (ECOWAS) and the international community, who could not have mounted an effective resistance in time. It is a tragic indictment of democracy that the military in Guinea got away with their sinister venture, making it the most recent victim of self-serving overlords. It now joins Mali and Chad, two other West African countries with military juntas.

But in most of the successful, mainstream models—those we find in the OECD and in other typical western democracies, representatives must *win a moral mandate,* granted by the people via an honest, transparent public ballot. Even then, elected officials remain subject to nationally elected assemblies—usually a house of representatives and a senate (or upper house of review), and are subject to the caveat that they are likely to be removed at the next ballot if they perform badly.

In the constellation of current, functioning democracies, the United States is almost unique in allowing a *parallel* power to operate *beside* the elected national assembly—the power attaching to the office of the US President. This single executive office can exercise a potent, sometimes overriding voice in the nation's democratic affairs and its power is only finally checked by a vote of *two-thirds of the Senate* to impeach, after an impeachment action has been initiated by Congress. Impeachment once required a *high crime or misdemeanour,* but now seems to have become so politically *weaponised* that a lesser event will do. Otherwise, many powers invested in this one office are relatively unconstrained.

As Australia considers moving towards a republican model, which it periodically does, it would be wise to reflect upon the US architecture and, in my view, to avoid its' pitfalls. Recent dysfunction in the US has cooled, rather than fanned, the coals of ambition for an Australian Republic, since our successful model—constitutional monarchy—still works very well, and our monarch is just a mirage.

The powers vested in a US President are unimaginable in Britain or Australia and would likely attract the ire of their more cautious electorates. Here are some of the powers conferred upon a US President, which I believe can operate corruptly or perversely to taint good government:

A US President can *'command the Army and Navy, and the Militia of the States'*. He (or she) can require the head of each executive department of government to report upon any subject relating to its office. He can *'grant Reprieves and Pardons for Offenses against the United States'*. He has the power to make Treaties with other nations, provided two thirds of the Senators present concur; and can nominate and appoint Ambassadors, public Ministers and Consuls, Judges of the Supreme Court, and *'all other Officers of the United States, whose Appointments are not herein otherwise provided for, and which shall be established by Law'*:

The President can also fill vacancies that may happen during the *Recess of the Senate,* by granting Commissions which will expire at the End of their Session. This Article allows a President to 'stack' his administration with his own preferred candidates and operates to politicise an administration over the heads of professional public servants, whose experience and judgement is then subject to new, partisan leadership. I consider this a serious flaw in the US democratic machinery.

Whilst there are modest checks and balances in the US model—most obvious in the electoral consequences for a rogue President, since he, too, is an elected leader, I would argue that this overlay of powers residing not *outside* by *alongside* the nationally elected assemblies, the Congress and the Senate, makes the US model volatile. As we look with hindsight at 'Trumpian' dysfunction and its associated toxicity in the US, it may be time to ask whether a parallel executive power enhances democracy or increase its dysfunction.

While respecting that many may disagree, I think the Australian, Canadian, New Zealand and British models have been more effective in their functionality and stability than the US model, because of the checks and balances which give them stronger moral authority and public suasion to remove a rogue politician from office. Their architecture makes the exercise of all power, excluding the power of the High Court, subject to the elected assembly and, by extension, to the voice of the people.

Can A Coalition of Different Regimes Speak with One Voice?

The coup in Myanmar on 1 February 2021, when the military toppled the civilian government of Aung San Suu Kyi and turned its guns on peaceful protesters, provides an insight into whether regional bodies, like ASEAN, whose systems of government straddles democracy, pseudo-democracy, presidential rule and even monarchical rule, can act in harmony and speak with one voice. The possibility of coalescing with other political systems is important in our rapidly changing world, as many nations watch the rise of China with a combination of fascination and angst. The Myanmar coup gave us a chance to test that possibility. Alas, the best ASEAN could manage was a joint call for… "*all parties to exercise utmost restraint as well as flexibility … and to seek a peaceful solution.*"

According to the '*Australian*' newspaper… "*the crisis officially blew the lid off ASEAN's existential flaw—a 10-nation bloc of nominal democracies, illiberal states, military juntas and an absolute monarchy—all lumped under one umbrella whose charter theoretically but clumsily tries to commit each member state to democratic values and the rule of law.*" It was nothing short of miraculous that ASEAN was able to craft a joint statement, since the ASEAN charter requires agreement from all member states, including Myanmar, before an agreed position is adopted.

After the release of the joint ASEAN statement, a number of more tersely worded, separate statements were released by ASEAN's four, albeit nominal, democracies—Indonesia, Malaysia, Singapore and The Philippines—demanding a reversal of the coup, an end to violence and the release of all political detainees. The non-democratic states remained mute. It had been necessary for the Indonesian Foreign Minister to drag member states screaming to the table after three weeks of dogged diplomacy. As we consider the different systems of government which inform, swirl around, or compete with democracy, the ASEAN example demonstrates, I think, that government architecture is not just influenced by events like Magna Carta and the Bill of Rights, which shaped our western democracies, but is also strongly influenced by surrounding regional, or inherited cultural influences (e.g., such as the reverence in which the King of Thailand is held by his people) and by the disparate systems of government of close neighbours, with whom we each must deal on a daily basis.

Since the four ASEAN democracies were unable to persuade their other ASEAN partners to adopt stronger positions—to force the Myanmar military to review or moderate its actions—the ASEAN bloc was condemned for its lack of unity. The flaw in its structure was described thus: '*A finger pointed at the democratic or human rights violations of one member state could result in four fingers being pointed back at your state, citing similar offences*'. Thailand is a case in point. Should it have condemned the Myanmar coup, it would inevitably have faced accusations over its own government's behaviour, since Thailand's present government is basically a rebadged version of the military junta that seized power in 2014, and which stands accused of rigging elections in its favour.

In the same way, 'one party' states, like Cambodia and Vietnam, would be hard pressed to demand that Myanmar abide by its democratic charter. The Philippines, which is facing charges in the international criminal court for crimes against humanity over the killing of thousands of alleged drug dealers, would be hard pressed to demand that the Myanmar junta abide by the rule of law. Moreover, according to an Oxford University study, even when regional groups mostly comprise democracies, as for example the European Union does, internal differences complicate their ability to find one voice for all member states. Despite national differences, the EU manages to approach some sort of unity, although its dogged and sometimes supranational power irks many member states. In each of its 5-year terms, it... '*proposes about 2000 binding legal acts and thus crucially shapes the form and substance of surrounding democracies and the daily lives of more than 500 million European citizens*'.

Despite the European Commission's mostly outstanding work in setting the agenda for over-arching European policy, it still blunders. It occasionally circulates legislative drafts that anger some Member States, sometimes introduces strikingly different rules and / or standards for members states, and even produces standards which contradict each other. In a recent study, academics Miriam Hartlapp and Julia Metz saw the internal processes of the European Commission as motivated by *technocratic problem-solving, competence-seeking utility maximisation*, or *ideological policy-seeking...* whatever those words mean. But in short, they describe a massive regional bureaucracy, larger than any of the individual member states it claims to represent, that holds sway over the lives and democratic rights of citizens who are also subject to their own, domestic political system—a sort of double overlay of government, which shapes and reshapes surrounding democracies.

Chapter 28
Is a Democratic Person a Capitalist or Socialist?

Measure welfare's success by the number who leave welfare, not the number added to it.
Ronald Reagan

Halfway through writing this book, I returned in a mellow mood from a sunset BBQ at the home of a well-to-do local farmer. A self-made man with a huge work ethic who breeds fine wool sheep and has a passion for vintage cars he is, by his own admission, an uneducated man who made good. An entrepreneur. As well as farming, he had established several businesses. He had become President of the Rolls Royce owners' association (he owned several *Rollers*). But he had also donated a large acreage of his land for the '*Children First Foundation*', which established a recovery farmhouse and dormitory for some 16 to 20 children at a time from all over the world, who were deformed, maimed or otherwise disabled. They included Olympic gold medallist Ahmed Kelly.

Most of these children were injured in warzones, by unexploded landmines and the like. This charity flew kids from places like Afghanistan, Iraq, Bosnia and other warzones to a 50-acre farm, donated by my friend, on the outskirts of Melbourne, Australia. The Foundation, assisted by pro bono surgeons, provided for their medical treatment, local schools sponsored their education and they cohabited as a group of happy, similarly disadvantaged children on the farm, helping with feeding the animals if they could, while their surgical procedures were finished, and their medical recovery completed.

What is the point of this story? Well, this man was a capitalist, but a good one with a social conscience, who *gave back* to society in manifold ways. He was only able to do good works because the capitalist free enterprise system in his native Australia had allowed a man of his talents to prosper. When I consider this example, I think how unfairly many people characterised these two ideologies—capitalism and socialism ... according to their socialist or conservative prejudice, to divide us and how this ideological divide, in our parliaments and in our civil discourse, influences the economic, social and other policy levers we use in the service of democracy. Clearly, all capitalists are not evil people, nor are all socialists Marxists.

At the BBQ, I found myself sitting beside a young woman who had just completed her Masters. When she asked me what I did, I explained that I was semi-retired and was writing a book about democracy. The discussion drifted to a view she held that capitalism was a cancer that concentrated too much wealth in too few hands and was a blight upon democracy. I agreed with her general thrust but found it much too simplistic. As a former businessman and lay-economist, I think of myself as a capitalist, free-market sort of guy rather than a socialist. But I think I have a modest dose of each philosophy, favouring a balance, like salt and pepper in a good stew—of market efficiency with a social conscience—as was reflected in the wonderful philanthropy of my friend, the wealthy farmer. The evidence seemed overwhelming that western free-market capitalism had demonstrated that it was the most effective system for delivering wealth and prosperity, for raising all boats on the same tide and for improving the human condition. But I absolutely agreed that an obscene amount of wealth in few hands diminishes social equity and breeds corruption.

In my discussion with the young lady, I dared to suggest that there was also a *benevolent capitalism*, for example, the private capital which was invested in hospitals and schools. I also commented that the private sector was more efficient at delivering public infrastructure than the public sector, so private capital was important because it delivered economic prosperity more efficiently than the bureaucracy, not just for a few, but for a whole nation. Public works are financed by taxpayers who expect that public funds are invested wisely and maximise the bang for their bucks.

As I sought to defend *benevolent* capitalism, her body language became increasingly defensive. In her mind, all capitalists were bad. She would truck no defence of them, or of the capitalist system more generally. I shared with her my view that, in a free and open democracy (like most OECD nations), we should not think of people as either capitalists or socialists, but rather, as left of centre or right of centre (i.e., in their thinking about politics and public policy). It was a matter of degree.

Democracy, I suggested, had already won the argument that free-markets and free enterprise deliver the highest standards of living and social benefits to people. It was a question of economics—the way a government motivated people and directed land, labour and capital, the three fundaments of every economy. The word 'capital' was just another word for assets, like a home, or the money our kids saved in their money boxes until they had enough to buy a video game. There was another, more critical form of capital, I argued—human capital—which valued the contribution people made to an economy. What mattered most was how the capital was developed, controlled and spent. These thoughts reflected a philosophical view I had developed as a Uni student, studying economics. In a fortunate twist of fate, I had also studied, as a voluntary elective, a subject called *The Economics of Industry and Labour*, which included a requirement that I read Karl Marx's *'Das Kapital'*.

As we know, Marx held that distributing capital equally would advantage most citizens until a popular majority rose-up and overthrew a few bloated plutocrats, who were corruptly running the show and taking all the dough. That thesis sounded quite plausible, but it was utopian in its expectation of human behaviour. Economists talk about the propensity to save, or to invest, but there is no theory of *'propensity to pinch public property and profits'*, to balance the equation. In the Soviet Union, in Putin's communist Russia, and in other communist states, communism has demonstrably failed for that reason. Instead of distributing wealth equitably, oligarchs and kleptocrats have misappropriated large swags of public money and denied the common people their proportionate share, or social dividend.

China is a notable exception. It has arguably managed this aspect much better than most communist states, begging the question whether it is really a communist state or, instead, a clever hybrid of communism. *Communism with market characteristics* recognises the value of working capital and of business profits as planks in building public wealth and prosperity, which must then be distributed equally. Indeed, over recent years China has consistently delivered increases in GDP of around 7%. Xi's regime claims to have purged corrupt officials (though many of them were also Xi's political opponents) and anti-corruption remains a major focus of Xi's administration. Indeed, his rise to prominence owes much to his anti-corruption campaigning in Fujian, Zhejiang and Shanghai, where he became known for his honesty and integrity, for his opposition to corruption and for his transformational work to encourage new investment and development in those provinces.

Returning to my discussion at the BBQ, I explained to my dinner companion that I was writing this book because I believed good public policy should triumph over political toxicity and that I was persuaded that the capitalist free enterprise system was the best public policy model for a modern state because it delivered the greatest improvements in the human condition. She frowned, so I ploughed on more carefully. I didn't want an argument or to appear patronising, so I apologised if that was how I was coming across. I only wanted to explore what system worked best for people. However, my explanation failed to lighten her mood or elicit a warmer response.

"The industrial revolution lifted millions out of poverty and out of subsistence agriculture," I said. "It took children out of coal mines, educated the masses, improved our health and longevity and vastly improved social amenity," I said.

As soon as I offered this view, she grimaced, stood and marched off in a huff. Why had these comments so offended her? This prompted me to question whether they had been a fair, whether they remained true today or whether things might have changed since I was a student or had worked in trade and commerce. Did I have it wrong? Had capitalism gradually become evil over time—at least in the eyes of her younger generation? As I processed these thoughts, it occurred to me that capitalism and socialism were like the invisible forces of repulsion in magnets—the forces that repel rather than attract when two magnets are brought together, causing a repulsive force. That, it seemed to me, was like the toxic force that was now flowing through American politics. Finding a middle ground of reason would be harder than I imagined. Indeed, two ideological armies appeared to have dug in. So, I turned to *Wikipedia* for a definition of each ideology and found the following information:

The virtues of capitalism are that it creates opportunity for those without their own wealth to acquire wealth and for those with wealth to expand it. Supporters of a free-market economy hold that it contributes to political and civil freedom since everyone has the same right to choose what to produce or consumer. It contributes to economic growth and transparency. It ensures competitive markets and thus lowers prices, thus lifting people's welfare.

Opponents hold that, as it encourages self-sufficiency and personal enrichment with limited government intervention, capitalism can cause inequality, market failure, materialism, and boom and bust economic cycles. It can also damage the environment.

Neither definition seemed to satisfy the dichotomy, so I decided I must feel my way forward, balancing my wealth creation and social justice instincts without choosing sides. On balance, I see more positive than negative benefits for mankind in societies which allow free and open markets and reward hard work, enterprise and innovation. Open market economies, unlike protected or highly regulated ones, have demonstrated, even in China, that they can vastly improve the human condition.

Under Mao, China's closed doors and its dogmatic conformity with a script for life—detailed in Mao's 'Little Red Book'—reduced everyone to an unremarkable, beige; a Mao-suited comrade, almost a '*Robotron*'. No individual was allowed to stand out, no woman to wear lipstick or a skirt, no man to ride a flashy motorbike instead of the ubiquitous *Flying Swallow* bicycle, available in only one colour—black. Individuality was discouraged. Individual excellence was not sought or celebrated, but rather condemned as rebellious.

The only way in which comrades were equal, it seemed to me, was in their equally drab apparel and their equally downtrodden condition. There was a dull glaze—a look of defeat—in every comrade's eye, with no incentive to lift oneself above a sense of futility or out of poverty. I know. I lived there.

When Deng Xiao Ping opened China's doors, the transformation was instant, and dramatic. Having lived in China through that transformation and witnessed it first hand, I am persuaded that 'good' capitalism lifts people out of poverty and, if it includes a social conscience, gives democracy the fiscal and other resources needed to protect the weak, the poor and the disadvantaged.

Capitalism is not easily dismissed as a selfish, untamed beast because it can also have a benevolent character. It is also not an untamed force because it is tightly regulated, not by governments or bureaucrats so much as by the *invisible hand of the market*. The 'invisible hand' theory, first described by economist Adam Smith in his '*Theory of Moral Sentiments*', in 1759 holds that fierce competition promotes a sort of Darwinian survival contest, breeding innovation, creating opportunity and producing efficiencies. Its public dividend is that it makes producers meet popular demand, which is the same as meeting the needs of people, so it *must* be beneficial to society.

Is it possible to defend both a business-oriented, conservative polity and a socially conscious, welfare-oriented polity? Can the two coexist in harmony? Where lies the common ground, in public policy terms, between the socialist view that capitalism corrupts and the capitalist view that free markets deliver national prosperity and happiness by promoting innovation and creating jobs and wealth?

History provides abundant evidence that national prosperity is a reliable indicator of national wellbeing. Societies where want and deprivation are minimised tend to be happier. Evidence also supports the idea that national prosperity improves the human condition, particularly when the benefits of national prosperity are shared across the social divide. Since high levels of welfare dependence lower individual esteem and happiness, the converse is true. I would argue that governments which manage to combine fiscal responsibility (that is, careful public spending) with tax and other incentives to encourage new business development and wealth creation, are also able to exhibit a strong social conscience. Higher GDP delivers higher returns to government and permits higher levels of spending on public amenity and social justice. Where there is a confluence of wealth creation and social conscience, democracy arguably operates at its finest and governments which find this balance tend to occupy the middle ground of politics, where good sense tends to prevail ideological extremes. That sounds like easy logic but is rarely found in practice.

When we think of superpowers, we think of the US and China, but consider this: in 1913 the British Empire held sway over 412 million people, 23% of the world's population at the time, and by 1920, covered 24% of the Earth's total land mass. As an empire, Britain was able to positively use its political, military and economic sway to do some good things. With the Slavery Abolition Act of 1833, it ended slavery and Britain's industrial revolution (1790—1870) hugely advanced and elevated the human condition. Its railways united people and greased the wheels of commerce, much as the internet and modern telecommunications have done. But its hegemony and gunboat diplomacy were negative elements (the Opium Wars, a state sponsored drug trade with China, left an indelible stain on British morality) and were actions which look strangely similar when compared with some of America's foreign military adventures in the 90's and the present territorial ambitions of a rising China. Despite its patchy record, British capitalism was, indeed, the major reason why kids were taken out of coal mines, why steam engines drained and ventilated mines, why subsistence farmers, with working-man's hands, were able to transition to much more efficient farming, using new-fangled things like tractors, ploughs and harvesting machinery to grow grain and feed the masses, and why farmers who were once restricted to small, village market places, were able to greatly increase their production and then find global markets for their surpluses.

However, there is a tragic timing problem for humanity when comparing British and Chinese ambitions, and a dark side to China's rapid development. The reason China is allowed much higher carbon emissions than the West is because it calls itself a 'developing country' and demands the same right as Britain and other developed nations to have its own industrial revolution.

Why should China not enjoy the same *leap forward* that its western counterparts enjoyed two centuries ago?

A little over a decade ago, China could still claim to be a developing country, with over 700 million of its people still living a basic, subsistence lifestyle. They made up 65 % of the population compared to 2.5 % in the US. But that figure rapidly declined with the introduction of modern machinery and practices, to about 30% today. In 2,000, China's middle class was just 2% of its population, but is now estimated to be over 770 million, or 55% of the population. Socialism is supposed to help all people; to lift all boats on the same tide, as waves of economic development roll in. But China's unique brand of 'socialism with market characteristics' has been wildly successful in creating a rich class. China now has some 700 billionaires, (roughly the same number as the USA) and the fastest growing luxury car market in the world. How much longer can the World Trade Organisation (WTO) continue to call China a developing nation? It is the world's largest manufacturer and exporter of consumer goods and embraces a large and growing middle class. Clearly, that must change—both for the sake of reining in the world's largest carbon emitter and to re-align its tariff and other market preferences with those of other developed nations.

Paradoxically, unlike the socialism which failed so spectacularly in the former Soviet Union and oppresses rather than elevates the human condition in Cuba, China's hybrid model borders upon 'misrepresentation'. China may be autocratic in its control over people's lives, but it is a good capitalist when it comes to dominating supply chains by investing in them and commanding global markets.

Indeed, latent capitalism may be the greatest lurking danger faced by the Chinese Communist Party, whose faux socialism coexists with capitalism, elevating the human condition of its people and making some wealthy. As it enjoys the fruits of its industrial revolution, can China combine prosperity with a social conscience? Its treatment of minorities in Xinjiang, Tibet, and Hong Kong suggest otherwise. China has already failed that test, and Xi Jinping is now moving to crackdown on individual wealth, pulling entrepreneurs into line and requiring them to redistribute their wealth.

In November 2020, the outspoken Chinese billionaire, Jack Ma, went missing. Ma's company, Alibaba, had risen from an online store run from his apartment, to one of the world's largest tech giants. On 24 October, his *Ant Group* was ready to launch the world's biggest initial public offering on the stock exchange. Ahead of this, Ma addressed an assembly of high-profile figures with a controversial speech that criticised the Chinese financial system. He was not seen in public again until late January. The Alibaba founder had accused Chinese banks of operating with a '*pawn-shop mentality… using the way one manages a railway station to manage an airport*' …when it came to regulating the new world of digital finance.

These statements so angered the banking establishment that they brought them to the attention of President Xi Jinping. It was not long before Ma and his close colleagues were summoned for a meeting with the regulators, and his *Ant Group*'s float was halted in its tracks. Shares in Ma's companies fell, wiping nearly $76 billion off their value. Ma had crossed an invisible red line for what can be said and done in Xi Jinping's China. Christina Boutrup, a China analyst who had interviewed Ma said …"*I believe it was a big surprise for him. He would never have crossed that line if he had known how bad it could go for him.*"

Eventually, on 20 January 2021, Ma resurfaced, but has since kept a very low profile and watched his 'p's and 'q's. The Chinese government is reconsidering its approach to regulating tech giants, launching an anti-monopoly investigation into *Alibaba*. Since then, the Chinese regulator has fined many companies, including *Tencent* and *Baidu*, over deals it says violate anti-monopoly rules. The move to rein in the tech giants is seen as placing central control above commercial success and has established a new barrier between capitalism and communism in China.

Chapter 29
Welfare Versus Self-Reliance

The nature of humanity is to feel another's pain and to act to take that pain away.
John Connolly

An important test of democratic integrity is the way a government delivers social justice for its people, cares for those who fall through the cracks and promotes happiness and self-reliance.

Universal suffrage—that is, the right of *every* adult to vote—is surely the first and most fundamental element of social justice, probably followed by free speech and then a declining constellation of other social justice rights. In many undemocratic or pseudo-democratic nations, citizens are denied a voice in the affairs of state, and on issues important to them and their families.

Democratic legitimacy will also be measured by the way a nation protects those core democratic values—freedom of speech and expression, freedom of movement, human dignity and the sanctity of family, the level of health services provided, the way a nation cares for its aged and disadvantaged and the way it provides access to education. Together, these things create an environment in which every citizen has an opportunity to live a happy life and to maximise their human potential. And in a free and open society, each person should be afforded an opportunity to excel—in business, in a trade or profession, in the arts or in any other field of endeavour. Above all of these is the way a government protects one's freedom to dream, to hope, to aspire and to achieve. That, in turn, requires ...

- a fair and balanced contract between people and their government, with both parties contributing to, and bearing responsibility for, the society they create.

- government processes which are fair, open and transparent.
- A government's accountability to electors, for the way its government governs.

Those ideals are a bit utopian and sometimes difficult to find as voters become increasingly cynical about politicians—particularly those who think they work in a rarefied atmosphere or stand above voters in the social hierarchy.

Another good barometer of democratic legitimacy is the way a nation cares for its downtrodden—its poor, its sick, and its genuinely disadvantaged. These qualities are evident in all of those nations with a genuine concern for the human condition, that is, for the well-being and happiness of its people. A good government protects such values, which ought to be universal, and underpins them by the rule of law to ensures that those values are shared across the political divide.

While the values which underpin democratic integrity *should* be shared across the partisan divide, I acknowledge that they are often interpreted differently, according to a party's ideological view and the exquisite tension which exists between self-reliance and creating an attitude of entitlement. The importance of social services, for example, is often weighted differently by socialist rather than conservative governments, as are spending priorities across other portfolios, like health, education, immigration, business investment and development, taxation, and defence. Spending in these portfolios is often ranked differently by socialist-leaning, compared to conservative-leaning, governments.

Australian budget papers show that, over time, the right has tended to be more constrained than the left, when it comes to funding social justice outcomes. The fiscally more conservative right has tended to spend more on economic stimuli and deficit reduction than on social programs (although this trend was reversed by the Morrison—Frydenberg budget in May 2021, which saw record spending, albeit by a government striving to address the Covid-19 pandemic). Whitlam's iconic reforms of higher education and wage inequality, and his no-fault divorce legislation were visionary, but their profligacy and budget consequences led to his questionable dismissal. So, there is merit in both approaches and they even out over time.

When adjusted for present values, conservative Treasurer Josh Frydenberg's May 2021 budget eclipsed Whitlam's alleged 1972 profligacy. It is thus fair to say that differences in spending (i.e., profligate or restrained) and in budget priorities (guns or butter) don't make the left Bolsheviks or the right Fascists. In a democracy, each party—whether left-leaning or right-leaning—has a right to deliver social justice outcomes its own way, to use different monetary and fiscal levers to do so, and to address policy challenges (e.g., long-term structural or short-term fixes) differently.

But unlike autocratic regimes, where there is no public contest of ideas, democracy requires both the left and the right face the same exacting master—the electorate—and are compelled by public sentiment, and political pressure to deliver the same outcome—a generally happy, prosperous, and caring nation and above all, a sense of familial and community security. If they fall demonstrably short of those standards, the *'invisible hand of democracy'* will make them pay at the next election.

In Australia, the US and the UK, for example, *boat people* and *border jumpers* are treated differently by conservatives than by socialists, not because one or the other is necessarily less caring, but because public policy is viewed through different lenses. In every instance, this difficult public policy issue has finally been settled by voters. The left has generally tended to grant boat people more generous entry provisions, while the right has argued that porous borders reward people smugglers, whose business model relies on that policy setting. Conservatives generally make illegals subject to prolonged detention, to deter them and to disrupt the people smugglers' business model. Both views have legitimacy in a democracy so long as the final policy settings are determined by voters, via the ballot box.

A political contest about how to address this challenging humanitarian issue is playing out in the United States right now, where a radical change in policy settings by the Biden administration has sparked a new wave of so called *illegals* seeking refuge in the United States. In April 2021, the media summarised the situation thus:

Biden administration officials have repeatedly stress that they inherited this disaster from Trump and say that any solutions would not be painless or quick. White House Democratic officials insist that the real crisis is in Central America. Indeed, the Biden administration claims that the cause of the migration surge is the failure of diplomatic efforts with Central American countries, which lapsed under the Trump administration. But objective observers say the problem is more complex. Trump did not create it. It has been going on for decades.

As all politicians do, a socialist Biden downplayed the surge, just as Germany's conservative leader, Angela Merkel did, in relation to a huge surge of immigrants escaping Middle Eastern wars, especially Syria's. Whether the leader was a conservative, like Merkel, or a socialist, like Biden, the bow-wave of illegal migration and the public policy challenge to address it, was the same. The number of unaccompanied children arriving at the US border hit a monthly-high in March 2021, exceeding the previous high in May 2019. In total, some 170,000 people were apprehended by border patrols in March. About 100,000 of those were single adults, who had been routinely removed from the U.S. by the Biden administration under a Trump-era public health authority. There is also simmering Democratic and activist frustration with Biden's use of the Trump-era authority — known as Title 42 — to expel the majority of those intercepted at the border. Privately, the White House has told reporters and Hill staff that they have no timeline to stop using the Trump-introduced authority (because it is working!)

Biden wants to house illegal immigrants in churches, stadiums, and summer camps. His administration is also racing to expand capacity to humanely house a growing number of illegal child migrants in emergency intake sites, like stadiums, church facilities and summer camps, rather than keeping them in tightly-packed border patrol facilities—the current situation—which flies in the face of a more humanitarian policy approach… the report concluded.

Just as we saw when well-meaning legislation was introduced to protect boat people in Australia, the current US scenario demonstrates that policies which are based upon emotion, or driven by a need to expiate an esoteric, humanitarian guilt, rather than to deliver a sober, pragmatic outcome, though well-meaning, can have dire human consequences. We saw this in Australia when people smugglers immediately responded to Labor's freer policy settings around *'illegals'*. A surge of boat arrivals occurred, along with an increase in deaths at sea and queue-jumping by illegals, admitted ahead of bona fide refugees in foreign camps who had been waiting years for relief. Both policy approaches indicate a strong social conscience and support for a humanitarian solution, but in the final event, the situation called for an almost callous pragmatism, to stop illegals and save their lives. The electorate finally decided the issue by returning Howard against all odds, resulting in Labor finally, grudgingly, altering its immigration policy to one which also *'controlled the boats'*.

Sometimes social conscience so overwhelms rational thought that the root causes of a public crisis is misunderstood. One could argue that this was the case in respect of the 2021 resurgence of illegal immigrants entering the US from the south. Consider this. In 2020, the average annual income in El Salvador was $4,000; in Guatemala $4,610; and in Honduras $2,310. People were clearly leaving those countries for the US because of the extraordinary disparity between income and living conditions in Central America compared with those in the US. But while that root cause was obvious, the policy response was not directed at resolving that issue.

In December 2020, Biden told reporters he would *'establish a more humane policy at the borders but would need six months to rebuild a system to process more migrants'*. While those policy solutions may have ultimately enabled faster processing of illegals, they failed to address the root cause of the problem—income disparity—a challenge for the Central and South American governments (albeit with assistance from the developed world, including the US, through humanitarian programs).

Human cargo is now flowing, like so much flotsam and jetsam in a flood, towards America's southern boarders where it piles up like flood waste caught in a wire fence. If the consequences of bad border policy are the destruction of life and limb and the dashing of hopes and dreams, those policy settings must end. Democrats, who are captured—in a policy sense—by their emotional speeches about compassion for the poor, still refuse to admit a catastrophic public policy failure—one which has been affirmed, again and again, by identical experiences in southern Europe and in Australasia, where identical policies were reversed because their inhuman consequences were too dire. Once again, emotions like compassion, pride and the loss of political face have paralysed good public policy.

If this political stalemate continues, it will probably fall to the next US administration to review Biden's border policies. Meantime, the cruelty of holding thousands of kids in detention must be recognised as a greater crime than assertive action to close borders.

Does A Bill of Rights Guarantee Social Justice?

The defence of social justice is a character unique to democracies and sets them apart from more authoritarian regimes, but the term 'social justice' itself is subject to wide interpretation and can differ with accepted social and cultural practices, which evolve and change over time. Men now have the right to *'chest-feed'*, while women can now vote and demand income equality, which were never contemplated or included in the old British or American Bills of Rights. Imagine a medieval knight being openly gay or removing his armour to chest feed!

We have seen that social justice is another measure of the way a government protects important values, like 'life, liberty and the pursuit of happiness'. In many democracies, social justice is formally protected by a *Bill of Rights* (sometimes called a *Declaration ... or a Charter of Human Rights)*. A Bill of Rights is defended by its advocates as necessary for *enshrining the most important rights accorded to every citizen of a country*, to *protect those rights from infringement against them by public officials or private citizens*. But not everyone agrees. Sometimes a Bill of Rights can be apposite to a particular era but quickly become out-of-date. For that reason, not every democracy has a bill of rights. Australia has never had one, and there is a good reason for this. Many Australians prefer the primacy of their parliament to having standards imposed upon them which may change over time.

Evan without a Bill of Rights, Australian rights exist under laws enforced by the Australian Human Rights Commission and the High Court, and there is a raft of other remedies available to those who feel their rights have been abused. But most offer legal remedies, and these can be expensive. An Australian bill of rights would enshrine rights for all individuals, regardless of their background, but at what cost?

In September 2019, an Australian Bill of Rights was sponsored and read for the first time by Andrew Wilkie, MP.

It 'gave effect to certain provisions of the International Covenant on Civil and Political Rights, the International Covenant on Economic, Social and Cultural Rights, the Convention on the Rights of the Child and the Convention against Torture and Other Cruel, Inhumane or Degrading Treatment or Punishment by 1 declaring an Australian Bill of Rights 2 providing that any Commonwealth, state or territory law that is inconsistent with the Bill of Rights is invalid to the extent of the inconsistency 3 specifying that Commonwealth, state and territory laws must be interpreted consistently with the Bill of Rights; and 4 providing the Australian Human Rights Commission with a range of additional powers and functions in relation to the rights and freedoms in the Bill of Rights'.

On 24 March 2020, having failed to gain support in the Australian Parliament, the draft legislation (draft Bill) was withdrawn. Why? I cite the reason, again, as the desire that the Parliament have primacy over words forged in a bygone era and the reality that cultural, moral and social values and standards change over time.

Rights enshrined in a Bill of Rights become so chiselled in stone that they cannot easily be changed or removed, even when they become outdated. The most obvious of these is the Second Amendment in the United States Constitution, which protects the right to keep and bear arms. Some would argue, with good cause, that they a directly responsible for murder and gun-related crime statistics in the US which are significantly higher than in comparable democracies. The right to bear arms was introduced way back in December 1791, in a totally different context. In Columbia v. Heller (2008), this right was reinterpreted by the courts as *a right that belongs to individuals, for self-defence in the home*. The US Second Amendment, in turn, drew upon a precedent—the right to bear arms in English common law—and was influenced by the English Bill of Rights of 1689. Sir William Blackstone described this right as *an auxiliary right, supporting the natural rights of self-defence and resistance to oppression, and the civic duty to act, in concert, in defence of the state.*

However, this US right had its genesis in a war of independence in which the common citizenry was encouraged to take up arms to overthrow the British Crown, who was seen as a foreign oppressor. The legacy of that right, enshrined in legal stone, is the abominable tally of deaths by shooting in the US. This obscene right is thus viewed by most foreign administrations as crazy public policy. And the remedy is simple. Just as there is a vaccine for starvation—one which we call *food*—there is a vaccine for senseless shootings in the US—it is called '*take the gun rights away*'!

A wonderful example of how US deaths by shooting could be much reduced by a changed public policy setting is offered by the Howard Government's response to the Port Arthur Massacre in Australia, which saw bipartisan support for strict controls over owning and using guns. All guns had to be licensed and noted on a state register. All had to be locked away, at a distance from a household so that crimes of passion could be eliminated. Guns had to be kept secure from access by criminals and children. No automatic weapons could be held in private hands without a demonstrated, court approved need or cause etc.

New laws granted an amnesty for people with unregistered or unlicensed arms to surrender them without penalty. If they failed to declare that they had undisclosed weapons, or to apply for a licence, they could be criminally prosecuted. Millions of weapons were surrendered by quiet, civilised Australians who saw the logic in these laws. Guns were crushed and destroyed so they could never be used again. The main opposition to the legislation came, understandably, from farmers who needed weapons for the legitimate purpose of controlling vermin, and laws were quickly fashioned to address those legitimate needs. There have been no mass shootings or public massacres since then, and the much tighter regulation of gun ownership has been reflected in much lower crime statistics (although it remains true that a determined criminal will always find a way to get a gun).

What About Shelter from The Cold?

Another social justice issue which is rarely ventilated is the right of every citizen to a roof over his or her head. The presence or absence of laws which show compassion towards those who find themselves living on the street will tell us something about the quality of a nation's conscience and social justice institutions.

I had not considered this issue until recently, when it became glaringly transparent to me because of an accident of fate. Following a health incident, I was encouraged by my doctor to walk regularly, to rebuild aerobic strength. As it happened, the following weekend my wife and I left for Paris. We would travel on through Berlin, Vienna, Madrid, Barcelona, Dubrovnik and Sofia, returning to Australia via Toulouse and Singapore. I began my new, early-morning walking routine in Paris, walking for an hour in a different direction each day. I repeated the ritual each morning, throughout our tour, in each of the cities and towns we visited.

I am a light sleeper, so I would usually wake around 5 am or 6 am, slip into my joggers and sneak out of our dark hotel room, so as not to disturb my wife. As dawn broke over each city, I was staggered to discover how many street people I chanced upon, sleeping rough—some under bridges, but most in parks or under cardboard cartons on a hard footpath—sometimes alone, but more frequently with a partner—a faithful dog, perhaps, or another street person. I had often to deviate from my route, step over them or go around them.

In heroic cities like Madrid and Paris, the contrast offered by destitute people sleeping rough while surrounded by regal buildings, manicured public parks, opulent public statues and fountains was stark. The incidence of people sleeping rough seemed higher in those anonymous cityscapes, than in more agricultural landscapes, like Bulgaria, where the average family home was much more humble and plainer, but where families looked after each other or social housing had been provided—a metaphor, perhaps, for a more humane society. I was so affected by this experience that I began taking loose change with me to give to street people. Surely each of us has the right to a roof over our head; particularly those of us on the street because of a mental illness or some other incapacity to cope with the crushing vicissitudes of life. I decided to research housing affordability, to better understand that related issue, but was confused, rather than enlightened, by the published information, which may have been meaningful to an economist, but failed to explain much to me. To my great surprise, the published data suggested that one's chances of owning his own home were much higher in an under-developed country than in a prosperous, developed country. In Romania, Croatia, Bulgaria and Lithuania, about 80% of people owned their home outright, while in Australia, that percentage was much lower, only 32% and lower again, only 23%, in the USA. Traditionally, Australian's have seen their home as their principal asset, and as a sort of safe deposit box, where wealth was secreted, immune from tax and other imposts, to vouchsafe one's geriatric years, but this culture is changing.

Self-Reliance Versus Welfare

What happened to self-reliance? The damning evidence is there, not in our opulent western lifestyles, but in refugee camps where mothers nurse emaciated babies, in poor streetscapes, albeit where kids still laugh and play using an old stick for a bat, because they have no money for a proper cricket bat or for an iPad or a Gameboy. They innovate and are self-reliant. We see this frequently in subsistence farming villages where boys manage the water buffalo while girls collect the firewood for the evening meal. Yes, those families are deprived compared to their self-indulgent, western counterparts, but their deprivation welds them together in a tight familial bond and gives them courage to solve daily issues themselves, without waiting for a government official to drop by or a financial subsidy to appear.

In lesser developed countries, deprived families *must* look after each other as an imperative of survival. In many of them, three generations live under one roof. Familial support and self-reliance are in their DNA. Every family member has a job—planting the rice, fetching the water, feeding the buffalo, collecting the firewood and so on, precisely so that the family has food and shelter. If a family loses a roof over its head—another family member, or perhaps a caring neighbour, will take them in. If you find yourself born under a sheet of iron in Kolkata (Calcutta) or in the poorer parts of northern Bangladesh, housing responsibility is with the family, not the state.

By comparison, affluent western democracies appear to have lost the self-reliance of the nuclear family. Before the industrial revolution and the rise of western affluence, welfare payments were a myth, not sweetmeats to be plundered by those who knew how to game the system. Was Plato right in his assertion that democracy breeds a sense of entitlement? Does a generous system of social welfare strengthen or weaken a society? Should the provision of welfare stop short of encouraging reliance upon the state rather than encouraging an attitude which says ... *"Let the state look after me. Give me a welfare payment ...or I will vote you out of office!"* Is that the kind of society we want to be?

The answer must surely be in determining a *'balance of social justice'*—that is, in balancing contrived need against genuine need and in policies which reward self-reliance over contrived dependency. Policies which encourage hard work and enterprise work to lift all boats on the same tide and must therefore be better policy settings than those which confirm Plato's view that ..." *democracy will not last ... it will create an attitude of entitlement."*

Affordable Housing

In addition to protecting those who fall through the cracks, a caring society should have policy settings which support the aspirations of people to own their own homes. Homes are not just buildings. They are the bedrock of a civilised society, the place where young and aged people alike are nurtured, and centres where families can come together. In most western democracies, a family home is a pretty good investment. In fact, according to Australia's Housing Industry Association (HIA) and to its Treasury data, housing is a preferred source of capital gains in Australia, and thus a preferred vehicle for personal investment. Since 1980, Australian house prices have risen faster than in any other developed country. But despite a strong cultural bent towards home ownership, housing appears to be less affordable for the typical Australian now than it used to be and more expensive than in comparable countries. Mortgage servicing (housing) costs have progressively risen and now consume 43 % more of a typical household's income than they did, averaged over the previous 35-years. This level of unaffordability is significantly higher than in comparable nations.

The ratio of house prices to rents is now also 63 per cent higher than the long-term average, making the yield on investment in rental housing very poor—only about 3 per cent before expenses (maintenance, rates and taxes etc.) are deducted. So, unless strong capital appreciation continues, investments in rental housing are not attractive. In this respect Australia is an 'outlier' compared to other countries.

The IMF and the OECD have stated that the Australian housing market is over-priced (over-heated) and warn of risks to the Australian financial system if there is a strong market correction. Australia's Reserve Bank is more sanguine, pointing to supply constraints on land for urban renewal and urban expansion, and holding that a shortage of supply has had held the market up. Moreover, Australian housing debt is only 28 per cent of total housing asset value, so a major fall in prices would not affect loan security much. Analysts say the answer is probably more and cheaper new land.

Policy initiatives on the supply side are less-complex levers for keeping housing prices in check than the demand side, which is relatively inelastic, being determined by a mix of things like population growth, net migration, investment—including local and foreign—taxation and other monetary and fiscal constraints, the availability of finance and other elements external to the industry.

The Reserve Bank has expressed concern that generous negative gearing has contributed to the over-valuation of house prices. Is this tax concession a public policy failure? The answer to that question depends whether you are a millennial who wants to cash in on the capital gains bonanza that was available to your parents, or one who believes that home ownership is not as important as personal consumption—enjoying life now rather than sacrificing to own a home. But that change in attitude makes housing less of a market-driven, wealth-creation issue and more a social justice issue, requiring great government subvention and less self-reliance.

In public policy terms, traditional policy settings probably need to change to reflect with this apparent change in attitude (propensity for home ownership). New policy settings would ideally continue to give all young people an equal opportunity to enter the housing market while ensuring that those who do not choose to own the roof over their head can rent one, equitably, so as to meet the needs of each group.

So, in policy terms, has there been any move towards addressing that new propensity? Surprisingly, it was a conservative, rather than a socialist government, which first introduced an affordable housing policy. In his 201718 budget, the then Treasurer, Scott Morrison, announced a comprehensive housing affordability plan to improve outcomes across the housing spectrum. His plan for housing affordability included measures to unlock supply and create incentives to improve outcomes for those most in need. Measures to boost the supply side included (a) $1 billion through the *National Housing Infrastructure Facility* to fund critical infrastructure that will speed up the supply of housing, (b) the *release of Commonwealth land* for housing development and (c) *specifying housing supply targets* in a new *National Housing and Homelessness Agreement (NHHA)* with the States and Territories.

Other reforms designed to create incentives to improve housing outcomes included helping first home buyers save a deposit through voluntary contributions into superannuation, salary sacrificing, reducing barriers to downsizing to free up larger homes, tightening capital gains rules for foreign investors, better targeting of housing tax concessions and changing foreign investment rules to discourage foreign investors from leaving their properties vacant. These were social justice reforms.

Housing Finance and Homelessness

The Australian government also established a *National Housing Finance and Investment Corporation* to provide low-cost finance for housing providers. This was to incr5ease institutional and private investment in community housing and provide more Australians with access to affordable rental housing. The Government's National Housing and Homelessness Agreement with States and Territories was to increase the supply of homes and improve outcomes for

Australians in the most need, with an additional $375.3 million to be permanently indexed to provide certainty of front line services for people who are homeless or at risk of becoming homeless.

In other countries—continental Europe, for example—attitudes about housing affordability are muted by the long-standing practice of the extended, nuclear family considering a family home an asset for all generations of a family needing a roof over their heads, at least until they become financially independent. The European property culture is older and the propensity to invest in new domestic housing has been dampened by an expectation of inheritance. We see evidence of this 'inheritance' culture seeping into the psyche of young Australians. European households typically accommodate a wider family cohort, from aging grandparents to younger family members starting out, who thus enjoy a financial hiatus while saving for their first home. Those cultures do not share Australia's albeit rapidly weakening obsession with individual home ownership. Many Europeans rent rather than buy, since new land is much scarcer and newbuilds are thus an expensive option.

For those young Australians who rent rather than buy, wealth capture is only neutral if the savings afforded by renting are invested in other classes of assets. But many choose to consume the difference, rather than investing it in another asset. This propensity to consume is an example of the *'sense of entitlement'* Plato warned us about. If one accepts the premise that any fair and compassionate society will ensure that every citizen has a roof over his or her head, democracy has three moral obligations. First, to develop policies which maximise the availability of new housing stocks, starting from first principles, by ensuring an abundant supply of development land or airspace and supporting infrastructure for new housing. In other words, by lubricating or ramping up the supply side, to maintain downward pressure on prices.

Second, as our major cities become more congested, we will increasingly need policy settings which shift populations from CBD to peri-urban or regional concentrations, where abundant land is available. This will require contiguous policies around better transport connectivity, regional employment opportunities and social infrastructure. Having the courage to get ahead of these policy challenges, rather than playing catch-up, and to do so in a market-based system, is one of the greatest challenges faced by democracies with capitalist free-market economies.

Policy settings should also encourage a competitive housing market. That may require some policy subtlety, for example, ensuring adequate trade training and apprenticeships in a world which now seems to push everyone towards a university education. Training policy must be supported by regulations which encourage the industry and support the sector's important contribution to employment and GDP.

And finally, investment and development incentives should continually be fine-tuned to allow the invisible hand of the market to deliver land and housing packages competitively (policies which maximise market competition will help to contain or push down construction costs and maximise housing affordability).

Chapter 30
Reaching Across the Aisle

Civil discourse will not come from watching our tongues. It will come from valuing our differences.
Parker J Palmer

Two thousand years after the achievements of Rome, one hopes that man might have learnt something about public policy and politics. Alas, in modern times, good public policy rarely survives the swirling rapids of political toxicity. In their zeal to be *all things to all men,* when in government, and *pugnacious opponents,* when in opposition, politicians routinely bend good public policy out of shape—to *get* elected or to *stay* elected. Each party's followers, (i.e., voters), being tribal, do the same.

This dysfunction inspired me, some 15 years ago, to establish the *'Quarterly Assembly of Fine Fellows, Epicureans and Raconteurs—Quaffers'*—a public policy forum which meets quarterly to debate pressing issues of our times. I have dedicated this book to those who joined me in founding *'Quaffers'* and who share my view that, if we are to rescue democracy, we must start by championing a more civil discourse—that is, rescuing democracy from the political spin, partisan bias, and media hype which bedevils it. I honour their contribution and salute the many excellent guest speakers who have informed our debates. Each has become a valued friend.

Quaffers is grounded in the belief that we are losing our *civilised discourse* and can no longer agree to disagree. That we have lost the ability to find common ground or apply common sense. We saw evidence of this in Trump's America and we see it now in the rise of a new, 5th column which dares to tell us how to think and act, imposes its political correctness upon us, and censors our language to limit our free speech. Its practitioners do not support democracy. They seek to bring it down.

The social psychologist *Jonathan Haidt* wrote a book called *The Righteous Mind* in which he identified six moral values which determine everyone's behaviour. He describes them as *'tools for understanding the views of others ... tools which prevent us from feeling superior and allow us to imagine what someone else might be thinking and why they believe what they believe'*, he said. *'These tools work universally, because each of us either shares the same human values or opposes them, practicing the opposite'*. Here are Haidt's six values (and their opposites):

1. *Care / Harm.* We are all one family and should have compassion for everyone else. We should try to eliminate suffering, and not harm others.
2. *Fairness / Cheating.* A society should strive to be fair. Justice should be equal for all of mankind. Cooperation is better than disagreement. The reverse is true: cheaters and free riders should be scorned or punished.
3. *Loyalty / Betrayal.* Loyalty is essential ... to one's family, community, team, business and nation. It holds everything together. Betrayal is unforgivable.
4. *Authority / Subversion.* Abide by the law, whether you agree or not. Our collective agreement to obey social and legal institutions makes us function as a society.
5. *Sanctity / Degradation.* Purity, tolerance, restraint and moderation stabilise our world. Malevolent behaviour is immoral and must be shunned.
6. *Liberty / Oppression.* People should be allowed to be free in their speech, thought and behaviour, so long as they don't hurt others... free to speak their minds.

In the interests of attracting members to its ranks from across the political divide, Quaffers adopted similar values and asked members sign a 'Charter of civil discourse', pledging to respect the views of others and to strive to find good public policy from the slurry of vitriol and spin coming from politicians and the popular media. (A copy of the Quaffers Charter is provided at the end of this book).

Over the past 15 years, the *'Quaffers'* Public Policy debates have grown in popularity and profile. Held at Melbourne's Royal Automobile Club, they are constructed around a luncheon format, to bring contributors together in a convivial atmosphere and, above all, *across the political divide.* Members understand that they must honour traditions of civil discourse and that personal animus is forbidden. They are asked to research the topic for debate before each luncheon, focussing upon available science and facts, and to shrug off personal political or other prejudices (though each of us inevitably finds this difficult).

A guest speaker, recognised as an expert in the field, is invited to open each session with what we call a 'road map'—salient facts, to better inform and direct the debate. Members are drawn from a range of social and professional backgrounds, mostly outside of politics. They meet in a warm, gregarious setting, dine together, develop a policy view by consensus and publish their views on a range of public policy challenges. *'Quaffers'* members always try to achieve three things:

- to filter fact from fiction and reject political spin.
- To craft honest policies which maximise public benefit (including social justice, fiscal prudence, and efficient delivery of projects and services), and of course …
- To better inform the public on policy issues affecting their lives.

What does that mean? That truth, fact and science must rise above sectional interest, and political prejudice. That clever language which misrepresents fact must be exposed. That bureaucrats too—and the red, blue and green tape they apply to restrain action—are held to public account. Why? Because bureaucratic red tape is a democratic malaise, tugging at democracy and weakening it compared to more assertive, autocratic regimes. Indeed, western bureaucracy, though intended to bring administrative order to society, can often act as a handbrake on decisive government action, and be weaponised, as a tool of public oppression rather than liberation. Its rigid rules have become blinkers on creative thinking and efficiency—particularly in the area of planning approvals and project implementation.

If democracy is to compete with other systems of government, its' agencies must be at least as 'nimble' as those it competes with. In a democracy, politics should not weigh like a sea anchor on public decision making. The agencies charged with delivering government and shaping public policy should have but one, compelling mission—to serve the best interests of a nation and its people.

My need to sell this message was shaped by a visit to the United States in 2005 as a member of a professional study group. During that visit, I discovered *'Hands across the Aisle'*, a US policy forum comprising former Republican and Democrat politicians, which encouraged civil discourse on policy issues. I was so taken with the work of this group that, in 2006, I invited a group of colleagues—former diplomats, politicians and business leaders—to join me in forming *'Quaffers'*, in Melbourne, Australia.

I wouldn't describe that first cohort of founding members as a motley crew, but we had lots to learn. We were at pains to include academics, laymen and a wide range of professions not generally represented in our parliaments, like engineers and soldiers. We thus instantly became a non-aligned, broad church of thought. We chose to stimulate debate by making each topic *controversial* and met around a square or round, rather than a long, dining table so that there would be no hierarchy. We met in a bar to 'sign in', creating a warm collegiate atmosphere before lunch.

It was necessary, for that first debate, to establish some ground rules. We agreed that we must be at pains to eliminate background noises and subjective views which emanated from those with a particular axe to grind, that is, those with vested interests or biased motives. We agreed that our deliberations should be informed by science or fact, rather than fiction or uninformed passion. We agreed that our membership, as it grew, should attempt to straddle partisan and socio-economic divides, to reflect the thoughts of everyday people. For our inaugural debate, those rules required that each member research, and test objectively, current policy settings around the subject for debate, with a view to improving them.

Unlike the usual format for public debates, which assigns speakers for the affirmative and for the negative, we allowed individual views, from each member's research into the issue, to be expressed. Discussion and debate then followed, aimed at capturing a consensus. Each of the salient points made, for or against a particular proposition, was captured in a record of the debate, which would be the basis of a press release giving salient information and conclusions. If our objective was to better inform the public, we had better give all views on an issue—and all of the available science and facts—and allow people to reach their own conclusions.

The findings of that first debate, on the then emerging controversy over *Climate Change*, were prescient. I have included that and other debates as case studies on public policy development and offered some observations on the direction public policy has taken, as it struggles to shape a more functional democracy.

For over a decade, Quaffers has been brilliantly accommodated by Melbourne's Royal Automobile Club, where its public policy forums have become signature events. I thank the RACV most sincerely for their wonderful support. Some 15 years later, Quaffers continues to go from strength to strength. Indeed, in addition to the Melbourne based institution, a Sydney chapter has been formed and work is in train to expand further. I am proud of this legacy and delighted to share excerpts of some Quaffers debates in the hope that they might illustrate the way we have sought to distil good public policy from prejudice and political spin.

Chapter 31
Climate Change—A Case Study in Public Policy

Wishful thinking is not good public policy.
Bjorn Lomborg

This book was inspired by a passion for public policy, which had its genesis in studying the life of Marcus Aurelius, the magnificent Roman emperor—philosopher who developed public policy into a science. I blame him, and a visit to the US sixteen years ago, for inspiring the establishment of *Quaffers*, a Melbourne-based public policy forum. To be honest, *Quaffers* was really inspired by discussions I had with Democrats and Republicans during an exchange visit to the US, which made me aware of the need for people of good conscience to *reach across the aisle.* Indeed, a US women's group called *Hands across the aisle* encouraged me to set up an equivalent group in Australia. *Quaffers* honours three ideas. One, that the pen is mightier than the sword. Two, that civil discourse must always rise above political toxicity if we are to find common ground. And three, that freedom of speech, even when it offends, is the cornerstone of democracy and reason.

For this penultimate chapter, I have thus chosen to share elements of some *Quaffers' public policy debates,* to explain the principles and processes which have guided its thinking. I have deliberately chosen a controversial theme, *climate change*, to illustrate the exquisite tensions which can arise between political passion and fact. I have added some spice, by contrasting two different debates, one which revolved around global warming and one which considered the next ice age, for the word climate, as loosely as it is used, covers both contingencies but rarely explores both. What differs about these threats is not their truth, merely the timing of their likely occurrence. Both are existential threats but there is no Greta Thunberg railing passionately about the dangers of an approaching Ice Age.

These juxtaposed climate threats illustrate how difficult it can be to craft good public policy when the premises are myopic, when the policy lens through which they are viewed is too narrow, or when there is no balanced perspective or context. Relying upon facts and science only works if one keeps things in perspective. If freedom, justice and equity rely upon truth, and social cohesion relies upon honest public policy, that quality is often lacking. True servants of democracy allow science and fact to rise above self-interest and political spin. As Marcus Aurelius teaches us, only this way can great nations rise to greatness and then remain great.

I have dedicated this book to two servants of public policy, the late Paul Barratt AO, former Australian Secretary of Defence, Secretary of Agriculture and Deputy Secretary of Trade, a special friend, and another dear friend, Rob Hobart, who I met when we two, callow youths began the adventure of our lives, in the Australian Trade Commissioner Service. These two men supported my dream to establish *Quaffers*—a public policy forum which meets in a gregarious luncheon context to ensure civil discourse and is informed by fact and science, contributed by a guest speaker with expertise in the field. Now boasting chapters in Melbourne and Sydney, Quaffers is a wonderful institution. I encourage those who share its ideals to demonstrate them in the way they interact with others, and in their lives.

Will Global Warming Kill Us, Or Will the Next Ice Age?

Aristotle was a great philosopher, but he owed much to his tutor, Plato, who taught him when he was still a boy… "Be a free thinker. Don't accept everything as truth. Be critical and evaluate what you believe in." This advice is key to a balanced view about a very broad subject, climate change, and to finding a policy path to deal with it. For climate change is a debate which struggles to reconcile what has become a religion for two generations of young people, whose passion sometimes glosses over or cherry-picks the facts which should honestly inform that fervour.

Followers of what has become a climate change religion may see themselves as saviours of our planet, but they follow their religion with such fervour that they scarcely draw breath to question the weather science, which is based upon chaos theory and which honest scientists concede is a work in progress. This dilemma became apparent to the Quaffers public policy forum when, in 2006, members met to consider what was initially called *'global warming'*. That terminology then morphed into *'climate change'* when its dire predictions failed to eventuate. Then someone said: *"Hang on a minute! Isn't the next Ice Age overdue?"* ... so we added that icy subject into the policy mix. Here's what our debate on *'climate change'* concluded:

Earth's atmosphere is shared across the political divide. The air that Angela Merkel and Joe Biden breath is the same air that Vladimir Putin and Xi Jinping breath. So why are there much tougher emission rules for western democratic countries than for Eastern countries, particularly China, the world's biggest emitter? What makes this debate interesting is the fact that our climate is politically neutral, indifferent to one's politics, but an extraordinary public policy challenge for mankind because the chances of getting a uniform, global compact to defeat it are zero.

At its inaugural meeting, back in 2006, *Quaffers* debated the proposition ... *That Climate Change is the Plaything of Alarmists*. Each of its subsequent policy debates have been framed the same way—that is, with a controversial statement, designed to stimulate a robust debate. This first debate opened with an exhortation from the chair that the debate should be guided by science and fact. That it should make transparent the available science, to better inform the public and then allow people to decide, rather than impose a rigid view. We agreed that informed public policy relied upon an open society, which allowed for freedom of thought and expression. Democracy, too, depended upon these things, so a free and open society and good public policy must work in unison to maximise public benefit.

Scepticism Is the Foundation of All Good Science

While they may not always agree about climate science, all scientists agree that differences of opinion are essential to the quest for new knowledge, albeit ultimately requiring peer agreement to verify good science. It turns out that differences are very important to finding consensus, but differences must be argued rationally, logical deviations respected, and each view expressed with civility. The *Quaffers* debaters noted that that the term *'climate sceptic'* had assumed a negative connotation. This was unfortunate, as all science depends upon scepticism—upon minds which probe and ask ... *"why is it so?"* Without scepticism, science can never advance. Blithely accepting dogma is not scientific. It entrenches ignorance.

From the outset, it became clear that a gap existed in the published information on climate change. As one member noted ... "all of the university-based and other scientific sources I have consulted have only identified negative consequences. There must be some positive ones."

He had searched for any serious research into *positive* impacts of climate change but had found no evidence of any research into that aspect having been undertaken. No one seemed willing to waste funds on research into positive aspects of climate change. That was not a very sexy science, even though it would give balance and positive information ought to be given an equal seat at the same table.

This random question ...*What about positive effects?* had thrown us a curve ball. We blinked and waited for someone to answer. Then a metaphorical dam burst, and a flurry of excited responses followed. Had we been conned by negative spin? Had we just identified an obvious flaw in the public discourse? We agreed that we should try to identify any positive aspects, if there were any, and we found many.

While we were in furious agreement that the industrial revolution was the main cause of a rise in man's carbon emissions, that same revolution was also responsible for man's drinking water being much cleaner, medical science being far better, longevity much greater, and man's quality of life much improved. Coal fired power stations were now 12 times more efficient than 100 years ago.

One member, a physicist, noted that carbon was a positive life-force. In fact, it is precious, and essential to all planetary life, as it fertilises soil, plants, plankton etc. Moreover, parts of our planet that are too cold for cropping, or for tourism may be beneficiaries of a warmer environment. In 1000 AD, Britain was much warmer and thus became a wealthy granary of supply for much of Europe. So, there were some positives after all. It just seemed no one wanted to discuss them. They were inconvenient truths.

Then someone posed a simple question: *"What is the largest greenhouse gas?"* No one seemed to know. We learned that, while CO2 made up just zero-point-zero four one percent (0.041%) of the earth's atmosphere and was the principal focus of media attention, water vapour was a far larger greenhouse gas, making up 70%. Ocean warming would likely raise this percentage and increase cloud cover. Heat reflecting surfaces—clouds, ice and snow—were important. If they were diminished and absorbed or reflected less heat (for example, if the polar ice caps melted) that would be catastrophic. The reverse—global freezing—was also true.

We agreed with the scientific consensus that, because man was *unnaturally* increasing CO2 and other greenhouse emissions, he must logically be *adding to global warming*. But there was an even more disturbing problem which rarely got any publicity. Man was soiling his own nest by overpopulating it, a major contributing factor. Climate had always changed, but never so rapidly, not just because of man's higher carbon emissions but because he was seriously overcrowding his planet. If overpopulation was the chief cause, why was this not the centre of media attention?

Many of the causal factors had always been there and most were natural, or beyond man's control. The earth's elliptical orbit, the *'earth tilt'* phenomenon, sunspots, volcanoes, continental drift, the oceans, which circulate heat between the poles and the equator, to moderate temperatures. Trees, vegetation and ocean plankton provide huge carbon sinks and rely upon carbon to grow. Carbon fertilises crops and plants and promotes vegetation. Carbon's photosynthesis is a miracle.

However, the planet would need millennia to absorb current levels of carbon emissions if its lungs were damaged—that is, if forest, soil and ocean sequestration were less secure, because of land clearing, reduced vegetation or other changes in carbon absorption. We reduce coal to ashes in nanoseconds, while the process of compressing carbon under massive geological pressure to form coal requires millennia. So, man's emissions must be adding to and running away from of our planet's ability to absorb them naturally. The words *natural* and *un-natural* are pivotal.

Scientists are divided about the capacity of earth, with its 'chaotic' variables, to restore climatic balance in the short term. They are also divided over the precise consequences for man's future. Philosophically, what is all the fuss about? After all, if man makes himself extinct, our planet will probably heal itself very quickly. But most scientists concede that a delayed policy response to climate change risks a rise in sea levels, hotter weather and an accelerated extinction of other species.

Over the past 140,000 years, man has adapted well to slow climate change. However, the faster pace of change makes the time frame for adapting much shorter, with serious consequences for man's survival, (particularly as negative impacts upon groundwater, food and fibre production and other key life supports begin to emerge). While a subject of some conjecture, there is support for the notion of a 'tipping point' being reached, triggering a chain reaction and accelerating global warming. There is evidence that this is what happened on Mars where water had once flowed.

Man's survival tools include better science and technology but paradoxically, his technical genius and avarice conspire to 'fuel' his emission problem, as he eats more, consumes more and produces more methane. In exporting his 'western lifestyle' to places like China, India and Africa, he is fuelling the demand side of the problem. Technology provides an escape. However, history shows that 'man fools with nature at his own peril' and is a feeble opponent in any genuine stoush with it.

On the balance of evidence, the Quaffers debaters found that concerns about climate change were *not* alarmists, but entirely realistic. That the stakes were too high for humanity to gamble with a catastrophic outcome, and that even action now may be too late. A range of public policy responses were within man's scientific, technical and legislative grasp, but, at five seconds to midnight, it was prudent to invoke all, not just some of them. Chief amongst these were taxes on emissions, and incentives for alternative energy development. However, promoting alternatives only makes sense if the carbon used in manufacturing alternative technologies is honestly accounted for and results in a genuinely lower carbon footprint.

Quaffers also found that untruths, repeated often enough by fervent climate warriors, distorted the debate. For example, the raw materials for batteries and wind turbines (aluminium, copper, lead etc,) are produced in energy-intensive smelters with very high carbon footprints. Similarly, the plastics used in solar panels are produced by the petrochemical industry. These technologies are, nonetheless, touted as 'saviours' in the alternative energy debate, but can only be so if their carbon footprint is honestly measured, to establish beyond doubt a *net balance of benefit*.

Engineers working for a leading US manufacturer of wind turbines, which use tonnes of copper and aluminium produced in energy-intensive smelters— recently conceded that, even if its turbines operated for their entire 'designed life', they could never repay the carbon used to produce them. Similarly, China is the world's largest producer of solar panels and of a host of other products reliant upon its massive coal consumption. To provide additional energy for its expanding manufactures of solar panels and wind turbines, China is building new coal-fired power stations, almost with reckless abandon, as debate in the west rages about how to rein-in such heavy coal consumption and related emissions. Using another nation's coal simply makes China a proxy emitter. If China's emissions impact all of humanity equally, including its own people, surely it has an equal moral responsibility to address the problem.

Electric cars, too, are touted as saviours of our planet, but they rely upon energy-intensive battery production, and upon all nations building an extensive network of recharge stations, many of which will have to draw their constant, based-load power from coal-fired powers stations. Smelters which produce lead, zinc, cadmium, graphite and other components for vehicle batteries will also leave a big carbon footprint, and a toxic mountain when they are discarded.

In 2019, a working paper from a group of German researchers at the Institute for Economic Research (IFO) found that *"electric vehicles will barely cut any CO2 emissions in Germany over the coming years."* This German research showed that *"CO2 emissions of battery-electric vehicles are, in the best case, slightly higher than those of diesel engines."*

Many who argue for carbon friendly battery vehicles fail to tell you that all batteries must eventually be recycled, lest they accrue as a mountain of toxic waste—and the only feasible means to do so is by energy-intensive re-smelting. Calculating their carbon neutrality is thus complex and so the story of their role in saving our planet tends to be plagued by media spin and often glides over inconvenient truths.

So, where did Quaffers come out on this vexing, complex issue. Well, in a prescient conclusion, considering it was reached 15 years ago, *Quaffers* found that political self-interest and legislative sloth would delay a timely, global response to this challenge. If mankind were to be responsible, risk-averse guardians of our planet, Quaffers recommended major changes in thinking and behaviour; the introduction of cost penalties; policies to restrain man's personal avarice, global strategies for planetary health (since we all share the same atmosphere) and initiatives on the 'demand' side, to limit excesses, such as recycling of plastics and use of organics.

However, Quaffers cautioned that this clear logic stood queerly juxtaposed to the Herculean task of persuading all governments, nation states and fellow travellers on our planetary ark to act in concert across man's political, geographic, religious and other divides. Looking back upon those early conclusions, reached when the debate was still in its infancy, I think *Quaffers* got pretty close to presenting a balanced position. The next great challenge would be to rein in global emissions.

How Come China Gets to Emit More Than the Rest of Us?

Between 2007 and 2020, action on climate change *ebbed,* rather than *flowed*. Then something marvellous happened—it *Zoomed*. The coronavirus forced people to isolate. They left their cars in garages, stopped flying around the world, freed-up our highways and byways and communicated via remote platforms. Vehicle and other emissions plummeted! Meanwhile, the 'Quaffers' prediction, made in 2006, that politics would be a massive sea-anchor on timely action proved correct. Attempts to set global reduction targets, in Kyoto Paris and Glasgow, were accepted by some nations but rejected by others, anxious about the impacts upon their economies or in China's case, hidden behind the specious argument that, since the West had been allowed an industrial revolution, China and India should also be allowed to have one. This had resulted in the West conceding that China's and India's emissions could be higher, despite the atmosphere they breathe being the same as ours. As Glasgow approached, climate warriors called for more ambitious reductions in emissions, but the governments they were hoping to persuade began blinking uncertainly. Some simply decided not to attend (China and Russia, without whom the whole event would become a farce) while others lost political conviction, as lights began to go out and energy resources were stretched. Zero targets might save the planet but freeze people to death while they did so. Passionate *'greenies'* would need to retreat into caves with thick blankets.

It is thus important, in public policy terms, to understand how present 'guilt' or responsibility for global carbon emissions is calculated. The scientific data which informs this work dates back to 1751, not the 20th century. Each country's cumulative contribution to atmospheric *CO_2* is measured, by country and by region, over the period from 1751 through to 2017. The distribution of cumulative emissions around the world is then mapped and then used to compare relativity to the total. Some key points emerge from this calculation: * The United States has emitted more CO_2 than any other country over that 266-year period. At 400 billion tonnes since 1751, it is responsible for 25% of historical emissions. This is twice more than China—the world's second largest national contributor. The 28 countries of the European Union (EU28)—which are grouped together here as they typically negotiate and set targets on a collaborative basis—is also a large historical contributor at 22%.

What Is the Ranking of Emitters in Actual 2021 Terms?

Many of the large annual emitters today—such as India and Brazil—are not large contributors in a historical context. Africa's regional contribution, relative to its population, has been very small. What becomes clear when we look at emissions across the world today is that the countries with the highest emissions over history are not always the biggest emitters today. The UK, for example, was responsible for only 1% of global emissions in 2017 and benefits from very low per capita emissions, both historically and currently.

PRESENT RANKINGS—2021

China (28%)
Rest of the World (21%)
United States (15%)
India (7%)
Russia (5%)
Japan (3%)
Germany (2%)
Iran (2%)
South Korea (2%)
Saudi Arabia (2%)
Indonesia (2%)
Canada (2%)
Mexico (1%)
South Africa (1%)
Brazil (1%)
Turkey (1%)
Australia (1%)
United Kingdom (1%)
Poland (1%)
Italy (1%)
France (1%)

*SOURCE: UNION OF CONCERNED SCIENTISTS

Some political commentators find this historical basis of calculation unfair because the climate issue is a real and present danger, not an historical one, and we should focus on reining in emissions from anywhere right now, not selectively. Some scientists also fear a loss of objectivity because of political fervour and are pushing back, in the interests of a more dispassionate approach. Bjørn Lomborg, President of the Copenhagen Consensus Centre and a former director of the Danish government's Environmental Assessment Institute, became internationally famous after publishing *The Sceptical Environmentalist*. In it, he argued that many of the costly measures and actions adopted by scientists and policy makers to meet global warming had a minimal impact on the world's rising temperatures.

Political differences around the world have poisoned rational scientific dialogue and divided sentiment, as those fearing rises in their energy bills join with vested resource businesses in calling for 'a gentle transition', while fierce climate warriors, like young Swede, Greta Thunberg, literally shake with indignation as she did when she railed at world leaders from her UN pulpit, becoming a symbol for youth around the world.

One thing is clear. An entire generation—a veritable army of young people—has now embraced the idea that we must act with urgency. They have been inspired by Thurnberg and tutored in sometimes unfiltered climate science by equally passionate, mostly lay schoolteachers. Thurnberg and her growing army of young supporters have created a bow-wave of sentiment, making any lasting push back by denialists futile and global acceptance of the need for action on climate change, an essential part of any mainstream political party's platform. Political point scoring may be paralysing good policy, but in a democracy, the public, whether you consider it educated or not, usually gets it right.

How Are Democracies Answering the Challenge?

Democracy has one fundamental advantage over other systems of government—its ability to progressively correct the course of public policy via the ballot box. So, a robust climate debate should be celebrated by those who support democracy, not silenced or opposed by those who cannot truck any opposition to their own partisan views. While western nations beat each other up over who is doing better at reducing emissions, one thing remains unchanged. China is easily the biggest emitter and is yet to impose any effective national emission limits. Research by the Australian Institute of Public Affairs has found that, in just 16 days, China produces CO2 emissions equal to Australia's total annual emissions and almost 10 times the emissions of Japan, a highly developed manufacturer.

In the build-up to the COP21 Paris talks, OECD policy strategists identified three main policy approaches, all market-oriented:

- a penalty price on carbon
- policies which encourage investors to reallocate their funds; and ...
- policies which greatly improve provision of so-called 'green finance'.

Way back in 1990, an unlikely climate saviour, George Bush Snr, introduced a tradable permits scheme to deal with acid rain caused by sulphur dioxide emissions from coal-fired power stations. A cap was imposed, providing incentives for power companies to switch technologies. If you polluted less than the binding cap, you could sell unused permits to someone else for a profit. It was a spectacular success. No more acid rain and the price of permits plummeted.

It seems that businesses always adjust to profit signals. Because of these, coal-fired power was disappearing in the US, while gas and renewables were being favoured. Displaced employees were moving to clean energy jobs, and these started to outnumber those lost in fossil fuels. However, despite growing evidence that this was the way to go, politics still got in the way of good public policy. In 2016, Donald Trump said: "*I will save coal.*" Hillary Clinton said the opposite. The '*Rust Belt*', swayed by regional job security concerns, passionately voted for Trump.

As with all decisions, there are risks and rewards, costs and benefits. Technology and taxes on carbon may eventually make coal, oil and even gas worthless. And there are new risks to environmental and public health. Bushfires in Australia and California are good examples. There are also huge liability risks for insurance companies, which might send premiums rocketing, and pension funds may lose value if portfolios are not diversified.

Once again, we need good public policy to come to the rescue, and that means overcoming political barriers to good logic. The problem, in a democracy, is this: politicians do not act solely in the international or national interest, but in the best interests of their local constituents. That is a political nightmare if one's electorate has a major coal mining or steel making enterprise which employs most local voters. Opposing coal will cost constituents their livelihoods and you, the politician, your seat. Moreover, if one country—let us say Australia—acts alone in reducing its carbon footprint, and other countries do not follow suit, that *good* policy becomes *bad* policy, because it unfairly taxes Australia's comparative advantage, making its people poorer. In this way, democracy is a curse.

However, a new light has appeared on the hill, offering an answer to this dilemma—a *carbon border tax (CBT) adjustment*. This policy was recently proposed by Ursula von der Leyen, who made it a priority as she took up her role as president of the European Commission. But it is a policy which will seriously penalise energy exporters, like Australia. A recent article in the Financial Review explained it thus:

"China is the biggest 'exporter of CO2 emissions in trade'. In 2015 this was about 2 billion metric tonnes. Australia imported 48.5 million tonnes of this (via its share of the polluted atmosphere). A CBT adjustment, should Australia properly price carbon while China does not, would tax these (emission) products at the border to remove any (Chinese) carbon subsidy. Job losses would thus be avoided. From China's point of view, if it has no trade disadvantage in pricing carbon—that tax having been sheeted back to Australia as the source producer— it might be persuaded to get on board and speed up its progress towards adopting an emissions trading scheme. This is a reasonable way to proceed, albeit at Australia's expense. It is not an antitrade tariff, but a sensible penalty if you believe it helps to meet the greatest existential threat facing our civilisation."

So Much for Warming. What About Global Cooling?

I chose the term *climate change* to demonstrate how difficult it can be to find a fair and equitable policy equilibrium—one which preserves truth, respects science and fact and meets the expectations of the vox populi. Climate change is a great subject to explore in that way because of its many contradictions in logic and the challenge it poses for policy makers, as it did for members of the Quaffers public policy forum, who learned the following:

"The moon stabilises earth's obliquity. The tilt varies between 22° and 22.5° and is enough to induce inconveniences like the occasional Ice Age."

These are the words of Seth Shostak, Astronomer. We worry about whether democracy can survive the rise of China and whether man can survive climate change. Our kids must feel their future is hopeless! But how trite do each of these threats seem when viewed against an approaching Ice Age?

Surely, when we speak about climate change, we must, in fairness, give all of our existential threats some sort of order of priority, some order of urgency for humanity, and keep them in some reasonable perspective!

Nobody seems concerned about *global cooling*, a subject any questioning mind would address to bring balance to the debate. A paper which inspired debate around the Ice Age was published in 2017 by learned Mathematician, Prof. Valentina Zharkova. A science journal then published Professor Zharkova's findings, bringing a new perspective to the climate debate. It began thus:

"When it comes to climate change, emphasis is put on human activity. But in our fervour to discover our culpability in this matter, we have missed a few things. What about the natural cycles of climate which our Earth has always experienced? It is a fact that fluctuations in the solar cycle impact earth's temperature, as do other massive bodies flying in and around our solar system!"

At a National Astronomy Meeting in Wales, Professor Zharkova presented a model that could predict what solar cycles will look like far more accurately than was previously possible. She stated that the model could predict their influence with 97% accuracy and was showing that Earth is heading for a mini-Ice Age in about the year 2032. The model suggest that solar activity will fall by 60 per cent during the 2030s to conditions seen during the mini-Ice Age in 1645. That ought to test democracy and public opinion! Zharkova believes the lowering of temperatures will be short lived and merely slow the process of global warming by a few short years, but she was surprised how much interest her research had generated.

But let us go back even further. Over time, meteorites hitting earth, and massive volcanic eruptions are thought to have had a significant impact on climate. In a recent scientific piece entitled 'On the Climate of Human Flourishing', there is an even more interesting perspective, which I now cite:

When we study the Climate of Human Flourishing, everything we think of as 'world history'—the beginnings of agriculture, the building of cities, the invention of writing and mathematics, the rise and fall of civilisations, the scientific and industrial revolutions—has occurred since the end of the last ice age. The next ice age should be upon us shortly. When it comes, it will have an apocalyptic impact on humanity. But there are other, hitherto unsuspected, dangers of a deep freeze. If you think global warming is a serious threat, consider conventional ice ages. The last ice age ended just 15,000 years ago. It lasted over 100,000 years and was preceded by a warm period, known by geologists and climatologists as the Eemian epoch, which lasted 13,000 years—about the same length as our current 'warm' period. Before that was the next to last ice age, which also lasted around 100,000 years.

Over the past three million years, the warm periods have averaged 10,000 years and the ice ages about 100,000—ten times the span of the warm periods. Since modern man has only been around for a bit over 100,000 years, much of which was an ice age, we can fairly say that man's tenuous survival in caves ended when the last period of warming began, leading to his ability to escape from his ice-bound cave existence, move around more freely, discover fertile valleys with plentiful food and water, and propagate his species. Cropping led to his staying in one place, establishing communities, developing laws, government, art and writing and was thus the platform for his higher evolution to the sophisticated species man is today.

Here is the rub. We have long since overshot the point at which the next ice age should have begun. While we think global warming is threatening us, we should see that we are close to the end of the warm period that has been the climatological precondition for the whole of 'world history', so the climate of human flourishing has nothing whatsoever to do with human agency, but with massive cosmological and geological cycles which overwhelm our species, indifferent to our intellects, religious beliefs, metaphysical speculations and secular ideologies of progress.

According to Calvin... *12,900 years ago, Europe cooled down to Siberian temperatures within a decade. Rainfall halved, and fierce storms whipped a lot of dust into the atmosphere. These conditions lasted over 1,300 years, whereupon things warmed, even more suddenly. The dust settled, the warm rains returned, within just a decade, and modern 'world history' began.* Such drastic, non-linear climate fluctuations have occurred hundreds of times since. Calvin says they had a rigorous and manifold 'sculpting' effect on our species, shaping hominids into 'canny survivalists' by making them 'canny generalists', with a suite of physical attributes and cognitive skills unmatched in the animal kingdom. This was a Darwinian process.

It seems a wide leap—from this evolutionary prehistory to the present public policy shaping our world and the way we inhabit it—but we should make that leap. For me, what this broader study of planetary and human evolution teaches is that we should focus on what we *can control*, rather than obsess over what we *cannot*.

So, Here's What The 'Quaffers' Climate Debates Concluded

Climate has always changed and factors which make it change are mostly beyond man's control. BUT, by un-naturally adding his own emissions to nature's, man is contributing (i.e., anthropologically) to the climate change, which is said to be heating, not colling our planet, in the geological short time scale. Two rarely acknowledge culprits of our planet likely overheating and experiencing a corresponding change in climatic conditions are man's avarice and his uncurbed reproduction. The stakes are too high for humanity to gamble, so we should be *risk averse*. A range of responses within man's scientific, technical and legislative grasp are available to manage CO_2 emissions, but probably not an encroaching Ice Age, albeit one most of us are unlikely to see. Policy and technological answers to address climate change carry political risks, but governments should invoke them all.

Chief amongst these are taxes on emissions and incentives to encourage alternative energy development and changes in personal behaviour. The task of persuading governments and fellow travellers on our planetary ark to act in concert the across political, geographic, religious and other divides is immense. Politics will likely weigh like a sea-anchor on real, timely progress. And finally, we should be honest about the science and not hide inconvenient truths.

At the conclusion of its second debate—about global cooling—the *Quaffers* debaters were rattled by guest speaker, Leith Doody's, shocking presentation. The fact that an Ice Age was just around the corner weighed heavily on our minds. Overpopulation was also a big problem. Multiple crises seemed to be unfolding at warp speed—in a geological nanosecond, so to speak. Depressed by these brutal realities, some of us adjourned to an adjacent bar to drown our sorrows. There, we decided that man, with all of his significant achievements, his affluence, intellect and self-indulgence, was merely a temporary resident on our planetary ark and, in the greater scheme of things, a minnow compared to the majesty and might of the universe.

The climate debates had been cathartic. We had been treated to good science and fact, not spin. The information had enlightened us, not confused us and helped us to see things in perspective. While we obsessed over '*parts per million of carbon*', we were also overpopulating of our planet and insanely consuming everything upon it. These other threats were rarely discussed and needed to be more transparent.

In the bar, one of our number, depressed by this reality, turned to me and said… "I think I'll have another drink. Can I buy you one?"

"I'll have another scotch," I replied. "No ice this time!"

Where to From Here?

This is the point in our journey where non-fiction—which presents fact and reason rather than fiction—leaps across the literary divide. For we could not end this narrative without attempting to answer the philosophical question this book leaves hanging … 'Will democracy prevail over autocracy, or is democracy dying, along with freedom of thought and expression?' This book would be pointless if it failed to imagine how our world, on its present trajectory, might look in 30 years' time … let us say in the year 2050. I attempt this in the next and final chapter, the epilogue, and invite you to write your own ending to our journey.

How the next few decades unfold will be shaped by a number of moving parts in our rapidly evolving international machinery. China's threatened invasion of Taiwan will be a central issue, as will the extent to which the free world can find new, charismatic leadership, to fill the present void and reignite its democratic engine. Should a messy reunification of China with Taiwan spark a military conflict, we will all need to strap in for a rocky ride, for today's military hardware, and software, is more terrible than any of us care to imagine and could write an extremely dark final chapter. For that reason, mine offers hope.

Epilogue
The Year 2050

Uncertainty is uncomfortable ... but certainty is absurd.
Voltaire

I board a shiny time machine. It whisks me at warp speed towards the year 2050. I arrive in a beautifully manicured city, where generous parks and gardens skirt the banks of a sparkling lake. Stately buildings line wide boulevards, reflecting the heroic architecture of a political capital. Just as the rings of a tree tell of its age, rings of architecture radiate outwards from the lake, the centrepiece of the city. Early colonial architecture lining its banks gives way to newer, more pragmatic structures which stretch to the surrounding hills, forming an amphitheatre and encircling the city. From the lofty heights of the hilltops, majestic towers reach skyward, their sleek pinnacles carrying rings, like the rings of Saturn. The rings are platforms, offering breath-taking views of the capital, but their purpose is to carry sophisticated communications arrays. As dawn breaks, a water geyser rises majestically from the lake's centre, as an orchestra of bird song welcomes the approaching day.

I am in Canberra, the federal capital of Australia. Long fingers of morning light creep across the lake as an attractive, 42-year-old woman, Sandra Cameron, wakes. As if to celebrate her return to the conscious world, kookaburras squawk a laughing welcome from the branches of eucalypts outside her apartment. A subtle vibration emanates from within her pillow. It is a built-in, high-tech alarm clock, telling her that it is time to get up. She fumbles under the pillow for a button to turn it off, rubs sleep from her eyes, rolls over and examines her new day.

Sandy has barely opened her eyes when her electronic Butler, *Fred-E*, announces: "Good morning, Sandy. It is 7.15 am. Your coffee is percolating, and the morning news will commence through your home media system at 7.30 am."

"Freddy," she replies, "Turn on the bedroom and bathroom lights and start the shower." This is the first of a series of voice commands which will activate domestic robots, dedicated to serving Sandy faithfully, reliably and without retort or complaint, as she prepares for her workday.

At 7.29 am, a familiar jingle signals the approach of the 7.30 am breakfast news, and an announcer says "Morning folks. Welcome to Radio 2CA, the voice of the capital. Now over to Nick West in the newsroom for this morning's stories."

"Morning all" opens Nick, in a cultured academic tone. "In the lead up to the election, Prime Minister Ellie Fletcher will today announce the signing of a trade pact with China under which Australia will supply wheat, barley and beef exports to the republic for ten years in return for duty free access into the Chinese market for its high-tech manufactures. Later, the PM will fly to Darwin with British Trade Minister Boyd McCleary, for the opening of the new Special Economic Zone and nuclear reactor there. The new nuclear power plant will support a smelter supplying local processing industries. The deal will be a bonanza for Australian commodity exports."

"In the US, President Elise Grant will announce a new mineral recovery mission to Mars, where rare earths for the communications industry were recently discovered. In other news, the Great Barrier Reef Underwater Hotel chain has announced a record profit, making the Australian tourism sector the second highest contributor to GDP. This newscast is proudly sponsored by 'Habitat Dome', the regional builder of the year and designers of award prefab, housing domes, providing open planning, geothermal temperature controls, on-site power generation, waste disposal and auto-composting. We cross now for today's weather forecast."

Sandy is single. She has lots of girlfriends and enjoys the occasional tryst with a bloke but prefers her independence. Starting a family at her age is impractical, particularly for someone like her. She has chosen a career in the Australian foreign service, so kids would have limited her career mobility. Moreover, because she has elected to remain childless, she qualifies for special tax and retirement benefits only available to those who meet the *no-child, adopt-a-child* or *foster-a-child* requirements for tax exemption. That is, only available to those who forego reproduction.

This population control measure has been in force for ten years and has been paired with a policy of providing universally free education, since research has shown a clear link between levels of education and lower birth rates. It is a policy which has been widely adopted across the developed world and has succeeded in lowering population growth in those countries to below zero. In less-developed nations, free contraception and medical intervention programs have been greatly expanded, funded under foreign aid programs to dampen population growth in those underprivileged environments, where overpopulation, poverty and illiteracy persist.

Policy gurus have learned from the experiences of China's *one-child* policy of the late 20th century, that a gender distorted society results from a 1child policy and is impractical. For those who elect to start families, 2 children, equal to zero population growth, are permitted, but additional children no longer attract family benefit payments. Instead, a third child will incur tax penalties. There is broad social acceptance that you can't have it both ways—demand a cleaner planet and lower carbon emissions while simultaneously ignoring population growth. Overpopulation is the root cause of both issues and requires a new, global social contract.

Back in Canberra, Sandy straightens her skirt and prepares to leave for her place of work. The sun is now climbing and showcasing a sparkling summer's day. Intense flashes of light dance across waves cresting in the light wind on Lake Burley-Griffin. Gulls soar and dip over sleek, aero-foil ferries, gliding smoothly on an invisible air cushion between lake-side drop-off and pick-up zones. *Car-o-drones*—lightweight e-hatchbacks with four, helicopterlike propellors—fly in designated air lanes, locked onto invisible flight paths as they travel like geese, in single file, between their suburban and CBD lift-off and set-down zones. Each carries up to 4 commuters.

Below them, on designated e-highways, driver-less busses, trucks, trams and other electric vehicles carry much heavier, human and commercial payloads from predestined pick-up points to pre-programmed destinations. Together, these marine, land and air highways have spread the traffic load evenly across the land, sea and air-scape, dramatically reducing congestion and lowering vehicle emissions.

In Canberra, as in most other capital cities, penalties have been imposed to restrict vehicular entry into the CBD. Bicycle and pedestrian access are free, but no other marine, land or air vehicle may enter the CBD without a permit, colour coded for days of the week, for essential services, like policing, medical services, construction and attendance at special events, like football matches or national days. These measures have calmed traffic and the three modes—marine, air and road—operate in harmony. There are no revving noises. Combustion engines are gone.

All major roads, thoroughfares and footpaths now feature smooth, hardwearing surfaces with lower bitumen and cement content. Those traditional materials are now bulked up with composites of granulated plastic and glass, produced from recycled waste. The carbon footprints of bitumen and cement production have been more than halved and so has the tonnage of plastic and glass waste going into landfill and oceans. Granulated plastics are also used in many other surfacing and material strengthening applications. In 2050, there is still plenty of plastic raw material to feed this program. Oceans and rivers still deliver a huge annual payload, which is now harvested by fleets of ocean-going barges charged with cleaning up those domains, some 20 years after plastics have been outlawed and replaced by bio-degradable paper, cardboard and bamboo products.

Flexible workplace legislation now encourages staggered working hours, permitting in-home and in-office workdays, spreading workloads rationally. Most people live outside of the CBD, in peri-urban or regional hubs—where cheaper land and affordable housing are abundant. This follows the linking of planning permits to demand and cost criteria, legislated to maintain an acceptable cost—price ratio and ensure a fair return for builders and investors, while preserving housing affordability. This important social justice reform also encourages a better work—life balance.

Timber house frames and timber cladding have replaced steel frames, brick walls and concrete structures, whose carbon footprint is too high. Timber homes source most of their materials from plantation forests, which sequester 200 tonnes of carbon per hectare over their 21-year growth cycles. Canberra is surrounded by dense plantation forests, which add to its rural ambience and give its air a pine freshness. Its plantation trees have, for 21 years, sucked CO2 from the atmosphere, but that is not the end of the sequestration cycle. Carbon-rich timber from the plantations is sequestered for a further 100 years in house frames and consumer products, like furniture, with a significant additional life and wide consumer appeal.

The air is now crystal clear. There is no trace of the smog or inversion which, some 20 years earlier, had routinely enveloped capital cities. Coal-fired power stations constitute a small fraction of base-load supply, having been replaced by hydro, tidal, wind, solar, hydrogen and micro-nuclear technologies. Freestanding homes are largely powered by on-site or community generators. Rooftop solar is now mandated for all new housing, and suburban solar farms are common. Local gas-fired power stations run on methane captured over rubbish tips and sewerage treatment plants. Domestic power bills have plummeted to a fraction of earlier levels.

Australia has enjoyed an economic rebirth. Coal exports have been replaced by hydrogen and uranium exports, as the world progressively switches to hydrogen and nuclear energy solutions, the safest and cleanest options, with strict safeguards. Coal still plays a role, but close to 100% of its carbon emissions are now captured in the coal stack (chimney) and redirected into agriculture, where they are sequestered in soil to improve pastures—another natural carbon sink. But the greatest economic contribution now comes from niche manufacturing and product value-adding. Elaborately transformed products have reduced supply chain dependence upon foreign suppliers and captured higher domestic returns in income and employment. Smelters powered by clean nuclear or hydro energy enable Australia to add value to its products rather than export them as crude materials—as bauxite, iron ore or rare earths. These materials are now further refined and processed at home and exported to global markets as finished aluminium, steel and other metallurgical products, as rods, bars or blooms, or as parts and components manufactured from them.

In 2050, Australia leads the world in sequestering nuclear waste. Initially burying waste deep below its geologically stable deserts, encased in a flux which accelerates atomic absorption and returns the waste to a naturally occurring uranium oxide, Australia's Space Agency has now pioneered *solar vaporisation* of nuclear and toxic industrials waste. Inter-stellar *space trucks,* developed in joint venture with investors at Australia's National Space Administration Space Port, now fly waste to the edge of space and *fire* it, using a space canon, towards the sun. Once caught in the sun's gravitational pull, the expelled waste pods accelerate to white-hot speed, finally disintegrating, vaporising and being sucked into the infinite furnace of the sun.

In 2050, philosophical acceptance of climate change has prompted major changes in social behaviour and thinking. There is universal respect for the planet. People care about climate and about pollution of land, waterways and oceans. They also care about the depletion of natural resources and about overcrowding of capital cities. Encouraged by clever new communications platforms and flexible work practices, Sandy Cameron's generation has seen a massive shift towards regional living. People now prefer a rural or peri-urban lifestyle to overcrowded, expensive cities. This closer interaction with nature has also, curiously, caused neighbours to demonstrate uncommon humanity towards each other. Where before there had been a kind of cyber-autism, particularly amongst kids obsessed with hand-held devices, people now talk, instead of text, drop by to check on elderly relatives and neighbours, play with other kids on the block, and sit as families around dinner tables.

Mobile phones and other hand-held devices, which had once mesmerised an entire generation and been so anti-social, have been replaced by fashion accessories with embedded micro-chips, worn around the neck by men and women alike. These provide connectivity with a host of public, business and private devices, to support and inform people. Their use, however, is constrained. Upon entering designated zones, like classrooms, public halls and boardrooms, devices are automatically muted, to minimise their intrusion into human discourse.

On this sunny, 2050 morning, Sandy is preparing to visit her office. It is a *central-desk* day, and she has been rostered-on to prepare papers for an ASEAN summit. She is a brilliant young diplomat, and despite having served just two postings abroad, in New Zealand and in Japan, has recently been promoted to the rank of 'Counsellor Political', with the public service title of 'Director, East Asia Branch'. Her home posting will last three years. While she waits for news of her next foreign posting, she will work closely with embassies in Beijing, Japan and ASEAN countries, monitoring regional political developments and recommending policy settings. Her work is made easier by the fact that China is now a more amenable partner and a more open society, following a successful containment strategy implemented by the West and a cultural rebirth from withing China's own society.

As Sandy settles into her pleasant Canberra office on this pleasant summer's morning, she reflects how close the world had come to war. Relations with China were now thoroughly affable, and a brisk trade had resumed. This contrasted starkly with the toxic state of the relationship 30 years earlier, when China's naval and air incursions into Taiwan's sea and air space had become so routine that it appeared the small island nation would simply have to capitulate and become a part of China. This seemed the only way Taiwan could avoid terrible bloodshed for its people. China's military had dwarfed Taiwan's, and western forces had seemed incapable of mounting a viable military response. But as the expected date for invasion had approached—the so-called 'Z-Day' nominated by China—something strange had happened.

China had massed its air, naval and ground forces, ready for invasion and was confident that a massive show of force would persuade Taiwan to simply capitulate. Then, suddenly, the Chinese High Command had lost all contact with its brigades, divisions and units. Communications across the region, both military and civilian, had died completely. An eerie silence had followed, as China's generals scrambled to understand what had happened. The invasion was cancelled, and in a humiliating post-mortem, Chinese intelligence had learned that the US Space Force had fried China's communications network with an electro-magnetic pulse.

In a triumph of US technical genius, war had been averted, and in a triumph of political genius, as China contemplated its reaction, western leaders had issued a joint communique explaining that a rare electrical disturbance in the upper atmosphere had affected all telecommunications over North Asia. Britain and the US had promised to work with China to restore services, a commitment which had served to de-escalated tensions and provide a face-saver for China. A new era of détente had ensued and had precipitated changes at the top of the Chinese Communist Party, favouring leaders seeking a more inclusive, open society.

An even more astounding ideological rejuvenation had come from within China. Its people had pressed home an opportunity they saw to chart a new course. Under pressure from China's middle class, which had developed a taste for western affluence, and from the Shanghai and Shenzhen business establishments, whose business success was lifting standards of living across China, the previously strict authoritarian rule had given way to a more relaxed style of government. The new Central Committee of the Communist Party, recognising a growing tide of pro-democracy sentiment, had soon changed its stripes, proposing a hybrid form of government— *'Communism with democratic characteristics'*. Pro-democracy voices within the central committee had at last won through. Warm diplomatic relations with the West had then been restored, ushering-in a new era of East-West detente.

Back in her Canberra office, Sandy finds herself reflecting that the West, too, has accepted the uncomfortable fact that China's command economy and autocratic system of government, despite its humanitarian flaws, has demonstrated that it can cut through red tape and achieve outcomes more efficiently that its western counterparts. The West has been forced to concede that democracy is sluggish and needs to change if it hopes to compete. Australia and Britain have established *'Democratic Reform Commissions'*, charged with identifying reforms to bring their Westminster systems into line with the requirements of the new digital age and to achieve more efficient, streamlined delivery of government functions and services.

The *Australian Democratic Reform Commission* has recommended that Australia become a republic, albeit with a President whose role is purely ceremonial, and has redrafted the Constitution to ... *'favour a new form of democracy, which guarantees freedom of speech, freedom of assembly and freedom of expression, while adopting a centrally regulated parliamentary and administrative framework described as 'democracy with national command characteristics'.*

The preamble to the Australian Constitution has been changed to recognise the first Australians, granting them a voice in government via their own 'Regional Councils'. But membership of a Regional Council requires unequivocal evidence of at least three generations of aboriginality and its role is to *propose* legislation for its own communities, not create it for all. Finally, the amended Constitution provides that *'No person born in Australia, whether indigenous or otherwise, shall enjoy benefits or privileges or suffer penalties or disadvantages greater or lesser than those of any other Australian. All Australians, whatever their colour, shall be born equal, be equal before the law and claim the same relationship with the land of their birth'*.

Sandy enjoys working in a vastly reformed *'public service'*, which encourages personal initiative and the removal of roadblocks. The directions from her political masters are clearer and government policies enjoy a stronger, more direct mandate from the people. That follows the introduction of three important reforms.

First, upper house rules have been changed to prevent the election of politicians with an unrepresentative voice. All members of the Upper House must now either belong to a party commanding 5% of the national (senate) vote, or themselves command a minimum 5% of the vote in their senate seat. This prevents rogue individuals filibustering or frustrating decisions on the passage of bills.

Second, elected governments now have the power to dilute unnecessary or unproductive bureaucracy. Public servants are no longer unionised. Instead, they are required to undertake work-placement or project-based exchanges with private sector organisations, to improve their efficiency, cooperation and business literacy.

Third, a new, national body—*'The Australian Future Commission'*, comprising leaders from the business, academic and scientific communities—is granted a commission by the Governor General, not the Parliament, to set desirable medium to long term targets for national growth and prosperity. Future Commission planning must set ten-, fifteen- and twenty-year targets, extending well beyond four-year election cycles. Governments of all persuasion are henceforth held to account, by voters and the media, for achieving, or falling short of, those aspirational targets.

It is late. My pen is protesting, and it asks to be rested. I conclude that my story is told, and my journey is at an end. I confess that this final chapter, like Orwell's 1984—written in 1945—is a fiction, but is offers a happy, rather than a sad ending. Tomorrow's dawn will light a new day and illuminate new pathways for each of us to follow. I have shared with you my picture of the past, the present turbulent times and an optimistic window into the future—one which is perhaps idealistic and only achievable in man's imagination. You may see a different future. Whatever each of you foresees, it is up to both of us, you and me, to shape that future, not simple to have it thrust upon us by indifference or idle observation.

For as Plato so deftly prophesised … *"The price of indifference to public affairs is to be ruled by evil men."*

If we can agree about that, we might hope to be ruled by benevolent, nor evil people. By wise men and women who put the public and the national interest ahead of their own self-interest, and by rulers who place humanity and happiness above vanity and avarice. We should aspire to be ruled by men and women who put people first and deliver public policies which rise above political prejudice and media spin. I thank you for sharing this journey with me and leave you with this final thought:

In Chinese, the word 'crisis' is a complex expression. The Chinese have laboured with the term for millennia and finally captured it in four characters, which express two different ideas … 'wēi'—危 meaning *danger*, and 'jīhui'-机 ; 機 meaning *change-point… dangerous point of change.*

How apposite those words are to our present, fast-changing world. They encourage me to conclude with my own philosophical statement …

"Change is not a random thing. It is certain. Embrace it. Make it work for you, or it will embrace you and make you work for it."

Bruce Nicholls—**Ni Ke Er Si**—尼克尔斯 (my Chinese name)

Annexure

Excerpts from Chinese President Xi Jinping's speech marking the 100th anniversary of the Chinese Communist Party—1 July 2021.

Comrades and friends,

Today, the first of July, is a great and solemn day in the history of both the Communist Party of China (CPC) and the Chinese nation. We gather here to join all Party members and Chinese people of all ethnic groups around the country in celebrating the centenary of the Party, looking back on the glorious journey the Party has travelled over 100 years of struggle, and looking ahead to the bright prospects for the rejuvenation of the Chinese nation.

On this special occasion, it is my honour to declare (that) we have realised the first centenary goal of building a moderately prosperous society... and are now marching in confident strides towards the second centenary goal of building China into a great modern socialist country.

With a history of more than 5,000 years, China has made indelible contributions to the progress of human civilisation. After the Opium War of 1840, however, China was reduced to a semi-colonial, semi-feudal society; suffered great ravages; endured intense humiliation, was subjected to great pain, and the Chinese civilisation was plunged into darkness. Since that time, national rejuvenation has been the greatest dream of the Chinese people and of the Chinese nation.

Through the Northern Expedition, the Agrarian Revolutionary War, the War of Resistance against Japanese Aggression, and the War of Liberation, we fought armed counterrevolutionaries with armed revolution, toppling the three mountains of imperialism, feudalism, and bureaucrat-capitalism and establishing the People's Republic of China, which made the people masters of the country. We thus secured our nation's independence and liberated our people.

The victory of the new-democratic revolution put an end to the state of total disunity that existed in old China, and to all the unequal treaties imposed on our country by foreign powers. Through a tenacious struggle, the Party and the people showed the world that the Chinese people had stood up, and that the time in which the Chinese nation could be bullied and abused by others was gone forever.

Through tenacious struggle, the Party and the Chinese people showed the world that the Chinese people were capable of not only dismantling the old world, but also building a new one, that only socialism could save China, and that only socialism with Chinese characteristics could develop China.

Through tenacious struggle, the Party and the Chinese people showed the world that by pursuing reform and opening up, a crucial move in making China what it is today, China had caught up with the times in great strides. To realise national rejuvenation, the Party has united and led the Chinese people in pursuing a great struggle, a great project, a great cause, and a great dream through a spirit of self-confidence, self-reliance, and innovation, achieving great success for socialism with Chinese characteristics in the new era.

Let us take this moment to cherish the memory of comrades Mao Zedong, Zhou Enlai, Liu Shaoqi, Zhu De, Deng Xiaoping, Chen Yun, and other veteran revolutionaries who contributed greatly to China's revolution, construction, and reform, and to the founding, consolidation, and development of the Communist Party of China.

On the journey ahead, we must continue to uphold Marxism-Leninism, Mao Zedong Thought, Deng Xiaoping Theory, the Theory of Three Represents, and the Scientific Outlook on Development, and fully implement the Thoughts on Socialism with Chinese Characteristics for a New Era. We must continue to adapt the basic tenets of Marxism to China's specific realities and its fine traditional culture. We will use Marxism to observe, understand, and steer the trends of our times, and continue to develop the Marxism of contemporary China and of the 21st century.

We must uphold and develop socialism with Chinese characteristics. We must follow our own path-this is the bedrock that underpins our Party. More than that, it is the historical conclusion our Party has drawn from its struggles over the past century. Socialism with Chinese characteristics is a fundamental achievement of the Party and the people ... and, we have pioneered a new and uniquely Chinese path to modernisation and created a new model for human advancement.

We must ... build up our country's strength in science and technology. We must ensure it is our people who run the country, continue to govern based on the rule of law, and uphold the core socialist values. We must ensure and enhance public wellbeing, promote harmony between humanity and nature, and take well-coordinated steps towards making our people prosperous, our nation strong, and our country beautiful.

The Chinese nation has fostered a splendid civilisation over more than 5,000 years of history. At the same time, we are also eager to learn what lessons we can from the achievements of other cultures, and welcome helpful suggestions and constructive criticism. We will not, however, accept sanctimonious preaching from those who feel they have the right to lecture us.

We must accelerate the modernisation of national defence and the armed forces. A strong country must have a strong military, as only then can it guarantee the security of the nation. At the point that it was engaged in violent struggle, the Party came to recognise the irrefutable truth that it must command the gun and build a people's military of its own... a powerful force for protecting peace in our region and beyond.

On the journey ahead, we must fully implement the Party's thinking on strengthening the military in the new era as well as our military strategy for the new era, maintain the Party's absolute leadership over the people's armed forces, and follow a Chinese path to military development.

We must continue to promote the building of a human community with a shared future. Peace, concord, and harmony are ideas the Chinese nation has pursued and carried forward for more than 5,000 years. The Chinese nation does not carry aggressive or hegemonic traits in its genes. The Party cares about the future of humanity and wishes to move forward in tandem with all progressive forces around the world. China has always worked to safeguard world peace, contribute to global development, and preserve international order.

On the journey ahead, we will remain committed to promoting peace, development, cooperation, and mutual benefit, to an independent foreign policy of peace, and to the path of peaceful development. We will work to build new international relations and a human community with a shared future, promote high-quality development of the Belt and Road Initiative through joint efforts, and use China's new achievements in development to provide the world with new opportunities. The Party will continue to work with all peace-loving countries and peoples to promote the shared human values of peace, development, fairness, justice, democracy, and freedom. We will continue to champion cooperation over confrontation, to open up rather than closing our doors, and to focus on mutual benefits instead of zero-sum games. We will oppose hegemony and power politics and strive to keep the wheels of history rolling towards bright horizons.

We Chinese are a people who uphold justice and are not intimidated by threats of force. We have never bullied, oppressed, or subjugated the people of any other country, and we never will. By the same token, we will never allow any foreign force to bully, oppress, or subjugate us. Anyone who would attempt to do so will find themselves on a collision course with a great wall of steel forged by over 1.4 billion Chinese people.

On the journey ahead, we must demonstrate stronger vigilance and always be prepared for potential danger, even in times of calm. We must adopt a holistic approach to national security that balances development and security imperatives and implement the national rejuvenation strategy within a wider context of the once-in-a-century changes taking place in the world. We need to acquire a full understanding of the new features and requirements arising from the change to the principal contradiction in Chinese society and the new issues and challenges stemming from a complicated international environment. We must be both brave and adept in carrying out our struggle, forging new paths and building new bridges wherever necessary to take us past all risks and challenges.

Comrades and friends,

We will stay true to the letter and spirit of the principle of One Country, Two Systems, under which the people of Hong Kong administer Hong Kong, and the people of Macao administer Macao, both with a high degree of autonomy. We will ensure that the central government exercises overall jurisdiction over Hong Kong and Macao and implement the legal systems and enforcement mechanisms for the two special administrative regions to safeguard national security. While protecting China's sovereignty, security, and development interests, we will ensure social stability in Hong Kong and Macao, and maintain lasting prosperity and stability in the two special administrative regions.

Resolving the Taiwan question and realising China's complete reunification is a historic mission and an unshakable commitment of the Communist Party of China. All of us, compatriots on both sides of the Taiwan Strait, must come together and move forward in unison. We must take resolute action to utterly defeat any attempt towards "Taiwan independence." No one should underestimate the resolve, the will, and the ability of the Chinese people to defend their national sovereignty and territorial integrity.

Comrades and friends,

A century ago, China was in decline and withering away in the eyes of the world. Today, the image it presents to the world is one of a thriving nation that is advancing with unstoppable momentum towards rejuvenation.

Comrades and friends,

Today, a hundred years on from its founding, the Communist Party of China is still in its prime and remains as determined as ever to achieve lasting greatness for the Chinese nation.

Long live our great, glorious, and correct Party! Long live our great, glorious, and heroic people!